Doing Foucault in Early Childhood Studies

The theories and analyses of poststructural thinkers such as
Michel Foucault can seem a long way from practice in early childhood services. However, in recent years many early childhood
researchers and practitioners have found this work important,
and this fascinating book brings together a range of research
and case studies showing how teachers and researchers have
brought poststructuralism to the classroom. The book covers such
issues as:

- becoming poststructurally reflective about truth;
- mapping classroom meanings;
- tactics of rhizoanalysis;
- becoming again in critically knowing communities.

Doing Foucault in Early Childhood Studies includes case studies and
examples taken from real situations and will be of interest to anyone
studying or researching early childhood practice and policy.

Glenda Mac Naughton is Associate Professor in Early Childhood and Director at the Centre for Equity and Innovation in
Early Childhood at the University of Melbourne.

Contesting Early Childhood Series
Series Editors: Gunilla Dahlberg and Peter Moss

This ground-breaking series questions the current dominant discourses in early childhood, and offers alternative narratives of an area that is now made up of a multitude of perspectives and debates.

The series examines the possibilities and risks arising from the accelerated development of early childhood services and policies, and illustrates how it has become increasingly steeped in regulation and control. Insightfully, this collection of books will each show how early childhood services can in fact *contribute* to ethical and democratic practices. The authors explore new ideas taken from alternative working practices in both the Western and developing world, other academic disciplines in addition to developmental psychology. They also locate theories and practices in relation to the major processes of political, social, economic, cultural and technological change occurring in the world today.

Titles in the series:

Unequal Childhoods
Children's lives in developing countries
Helen Penn

Doing Foucault in Early Childhood Studies
Applying poststructural ideas
Glenda Mac Naughton

Early Childhood Education in Reggio Emilia
Dialoguing, listening and researching
Carlina Rinaldi

Ethics and Politics in Early Childhood Education
Gunilla Dahlberg and Peter Moss

Doing Foucault in Early Childhood Studies

Applying poststructural ideas

Glenda Mac Naughton

Routledge
Taylor & Francis Group

LONDON AND NEW YORK

First published 2005
by Routledge
2 Park Square, Milton Park, Abingdon, Oxon, OX14 4RN

Simultaneously published in the USA and Canada
by Routledge
270 Madison Ave, New York NY 10016

Routledge is an imprint of the Taylor & Francis Group

Transferred to Digital Printing 2009

© 2005 Glenda Mac Naughton

Typeset in Baskerville by
Florence Production Ltd, Stoodleigh, Devon

British Library Cataloguing in Publication Data
A catalogue record for this book is available from the British Library

Library of Congress Cataloging in Publication Data
A catalog record for this book has been applied for

ISBN 0–415–32099–2 (hbk)
ISBN 0–415–32100-X (pbk)

Publisher's Note
The publisher has gone to great lengths to ensure the quality of this reprint
but points out that some imperfections in the original may be apparent.

For my mother, Joyce, from whom I continue to learn what courage means

Contents

Acknowledgements

Taking a political stance in early childhood education can be a tricky step. It is always an easier step when others take it with you. I would like to thank those early childhood educators who in contributing to this book have taken that step with me. I would especially like to thank them for their generosity in allowing their stories to shift from place to place as the book took shape and for inspiring me through their strength and good humour to continue to take the tricky steps in our field.

Sally Barnes always brings me questions I had not thought of, ways of thinking that intrigue me and reminders that early childhood teachers are powerful theory builders capable of thoughtful critiques of the knowledge base that informs their work. Sheralyn Campbell is a source of strength and inspiration in my work in early childhood education because of her determination to test the 'big ideas' in the daily life of early childhood services, the integrity with which she does this, and her willingness to share her dilemmas and struggles in it in order to further equity and social justice in our field. Karina Davis has taken a journey through her own whiteness and its effects on her work in early childhood with a political and intellectual honesty that has brought with it hard personal and professional times. Watching how this journey is etching new ways of thinking and being into her work has been a privilege. Miriam Giugni sparkles with ideas and with the love of seeing what they mean to hold and to use in her work with children. It is impossible not to be dazzled by her enthusiasm for holding only onto the ideas that matter for social justice and equity. Kylie Smith often tells me she doesn't know what she is doing. But, I have seen how her ways of not knowing provoke and inspire others to ask, 'Who is silenced and who is privileged in my work with children?' Her refusal to be the expert knower and her capacity to ask 'Why can't we do it differently?' are an ever delightful part of the benefits I gain from being her colleague.

This book's inspiration came from the work of these women and their commitment to make a difference in early childhood education. They are a powerful force for socially just change within our field.

I learnt much about what it takes to be critically reflective in early childhood education from a wonderful group of colleagues in North West Tasmania, who worked with me in the research project on Creating and Sustaining Critical Reflection in Early Childhood. To them my thanks for being there on those Friday afternoons and being prepared to take a journey in which power and knowledge were so much part of its fabric. The Margaret Trembarth Early Childhood Research Scholarship Fund and the Department of Education, Tasmania funded this work. Funding from the Australian Research Council and the University of Melbourne has also supported the research projects woven through the book.

Many of the contributers to this book, including myself, have tested ideas and understandings that weave through the book in what we know as the Postgraduate Support Group, embedded in the Centre for Equity and Innovation in Early Childhood (CEIEC) at the University of Melbourne. Sheralyn, Kylie and Karina were inaugural members of the group. My thanks to that group for being a place where new ideas can be shared and explored in a climate of trust and support.

The book also owes much to my partner Patrick Hughes, who, as always, supported me in myriad ways throughout its writing. His untiring belief that it mattered, his willingness to read and discuss it at points that it really mattered to me, and the time he gave to proof-reading made it possible to imagine the book would be finished. I want to thank him for his patience, intellectual engagement with the book and personal support for me throughout its writing.

I was both surprised and delighted to be asked by Gunilla Dahlberg and Peter Moss to write a book about 'Doing Foucault' in early childhood studies. I want to thank them for their encouragement to write this book and for their positive and timely comments on the manuscript. They have been generous in their offers of support from its conception.

Introduction

Beyond quality, towards activism

> What is the question that will help push this person's thinking that one step? Who is advantaged and who is disadvantaged? You can use that question in lots of situations.
>
> (Rana, early childhood district co-ordinator,
> South Australia)

> What are the means by which we can change ourselves in order to become ethical subjects?
>
> (Foucault, 1984b, p. 354)

Consuming and producing knowledge of children and of early childhood education is part of the everyday business of early childhood studies. The everyday language, ethics, routines, rituals, practices, expectations, ideas, documents and invocations of quality in early childhood services are formed through and motivated by very particular understandings of children and how best to educate them. Over time, some of this knowledge has settled so firmly into the fabric of early childhood studies that its familiarity makes it just seem 'right', 'best' and 'ethical'. Also over time, new understandings of children and how best to educate them have persistently emerged to unsettle the familiar. In between the new and the familiar are competing and contested understandings of what is 'best', 'right' and 'ethical' for children, and these understandings bring choices: choices about which knowledge is 'best' and 'right' to form and motivate the everyday business of early childhood. How can and should we make these choices?

The business of this book is how to establish knowledge(s) in early childhood studies that sustain ethical, democratic lives with children every day and that recognise the political processes and effects of privileging one form of knowledge of children and of early childhood education over another. It invites reflection on who selects which knowledge of children and of early childhood education is consumed and produced in early childhood studies, why, how and for whose benefit. It invites reflection on the politics of knowledge in early childhood studies and the shifting ways it advantages some groups and disadvantages other groups.

The politics of knowledge and the politics of this book

This book engages with the politics of knowledge in early childhood studies in order to create greater social justice and equity. It presents early childhood studies as a site at which to transform inequitable relations of gender, 'race', class, sexuality, ability and age. This is not an easy task nor is it one for which there are imple roadmaps showing routes to certain destinations. It is a task replete with complex ethical choices, unpredictable twists and turns, and never-ending possibilities. I have chosen to frame that task of transforming inequitable relations within poststructuralist perspectives on the politics of knowledge. These politics are part of a wider social project of education for emancipation and, as such, they have been influenced significantly by the work of French theorist Michel Foucault (1926–1984), by the transformational intents and activist politics of critical educationalists (e.g. Freire, 1970; Freire, 1972; Carr and Kemmis, 1986; Apple, 1989; Giroux, 1988; Greene, 1986; hooks, 1994), feminists (e.g. Luke and Gore, 1992; Kenway and Willis, 1997; Luke, 1996; Spivak, 1990; Butler, 1990) and critical race theorists (e.g. Sleeter and McLaren, 1995; Darder, 2002; hooks, 1996).

My understanding of what that wider social project of emancipation can mean in early childhood studies owes much to the work of anti-bias educators such as Louise Derman-Sparks in the US (1998; Derman-Sparks and the Anti-Bias Task Force, 1989) and Babette Brown in the UK (1998), who have advocated an activist stance in early childhood that seeks to recognise and confront discrimination, to celebrate diversity, and to build respectful and democratic early childhood communities with young children. I am indebted also to feminist poststructuralists such as Valerie Walkerdine (e.g. 1981; 1982) and Bronwyn Davies (e.g. 1988; 1989), who pioneered a turn to the poststructuralist in early childhood studies in their search to challenge the effects of patriarchy in young children's lives. Others have continued and expanded this work (e.g. Alloway, 1995; Campbell, 1999; Ryan and Ochsner, 1999; Cannella, 2000; Cannella and Grieshaber, 2001; Ochsner, 2001).

This book is written for those interested in doing early childhood studies differently to make the world a better place. It explores possibilities in a spirit of hope, yet it is full of doubts and uncertainties, especially about the knowledge base that should drive early childhood studies. Some of you who read this book may not share its politics and feel very certain about what early childhood studies should be. You may say that its explicit political stance is a weakness, influencing how I and other contributors to the book engage with the politics of knowledge. In reply, I invite you to reflect on how your politics affects your positions on the politics of knowledge in early childhood, because the recognition that knowledge is inseparable from politics is what 'Doing Foucault' in early childhood studies seeks to achieve.

This book is firmly grounded in contemporary early childhood studies. It introduces you to early childhood educators who are using the ideas of Foucault and poststructuralists to create and sustain critical reflection and activism in their everyday life in early childhood studies. Specific vignettes of this work have been provided by the following early childhood educator–researchers:

- Sally Barnes, South Australia
- Sheralyn Campbell, New South Wales
- Karina Davis, Victoria
- Miriam Giugni, New South Wales
- Kylie Smith, Victoria.

As you read this book, you will meet terms that may be unfamiliar to you, such as 'knowledge/power', 'discourse' and 'regimes of truth'. These terms are central to Foucault's work and becoming familiar with them is part of the work of 'Doing Foucault' in early childhood studies. If you are unfamiliar with Foucault's work, your familiarity with these terms should grow as the book unfolds and you make your own judgements about the benefits to the early childhood field of educators who are poststructurally reflective and activist. If you are familiar with Foucault's work, the book offers glimpses of how early childhood educators can draw on his ideas to rethink their pedagogical knowledge and practices as they seek to create equity.

Foucault and postructuralist politics of knowledge

Michel Foucault is widely regarded as one of the most influential thinkers of the twentieth century, whose work has challenged how people think about the police, schooling, welfare organisations, gay rights and care of the mentally ill. His ideas were shaped by diverse theories including Marxism, phenomenology, structuralism and psychoanalytic theories and the work of German philosophers Friedrich Nietzsche and Immanuel Kant (see Danaher, Schirato and Webb, 2000; Weedon, 1997; Rabinow, 1984). Those diverse influences on Foucault's thinking make it hard to readily label his work but he has deeply influenced the body of theories widely known as poststructuralism. He is often referred to as a post-structuralist thinker because of his affinities with poststructuralism.

Since the late 1960s and early 1970s, Foucault and poststructuralist thinkers have unsettled and reshaped the knowledge base of fields of study as diverse as law, economics, history, psychology, sociology, philosophy, criminology, medicine, art, public relations and education (McLaren, 2002; Danaher, Schirato and Webb, 2000; Weedon, 1997; McNay, 1995). In each one, they have challenged the assumption that knowledge is free of – and distinct from – politics. Further, they have argued that language is connected intimately with the politics of knowledge and that those politics are evident in the language we use to think of ourselves (our subjectivities) and to describe our actions and institutions. Poststructuralists have also challenged the idea that individuals can think and act freely outside of the politics of knowledge. The poststructuralist approach to the politics of knowledge challenges the Enlightenment notion of the rational and coherent individual telling a rational and coherent story about themselves (their identity) and their society. In contrast, poststructuralists believe that individuals may tell several – possibly competing – stories about themselves (identities) and about societies. The politics of our time and place influence which stories (of individuals or societies) are told, when and by whom, which is why some stories are heard more often and given greater status than others. Consequently, identifying the stories (of individuals or societies) that are silenced or marginalised and then sharing them is a political act.

Despite Foucault's deep and continuing influence in diverse fields of study, early childhood students rarely meet Foucault's work, or the work of poststructuralist thinkers. It's hard to find, for example, Foucault's ideas of 'disciplinary power', 'docile bodes' and 'power/knowledge' in a mainstream early childhood text. Perhaps this is not surprising. Foucault's ideas on the relationships between power, discipline, knowledge and our bodies are generally understood as radical because he, along with poststructuralist thinkers, claimed that truth does not exist. Instead, he believed that what we hold to be true about, for instance, child development or early childhood curriculum, is a fiction created through 'truth games' that express the politics of knowledge of the time and place (Foucault, 1997).

Much of Foucault's work explores the relationships between knowledge, truth and power and the effects of these relationships on us and on the institutions we create. The research interviews and vignettes in this book show that becoming poststructurally reflective often provokes educators to rethink and deepen their understandings of equity and its possibilities in their work by radicalising their understandings of power and knowledge in early childhood institutions. In turn, this radicalisation drives efforts to find new ways to act for equity. It serves activism.

An apology to Foucault and to Foucauldians

This book is unapologetic about its politics. However, I apologise in advance to Foucault and to people familiar with his work. This book is not a comprehensive introduction to his work – others have accomplished that task already (Danaher, Schirato and Webb, 2000; Popkewitz and Brennan, 1998; McHoul and Grace, 1993). Instead, this book presents ideas from Foucault and post-structuralists that can support activist educators. In doing so, the book has muted many of the complexities, contradictions and nuances of the scholarship of Foucault and of the poststructural-ists it draws on.

Tactics and strategies for activism

Activism arises for many reasons and the choice to actively seek social justice and equity is both deeply personal and politically inspired. Central to activism within education has been the process of conscientisation that Freire (1970) referred to as 'developing consciousness, but consciousness that is understood to have the power to transform reality' (Taylor 1993, p. 52). Concientisation directs a critically reflective stance on educational work towards action for social justice and equity. To grasp its significance for activist educators it is helpful to distinguish between being reflective and being critically reflective.

The politics of the reflective and the critically reflective educator

> [Reflection is] looking back on current practices and seeing how they fit in with how I thought about it years ago and how things are now and how I can change given what is happening now. I use it to attempt to change my practices with parents and families and take a different, broader approach.
>
> (Anna, early childhood educator,
> Trembarth Research Project)

Reflective practice has been characterised as a hallmark of quality teachers and as the bedrock of their professional growth (Wood and Bennett, 2000). At its simplest, being reflective means, as Anna says, 'looking back' at practices in order to rethink them. To do this, reflective educators need to be inquisitive and sceptical. They need to be inquisitive about what is happening in their classrooms and why. They need to be sceptical about whether they have the right answer for their current questions. They can use their inquisitiveness and scepticism to examine their specific classrooms and to build pedagogical theories that can inform their daily professional judgements about how best to act in their classrooms (Carter and Halsall, 1998).

Reflective practice does not just happen automatically. It arises as educators actively build and transform their pedagogical knowledge (Yost, Sentner and Forlenza-Bailey, 2000). It requires educators to take control of their own learning and meaning making about being educators, about education and about pedagogy (Wroe and Halsall, 2001) and it implies that they know how to drive innovation in their classrooms. To this extent, reflective practice is a means to discover and transform an individual's understandings and practices (Bleakley, 1999; Boud, Keogh and Walker, 1985; Mezirow, 1990; Brookfield, 1995; Cranton, 1996).

It is an important step toward working for equity and social justice, but it needs to attend to the social and political contexts to make a difference.

Inserting the 'critical' into reflective practice: a working definition

> Critical reflection means there are always far more questions than there are answers, that I cannot pretend that there are no power effects related to my actions as a teacher and that there are rarely, if ever, simple solutions to the incredibly complex task of teaching.
>
> (Sally Barnes, early childhood educator
> and researcher, South Australia)

Inserting the 'critical' into critical reflection directs attention away from the individual and towards, as Sally says, the operation and effects of the power relationships *between* people. In all educational relationships, critically reflective educators seek to analyse their implication in oppressive and inequitable power relationships with students and then use their analysis to work against that oppression and inequity.

Thus, critical reflection is the process of questioning how power operates in the processes of teaching and learning and then using that knowledge to transform oppressive or inequitable teaching and learning processes (McLaren, 1993). It assumes that there is no single, correct way to be an educator and that all teaching and learning can either contribute to or contest oppression and inequity:

> Consequently, one cannot speak of pedagogy but must speak instead of pedagogies which respond to particular necessities, interests and conditions.
>
> (Gaudiano and de Alba, 1994, p. 128)

The origins of the 'critical'

In everyday language, 'critical' is often associated with negative ways of thinking captured in words such as disparaging, carping, unfavourable and fault-finding. However, in the social sciences 'critical' has another meaning and heritage that derives from the work of theorists such as the German philosopher Jürgen Habermas. Habermas is referred to as a neo-critical theorist to acknowledge his debt to critical social theory of Karl Marx but to mark him as moving beyond it.

Neo-critical theorists, like the poststructuralists, have a deep interest in questions of knowledge and power. Specifically, they ask how particular ideas come to dominate our understandings of and actions in the social world and contribute to inequities in it; and their answers draw heavily on the notion of ideology. Ideology is often used to refer simply to the shared sets of ideas that guide our actions and enable us to justify them (Bayley and Gayle, 2003). However, not all ideologies have equal power and Marx (Marx and Engels, 1965) argued that the dominant ideologies are those associated with (and benefiting) the most powerful groups within a society. Dominant ideologies' power is often masked: we often hold ideologies implicitly, rather than knowing them explicitly. Consequently, we take for granted the power structures in social institutions, social structures and social expectations. We miss their effects on us all and we miss the fact that they serve the interests of those with most power. Macedo (1998) called ideology insidious because it can 'make itself invisible' (p. xiii). Discovering ideologies – uncovering the invisible – is the first step to challenging them and the oppressive and unjust power relations they hide and support.

Marx and Engels (1965) argued that in any society, the dominant ideologies hide the economic foundations of the conflicts between classes. For example, the ideology of individualism asserts that anyone can become rich and powerful, hiding the inbuilt advantages of the ruling class – wealth, high-quality education and health care, and ready-made connections with the powerful and wealthy. In this way, individualism hides the class-based distribution of advantage and disadvantage, leading people to believe that social success and failure are the result of individual responsibility, rather than the result of a class-based society. Critical theorists (following Marx) argue that individuals' belief that they think, choose and act for themselves merely expresses a 'false consciousness' that is the result of the ideologies of the ruling class (Bottomore, 2002). To act freely, we have to make explicit our implicit views about how society works and then engage in an 'ideology critique' that will bring us true freedom. Ideology critique involves making explicit the implicit ideologies that dominate our society, their power effects and the interests they serve. Ideology critique reveals how ideology has created our false consciousness. Only when we can choose to act outside of ideology is freedom possible. As MacIsaac (1996, p. 1) explained:

> Critical Theory agrees with . . . Karl Marx in that one must become conscious of how an ideology reflects and distorts reality and what factors influence and sustain the false consciousness which it represents, especially reified powers of domination.

Habermas sees both the process of ideology critique and the knowledge it produces (critical knowledge) as essential to social and political emancipation. Lovat and Smith (1998, p. 87) highlight the links in Habermas's thinking between emancipation and critical knowledge:

> For Habermas, it is only when we have reached . . . (critical knowledge) . . . that we are guaranteed true knowledge because true knowledge demands that we be free. . . . The so-called 'truths' which we receive . . . can be the result of ideology or 'unreflective action'.

The 'critical' in educational theory

Educational thinkers who draw on neo-critical theory (e.g. Freire, 1996; Carr and Kemmis, 1986; Giroux, 1991) are referred to as critical pedagogues. Paulo Freire (1921–1997), a Brazilian educational thinker, is considered to be 'the inaugural philosopher of critical pedagogy' (McLaren, 2000, p. 1) and he has had and continues to have a major influence on critical educational theory internationally. Critical pedagogues argue that adding 'critical' to reflection requires us to ideology critique educational goals, processes and effects, i.e. to examine the social and political factors that produce dominant educational knowledge and practices, and to ask whose interests they serve. In this way, critical pedagogues believe, ideology critique can create emancipatory and just transformations in social relationships and practices (McLaren, 2000; Darder, 2001).

Inserting the 'critical' into reflective practice therefore links education to a wider social project to create social justice and emancipation, and freedom for all through education. This project

is based on the belief that inequalities and oppressive power relations exist in contemporary educational institutions (Burbules and
Berk, 1999). The concern shifts from just changing an individual
educator's practices to changing individual educators in ways
that challenge oppressive and inequitable power relations in the
classroom. In recent years several early childhood scholars (e.g.
Alloway, 1995; Boldt, 1997; Campbell and Smith, 2001; Mac
Naughton, 2000; Cannella and Grieshaber, 2001) have shown how
early childhood institutions embody and express oppressive and
inequitable power relationships. For example, Cannella (1997)
pointed to how discourses of childhood and child-centred pedagogy limit how we understand younger people, and produce adults
as more privileged and powerful than children. In addition, the
institutions formed for children segregate them from being active
participants in the wider civil society and the professionalisation
of teaching disciplines, and regulate women and children 'within
a continuing patriarchal system' (Cannella, 1997, p. 159).

Early childhood educators could use critical reflection and ideology critique to reveal how these embedded forms of injustice and
inequality appear in the everyday world of teaching and learning;
and then use this knowledge to transform them. In this book,
several of the contributors have chosen to use collaborative action
research informed by critical reflection as a strategic change-
oriented process to support their efforts to transform injustices and
inequalities in their everyday world of teaching and learning.

Collaborative action research and activism

Action research comes in many shapes and sizes (see Grundy, 1982;
Swepson, 1995). However, all forms of action research have in
common a planned process of change in which individual and/or
collective reflection and action inform each other. Generally, action
researchers choose a target for change, review how they currently
act and understand their change target, reflect on what specifically
needs to change and why, plan a change, implement it and then
evaluate it. This process is then repeated in a never-ending cycle of
'reflect, plan, do, reflect, and so on' that is often referred to as the
action research cycle (Carr and Kemmis, 1986). Action researchers
aim to systematically and strategically implement changes based on
their current – but ever-changing – knowledge of what needs
to be done and why.

Collaborative action researchers work with others to implement systematic and strategic changes geared towards educational emancipation and social justice. Some collaborative action researchers (e.g. McTaggart, etc.) use Habermas's views on the power of ideology critique to link reflection and action (Mac Naughton, 1996). They use critical reflection to be sceptical of claims to knowledge and inquisitive about the relationships between social contexts, ideas, actions and effects in their lives (McTaggart, 1991).

Critical reflection that is informed by ideology critique can create social change because as we become inquisitive and sceptical about power in our daily lives, we weaken the dominant ideologies that hide power's support for the interests of those who oppress and discriminate. Once we understand how power operates through ideologies to oppress and constrain in our particular social and political contexts, we can begin to understand what needs to change and why. By asking questions such as, 'Who benefits from what I do and know?', 'How and why do they benefit?', 'Do I want this to continue?', 'Why do I take this particular action or use this particular knowledge?', or 'Whose interests does this knowledge or action support?', we can expand our choices about how to think and to act against knowledge and actions that oppress or discriminate.

In 2001, I facilitated a South Australian Department of Education and Children's Services action research project called the Critical Teaching Project (CTP) (refer to the Appendix for details). Several participants in that project talked about how these questions offered them new ways to see and understand their teaching that became linked to their choices to act for equity and justice:

> I really enjoyed the session on critical questions, which I think are really useful for me because I think I tend to work from a questioning basis. So actually looking at the sorts of actual questions, and listening, and trying to make connections with where people are at, and thinking about, 'What is the question that will help push this person's thinking that one step?', 'Who is advantaged and who is disadvantaged?'. You can use that question in lots of situations. For example, in assessment, 'Who's advantaged by this way of doing assessment? Who's disadvantaged? What do you miss?'
> (Rana, district co-ordinator, Critical Teaching Project)

I keep looking back on the questions, 'Who is the child? What type of child do you want? Do you want a child that just goes with the flow, or do you want a thinker and a doer and a changer?' That was in the first session and I'd never thought of that before. Then that made me start thinking 'Well, am I a person who just goes with the flow or am I a doer and a thinker and a changer?' That was a hard one. That also reflected in my question too. When I was looking at the word 'curriculum', I was thinking 'Well, who do we do curriculum for and how do we do them and what do we want as the end result?' It got all the way up to the Department and Government policies and reflecting upon what type of children and adults they want produced at the end? And that's scary as well because that's a really big picture, rather than just focusing on one little centre and one little curriculum.

(Heather, teacher, Critical Teaching Project)

Sarah, who was also a CTP participant, described as follows the difference between collaborative action research informed by these concerns, and individual action research that is not:

You know I've done a lot of action research projects, action research was more about the physical [things], the observation. This one felt to me that it was more about what was happening in my head, about my thinking, about words, about my values and ideals. I remember [in a previous action research project] we did something on who played where and we did things like, 'Oh, the alarm's gone off, 10 o'clock. Quick, who's in the home corner; Mary Jo and Sue. Oh, 11 o'clock, who's in the home corner, Wendy. Oh, no boys in the home corner. Gender bias right?' But with [critical teaching] I wouldn't have actually done the research like that, because I probably could have done that in 5 seconds. I would have gone into thinking about, 'Why are they playing there? Is it something that we are "setting up", the values we're giving', i.e. more about the thinking rather than, 'Let's put the dolls in the sandpit and see what happens'.

(Sarah, preschool director, Critical
Teaching Project)

As educators reflect critically on their work, they are able to share and debate their choices and make strategic, politically informed decisions as action researchers about how to act:

> Critical teaching is about not just reflecting on practice, but through that, uncovering what it reveals about what we think and believe and an opportunity to find out exactly who we are doing things for and why, and to change and adapt if you need. I know as an educator one of the main things I've got out of it is changing, and being able to change and knowing that you can. Whereas before, I went along thinking I had to do things because that's the way they were done, that's the way I was taught at Uni. And so you do them. But now I know that I can question, and I can change if I need to – it's quite a liberating experience. If anything, I've felt that I've actually got more out of my work because I'm looking at what I'm doing, the way I'm doing it. I've changed some things, and I've felt that I've got a tool that I can use with other things – even things outside of work, outside of education.
>
> (Shona, teacher, Critical Teaching Project)

Many contributors to this book have added poststructuralist perspectives on the politics of knowledge to the mix of collaborative action research and the 'critical' to open up a wider toolbox of possibilities to support transformational educational work for equity and social justice. Sally Barnes is one such early childhood educator. In what follows, Sally describes how her increasing reliance on poststructuralist ideas in her daily work led her to reject developmental truths of the child as the foundation of her teaching and to substitute issues of power, desire and privilege. Sally's reflection on her journey shows you this chapter's themes and issues through the eyes of an early childhood educator who sees the politics of knowledge as deeply embedded in her work.

SALLY BARNES
Unsettling and resettling pedagogical knowledges

My name is Sally Barnes and for the past fourteen years, I have been a kindergarten teacher and Director. In South Australia, that means that I work with four-year-old children in the year prior to their entry to formal schooling. This is a non-compulsory year of education that is provided by the state government. Nonetheless, more than 94 per cent of South Australian families ensure that their children attend a kindergarten when they are four years old.

I have always believed that a good teacher is a thinking teacher and in the past five years, I have become increasingly interested in the theories and beliefs embodied in action research. However, while my academic understanding of research has grown during this period, I believe that action research began to shape my teaching practice when I was a third-year undergraduate teaching student.

During the three years in which I trained as a teacher, I was influenced and taught by strong and confident women. Many of these women had worked in diverse communities within and outside of Australia and the knowledge that they had gained shaped the way that they taught a new generation of early childhood educators (of which I was one). Although the course that I studied was embedded in the traditional early childhood discourses of developmental psychology, I was also encouraged to think and question before making an assumption that I could know or understand someone else's child. As a third-year student, the idea that teachers need to think and question was crystallised for me when I was placed (for practicum) in a dynamic and exciting kindergarten with two highly reflective and critical early childhood educators. These women thought deeply about what they did and why they did it and did not hesitate to disagree with one another on the interpretation of a particular situation. They were passionate about equity and they questioned many of the taken-for-granted assumptions of kindergartens at that time (for example, Christmas as a 'universal' celebration). I guess that because their approach to teaching resonated my own political commitments to education, teaching from a critical perspective seemed the 'normal' thing to do.

Critical reflection means thinking deeply about what I do and why I do that. Once, I heard Lillian Katz (1996) say that teaching was about decision-making, but the skill was not in making a decision or in knowing why you had made that decision. Rather, the skill lay in knowing why you did not choose one of the 100 other ways in which it was possible to act. Critical reflection also means that I have to pay attention to who is advantaged and who is disadvantaged by my decisions. I think that this is the most difficult part because often I can make a decision on how to act and then in the same action advantage one and disadvantage another, when both were disadvantaged to begin with. I'm also conscious that what I may see or understand as disadvantage may be totally different for another person with another point of view. Critical reflection means that there are always far more questions than there are answers, that I cannot pretend that there are no power effects related to my actions as a teacher and that there are rarely, if ever, simple solutions to the incredibly complex task of teaching.

As a practising teacher, I was not drawn initially to poststructuralist theories or theorists, but the publication in the US of the Anti-Bias Curriculum in 1989 (coincidentally my first year of teaching) put me on a path toward post-structuralism. The Anti-Bias Curriculum introduced me to two key concepts – power and privilege. As I began to explore the issues that had been raised (initially race, then gender, sexuality, ethnicity and ability) I moved quickly beyond notions of the 'innocent child'. When understanding the individual became problematic, I was drawn to those like Alloway (1995), Cannella (1997), Mac Naughton (1999) and Burman (1994) who were questioning the 'developmental child'. With a particular interest in curriculum, I was influenced highly by Silin (1995) – in particular, his plea for a curriculum that spoke to the things that mattered in children's lives.

As I have proceeded with my own research on early childhood curriculum, I find that I am drawn increasingly to the work of Foucault. Concepts such as 'disciplinary power', 'docile bodies' and 'power/ knowledge' are helping me to rethink the spaces that we call kindergarten and the things that happen within those spaces. Through the notion of 'subjugated knowledge', I am developing an understanding of how and why early childhood understandings about education, curriculum and the child have been marginalised within mainstream educational discourse. In addition, Foucault's belief in 'productive power' is deepening my understanding of the bureaucracy in which I work.

Recently I read Ebbeck's (2003) argument that poststructuralism is useless to teachers if its critique does not tell them how to act. I suggest that Ebbeck's argument can only be valid if we accept that teaching is simply a technical task, and that in undertaking this task, teachers can *know* how to act. My experiences tell me the opposite – that teaching is unknowable, complex, contextual, unpredictable, contradictory, messy and intensely personal.

Some colleagues argue that, by embracing poststructuralism, I work constantly in uncertainty, but I disagree. I think that I am certain about many things, which is why I am able to act. However, while poststructural ideas acknowledge the complexity of teaching and enable me to delve more deeply into this complexity, I find it increasingly difficult to work with those who do not have the same understandings or desire to understand teaching in the same way.

In the initial stages of looking at my work through a poststructural lens, I was shocked and unsettled by what I saw (although I realise now that what I was seeing was always there). However, the process of looking at the landscape completely transformed it and to return to that original landscape would now be both undesirable and virtually impossible (although I have tried because it really would make working with others easier at times). As a teacher, developmentalism no longer drives my understandings of the child or my curriculum decisions, nor does it justify practices that discriminate, disadvantage or exclude. Instead, I see the kindergarten as a space where power and desire are woven in a myriad of complex relationships between child and child and between child and adult. This interplay between power and desire (e.g. 'You can't be the princess because you're too fat') goes to the heart of our experiences as human beings and seems far more important than whether a child can hold a pencil with a mature pencil grip. Without hesitation, I would say that engaging with poststructural ideas has enriched my teaching. I am more articulate and confident about my work, my understandings of the child are deeper and richer and my educational work is more intellectually stimulating than I ever imagined it could be or would be.

Adding the poststructuralist to the 'critical' mix

> Poststructuralist theories have changed the ways I 'do' everyday practice because I contest, I theorise and I reflect critically.
> (Miriam Giugni, early childhood educator and research, New South Wales)

In recent years, poststructuralist perspectives on knowledge have introduced an additional political edge to the 'critical' in critical reflection (eg. Parker, 1997; Ryan and Ochsner, 1999; Campbell *et al.*, 2000; Mac Naughton, 2000; Cannella and Grieshaber, 2001).

Poststructuralist perspectives on knowledge push you to contest existing relations of power and to refuse to 'naturalize' them (Keohane, 2002). To naturalise something is to accept it as part of the existing order of things. Thus, to naturalise the existing relations of power is to assume that they are as they are because that's just how it is. The nature of society, the nature of us and the nature of the world just makes them the way they are. There is nothing to be done about them because that's just how it is. For instance, as Sally became poststructurally reflective, she changed her everyday practices as an early childhood educator because she learnt to contest the inequitable and to theorise new possibilities for justice in her work with children.

This book's interviews and vignettes (generated primarily in collaborative action research projects informed by poststructuralist ideas) will introduce you to educators like Sally who are 'becoming poststructurally reflective'. Each project is introduced in the Appendix. They are:

- Creating and sustaining critical reflection in early childhood services, funded by the Margaret Trembarth Early Childhood Research Scholarship, the Department of Education, Tasmania and the University of Melbourne. It is referred to as the Trembarth Project in what follows.
- Creating and sustaining critical reflection and innovation in working with children under three, funded by the University of Melbourne. It is referred to as the CRIUT project in what follows.
- Preschool Equity and Social Diversity project, funded by the University of Melbourne and the Australian Research Council. It is referred to as the PESD project in what follows.
- Critical teaching project funded by the Department of Education and Children's Services, South Australia. It is referred to as the CTP in what follows.
- Reconceptualising observation in early childhood services, doctoral research, Kylie Smith, the University of Melbourne.
- Secret children's business, honours research, Miriam Giugni, University of Western Sydney.
- Reconceptualising indigenous perspectives in the early childhood curriculum, doctoral research, Karina Davis, the University of Melbourne.
- The Curriculum Club, Sally Barnes and colleagues, South Australia.

For educators such as Sally, pedagogical decision-making is political. It is a complex ethical and political endeavour borne of critical reflection informed by poststructuralist ideas of knowledge, truth and power. This can produce questions, doubt and uncertainty for early childhood eductors as they question what they took to be their pedagogical truths and learn to see truth as provisional and politically biased.

The ethical complexity of pedagogical decision-making is recognised rarely in research on quality pedagogical decision-making (e.g. Wolf and Walsh, 1999). Instead, a technocractic view of teacher decision-making and innovation dominates a majority of mainstream early childhood literature (e.g. Bredekamp and Copple, 1997; Honig, 1996; Mooney *et al.*, 1997; Munton and Mooney, 1999). The educators featured in this book directly challenge this view. They are able and willing educators who drive pedagogical innovation through engaging deeply with the politics of their pedagogical knowledge and practices. The book puts a case that the capacity to see how existing relations of power are embedded in our actions and our understandings and a refusal to naturalise them is the hallmark of a quality teacher who seeks social justice and equity in and through their work with young children.

In the following chapters, you will glimpse the educational richness and transformational possibilities that come from engaging with the politics of knowledge. In these educators' stories, with their refusal to naturalise the existing power relations, I see intellectual richness, political commitments and possibilities for social justice. I also see the pedagogical doubts and refusals that accompany the process of becoming critically and poststructurally reflective. However, I see them as points of hope for greater equity in and through our relationships with each other and with children, and I see them spurring action to bring that hope to life.

For reflection

- What does critical reflection mean to you?
- In what ways do you try to critically reflect on your work?
- What do you enjoy (if anything) about critical reflection?
- What have been the most helpful resources/people to you in practising critical reflection?
- Why do you critically reflect?
- Do doubt and uncertainty 'strand' educators?

Chapter 1

Journeys to activism

Becoming poststructurally reflective about truth

> I continue to remind myself that it is with political intent that
> I should choose my truths.
>
> (Kylie Smith, early childhood educator
> and researcher, Victoria, Australia)

> 'Truth' is linked in circular relations with systems of power
> which produce and sustain it, and to effects of power which it
> induces and which extend it.
>
> (Foucault, 1980a, p. 133)

Beginning with truth

This chapter introduces you to a poststructuralist position on
the politics of truth and its implications for activist educators.
Specifically, it:

- surveys how and why critical and poststructuralist theorists see
  truth as political;
- identifies how scientific truths about children are used in early
  childhood studies to establish facts about children and to build
  pedagogies;
- shows how truths about children are linked to culturally biased
  norms about how children should be;
- explores how truths compete with each other for positions of
  privilege in fields of study, such as early childhood;
- discusses how the 'winning' truths in this competition form in
  Foucault's (1977a and b; 1980a) terms a 'regime of truth';
- uses the case of a developmental 'regime of truth' of the child
  to highlight why disrupting regimes of truth is important to
  work for social justice and equity in early childhood studies;

- argues that the politics of truth in early childhood studies brings with it unavoidable political choices for activist educators.

Foucault argued that truths naturalise existing relations of power (Keohane, 2002), so understanding how truths naturalise discrimination and oppression in, for instance, education helps us to combat them. To contest 'naturalised' relations of power, we must understand the politics of truth that infuse and produce categories of power. For instance, to contest naturalised gendered and 'racialised' relations of power, we must understand the politics of truth that infuse and produce the categories gender and 'race' in education. To do so means using truth in 'the deliberate practice of liberty' (Keohane, 2002, p. 74). For Kylie Smith, the politics of truth is key to her work as a poststructurally reflective activist in early childhood studies. Kylie's reminder to herself to choose her truths with 'political intent' comes from her deep understanding of truth as political and from her desire to make choices between the truths that honour her commitment to social justice and equity and those truths that do not. Kylie reached this understanding by becoming poststructurally reflective about truth and by grappling with how truths join together into discourses that produce what Foucault termed 'regimes of truth' (Foucault, 1980a) to produce relations of domination.

Foucault (1972) understood discourse as a body of thinking and writing that used shared language for talking about a topic, shared concepts for understanding it and shared methods for examining it. The shared language, concepts and methods are found in everyday practices and decision-making and in diverse institutional texts, practices and decision-making processes in different societies and different times. For instance, there is a body of thinking and writing about children and childhood that could be found in early childhood textbooks, observations taken by early childhood educators, lectures in university courses for early childhood educators, parent newsletters and early childhood conferences in different societies. These texts form a discourse on 'the child' when shared language, concepts and methods are apparent. For instance, if developmental language, concepts and methods for working with young children are apparent in these texts they could be said to form a developmental discourse of the child. Discourses systematise (Foucault, 1972) and frame how we think, feel, understand and practise in specific areas of our lives. A developmental discourse of the child systematises and frames how early childhood educators think, feel, understand and practise being, for instance, an early childhood educator in an early childhood programme.

To understand how discourses within a 'regime of truth' operate and systematise thought, I start by examining a poststructuralist politics of truth.

Critical theorists, 'posts' and the politics of truth

Critical theorists and poststructuralists are concerned with the role of the politics of truth in the 'deliberate practice of liberty' (Keohane, 2002, p. 74), but each side understands the politics of truth differently. Critical theorists believed that we can achieve liberty by using ideology critique to strip truth of ideology. In contrast, the poststructuralists, following Foucault, believe that we can't strip truth of its politics, since truth itself is a political fiction. This challenges two beliefs about knowledge and truth that have dominated Western thinking, including critical theory, since the European Enlightenment (late 1600s to mid-1700s): the possibility of objective truth about the social world; and the possibility of establishing a single, universally applicable truth about social phenomena. Thus, the poststructuralists' position on truth unsettles the value of rational and scientific thinking in creating freedom and equality.

Challenging reason, challenging objectivity

Enlightenment thinkers believed that reason was the key to human progress and that reason, in the form of scientific thinking, could produce objective truths about our world. As Habermas explained, Enlightenment thinkers believed that in reason and in scientific thinking lay the promise of true happiness, freedom and equality:

> Enlightenment thinkers still had the extravagant expectation that the arts and sciences would promote not only the control of natural forces, but would also further understanding of the world and of the self, would promote moral progress, the justice of institutions, and even the happiness of human beings.
> (Habermas, 1981, p. 22)

Habermas challenged this view. He believed that we cannot find happiness, freedom and equality until we strip ideology from our thinking. True knowledge was 'critical' knowledge developed through ideology critique – thinking rationally about equality and class relationships to promote progress towards freedom for all. In contrast to the neo-critical theorists like Habermas, poststructuralists argue that is impossible to have 'undistorted' knowledge free from the interests of the people it serves. Knowledge can never be free from ideology, because all knowledge is biased, incomplete and linked to the interests of specific groups of people. Consequently, Danaher, Schirato and Webb (2000) argued that poststructuralist approaches to knowledge highlight the 'contradictions, unanswered questions and cultural prejudices' (p. 2) in all knowledge.

Poststructuralists also challenge the belief that reason (rationality) can fulfil the Enlightenment's hopes and promises. They see the production of knowledge as a politically competitive endeavour in which different truths about the world vie for power and for the status of being the 'real' (or universal) truth about it. Poststructuralists challenge the idea that we can ever find the real truth about anything in our social world. For instance, they challenge the idea that we can discover or learn the real truth about young children's development and about good (and bad) early childhood pedagogies. Instead, they believe that our knowledge about the world is inherently and inevitably contradictory, rather than rational; and, consequently, that many different truths about the world are possible. For instance, poststructuralists believe that our knowledge about childhood and about early childhood pedagogies is inherently and inevitably contradictory, rather than rational; and, consequently, that many different truths about the child and about early childhood pedagogy are possible. Thus, poststructuralists challenge the neo-critical theorists' view that ideology critique reveals the truth by removing ideology's distortions – indeed, they challenge the very belief in a universally applicable truth about 'freedom'.

Foucault had a particularly significant role in challenging the search for universal principles (structures) to explain social and cultural worlds. In the late 1970s and early 1980s, he elaborated the links between the production of knowledge, the exercise of power and its effects in everyday life. As Danaher, Schirato and Webb (2000, p. 29) suggest, Foucault argued that, 'knowledge and truth are tied up with the way in which power is exercised in our age ... and are themselves caught up in power struggles'. No knowledge is 'true' knowledge free from ideology. Instead, all knowledge is 'culturally prejudiced' (ibid., p. 2) and is, therefore partial, situated and local. It expresses particular knowledge/power relations and cannot be applicable universally. For instance, if developmental psychology is partial, situated, local knowledge then it cannot be applicable to all children at all times.

We shall now explore in greater detail these politics of 'truth' and their implications for equity and social justice using the case of 'developmental truth' in early childhood studies.

Exploring the politics of truth in early childhood studies: beginning with a truth

A truth is authoritative. Its authority lies in its claim to be a statement about a phenomenon that is factual and, therefore, correct. For instance, a developmental truth about a child is a statement about how a child develops that is factual and, therefore, correct. Western social sciences (including developmental psychology) build truths incrementally through rational scientific investigation; and Western social scientists in the capitalist, industrial countries (e.g. US, Canada, Australia and New Zealand, and Western Europe) that include a minority of the world's population often assert that their statements about people are factual and therefore correct. Their statements have the authority of science, but they ignore or silence Majority World views of the child, ('Majority World' refers to the poorer countries of the world, highlighting the fact that the majority of the world's people live in poverty (Ellwood, 1998).) As a reminder of this, I have chosen in what follows to refer to 'Minority World' truths of the child. When these truths combine to produce a shared language, concepts and methods of seeing the child that are circulated in different texts, institutions, daily practices and decisions, they form a developmental discourse of the 'Minority World' child.

'Minority World' truths of the child

Developmental psychology is a Minority World social science that seeks to build universally applicable, factual and correct statements about how children develop. Its truths include statements that explain and predict normal child development, enabling developmental psychologists to identify developmental delay and abnormal development. These include Gesell's (1952; Gesell and Ilg, 1943) work to develop detailed norms for physical development in the first six years of life; Piaget's efforts (Piaget 1944/1995a: Ginsberg and Opper, 1969) to detail universal stages of cognitive development; and the current work on diagnosing developmental disorders and predicting what improves development. Each and every approach 'normalises' the child. Consider how the following Minority World statements about children build implicit and explicit truths about the normal child:

> Pervasive Developmental Disorder – Not Otherwise Specified (or PDD-NOS) is a diagnosis given to young children who meet many, but not all, of the criteria for autism. Some of these children have fewer difficulties with socialisation, but many have quite severe language disorders.
>
> (Roe, 2001, p. 7)
>
> [*Normal children socialise and have ordered language.*]

> Children who attended any form of organized group preschool program when they were three and four years old showed improved cognitive development and academic achievement compared to children who did not.
>
> (McCain and Mustard, 1999, p. 47)
>
> [*Normal children are more likely to be normal if they attend preschool programmes.*]

> Children may delay, resist, or defy directions. Their behaviour is appropriate to their developmental level. They need to assert themselves to test how independent they really are.
>
> (Read, Gardner and Mahler, 1993, p. 176)
>
> [*Normal children obey directions and are independent.*]

Developmental truths express authoritative discourses (systematised ways of speaking, seeing, thinking, feeling and acting) about children and childhood. Within these discourses, the child is but an immature and irrational adult whose progress (development) towards adulthood and towards mature, rational adult behaviour follows predictable, pre-given pathways (see Woodrow and Brennan, 2001). By identifying and monitoring these pathways it is possible to identify which children are developing normally and which are developing abnormally. Expressions and reiterations of these ideas abound in early childhood professional texts (e.g. Henniger, 1999; Eaton and Shephard, 1998; Ebbeck, 1991).

Developmental truths of the child and early childhood pedagogies

In much of the Minority World (e.g. Europe, North America, Australia and New Zealand), developmental psychology's authority is established so well that it is a foundational discipline of study for early childhood educators and other professionals who work with young children, and it is a pervasive influence on early childhood pedagogies (Bloch, 1992; Burman, 1994; Walkerdine, 1994; Fleer, 1995; Cannella, 1997; Mac Naughton, 2001b; Ryan and Ochsner, 1999; Dahlberg, Moss and Pence, 1999). Its authority can also be seen in its power to make things happen. Developmental truths of the child have produced programmes for young children that can facilitate, enhance and maximise children's normal development (Woodrow and Brennan, 2001). For those children whose development does not fit the norm, special educational programmes, often referred to as early intervention programmes, are designed (Mallory and New 1994). Internationally, early childhood policy, curriculum and training documents demonstrate persistently this close link between developmental truths of the child and early childhood pedagogies (Alloway, 1997; Grieshaber, 1997; Dahlberg, Moss and Pence, 1999). For example, the US National Association for the Education of Young Children's (NAEYC's) guidelines on developmentally appropriate practice (DAP) for young children guide early childhood educators and providers on what are developmentally appropriate and developmentally inappropriate practices (Bredekamp, 1987; Bredekamp and Copple, 1997). There has been international debate over the developmental truths that underlie this document's view of appropriate and inappropriate practice (see Fleer, 1995; Mallory and New, 1994; Lubeck, 1998).

Bloch (1992) tracked the links in the US between scientific study of children's development and early childhood pedagogies. She showed that during the late nineteenth and twentieth centuries scientifically generated factual information about children's development was seen as hard data (accurate facts) from which to build early childhood pedagogies. Bloch argued that this desire for hard, scientific data about child development with which to generate early childhood pedagogies linked directly with the field's desire at the time to be seen as a profession:

> In an effort to be scientific and professional, early childhood education professors appeared to emulate child psychology, varying in the constancy of their attention to early childhood education and pedagogy issues.
>
> (Bloch, 1992, p. 15)

Early childhood educators' and researchers' century-old desire to legitimise their pedagogies using hard scientific data continues. The certainties of new truth about the child, such as those generated in the neurosciences (often referred to as 'the brain research') (see National Research Council and Institute of Medicine, 2000) are widely claimed to prove that the early years are significant to later development (see Thompson 2001; Fleer, 2002) in areas such as our capacity to learn, control emotions and be disease-free (McCain and Mustard, 1999; Thompson, 1999: National Research Council and Institute of Medicine, 2000). More specifically, neuroscience is seen as the source of hard, scientific data that supports the view that early experiences, including nutritional and emotional experiences, stimulate brain activity and influence how neural pathways develop. The ideas have considerable currency and authority. For example, they are being promulgated by key international institutions, such as the World Bank (e.g. World Bank Group, 2002), that link normal child development with effective economic development.

Exploring the politics of truth in early childhood studies: from truth to regimes of truth

> [The concept of a] ... regime of truth can be applied to discourses and practices that reveal sufficient regularity to enable their imminent naming.
>
> (Gore, 1993, p. 56)

Officially sanctioned truths about the social world are woven together into a discursive regime (or system of management) that governs what are held to be the normal and desirable ways to think, act and feel in institutions. They produce a 'general politics' (Foucault, 1980a, p. 131) or 'regime' (Foucault, 1980a) of truth in a society. From Foucault's and Gore's perspectives, developmental psychology discourses (e.g. about normal development, domains of development, developmental stages and causes of development) form a regime of truth that governs the normal and desirable ways to think, act and feel about young children in early childhood institutions (see Mac Naughton, 2000). For instance, if it is normal for young children to assert independence, then it is desirable for early childhood educators to allow them opportunities to be independent. To understand the implications of regimes of truth for activist educators, we will revisit and deepen our understandings of Foucault's ideas on power and knowledge, for within them, the significance of 'truth' for the practice of equity and social justice becomes apparent.

Seeing power as a battle for truth: social science and the 'normals'

Power is a central and recurring concept in Foucault's work (see for example, Foucault, 1977; 1980a; 1980b; 1980d; 1983; 1988). However, for Foucault, power is not a simple exercise of force in which one person, group or institution makes another do something – for instance, when a teacher makes a child sit quietly during a group discussion, or when one child makes another child cry. For Foucault, power is a relationship of struggle (Belsey, 2002) to dominate the meanings we give to our lives. It is a battle to authorise the truth, because truths don't just happen, they are *produced* in our struggle to decide the meanings of our actions, thoughts and feelings. More specifically, power is a relationship of struggle over how we use truths and build discourses about normality to produce and regulate ourselves (e.g. our bodies, desires and texts), our relationships and our institutions, especially our production of normality (Alvesson, 2002). This struggle plays out persistently in organised bodies of knowledge (e.g. discourses of social sciences such as psychology, medicine, psychiatry, sociology, pedagogy) as attempts to define, categorise, classify and organise people (Sarup, 1988); and to generate a set of truths about what is normal development and what is not, what is healthy and what is not, what is sane and what is not or what is normal learning and what is not. Contemporary child development journals present a plethora of ever more detailed maps of what normal child development looks like, but these norms are expressed most clearly in the scales used to measure child development. The Canadian government used such a scale to assess a child's social and emotional behaviour in their 'Understanding the Early Years Early Childhood Development in the Montreal study area' (KSI Research International, 2003). This study asked parents in Quebec to report on their children's behaviour in these domains of development using the following elements:

Positive social behaviour: children who exhibit higher levels of positive social behaviour are more likely to try to help and comfort others. They may offer to help pick up objects that another child has dropped or offer to help a child who is having trouble with a difficult task. They might also invite their peers to join in a game.

Indirect aggression: this element identifies children who, when mad at someone, try to get others to dislike that person; who become friends with another for revenge; who say bad things behind the other's back; who say to others, 'Let's not be with him/her'; or who tell secrets to a third person.

Hyperactivity: hyperactive children cannot sit still; are restless and are easily distracted; have trouble sticking to any activity; fidget; cannot concentrate, cannot pay attention for long; are impulsive; have difficulty waiting their turn in games or groups; or cannot settle to do anything for more than a few moments.

Emotional disorder/anxiety: this element identifies children who seem to be unhappy, sad, or depressed; are too fearful or anxious; are worried; cry a lot; tend to be rather solitary; appear miserable, unhappy, tearful, or distressed; are not as happy as other children; are nervous, high strung, or tense; or have trouble enjoying themselves.

Physical aggression and conduct disorder: these children get into many fights. When another child accidentally hurts them (by bumping into them, for example), they assume that the other child meant to do it, and then react with anger and fighting. Also included are children who kick, bite, or hit other children; who physically attack people; and who threaten people, are cruel, or bully others.

(KSI Research International, 2003)

These elements were then used to judge the Montreal sample of children's development against national norms. (Children in the Montreal sample showed higher levels of hyperactivity.)

Over time, the social sciences have categorised people by age, by sanity, by gender, by ability, by 'race', by ethnicity, etc. In each category, they have specified normal ways to look, feel and think about gender, 'race', class, ability, age and sexuality. Child development scales, such as the one used by the Canadian government, sanction truths about normal ways to comfort people, to relate to peers, to concentrate on tasks and to deal with disappointment, sadness, hurt and anger according to your age. Such categories and norms matter because we use them as we create and maintain social relationships (e.g. families and friendships) and as we organise institutions (e.g. early childhood services, schools, hospitals, clinics, etc.). For instance, insane people spend time in different types of institutions and have different types of relationships in those institutions from people who are considered 'sane'. Definitions of insanity may have shifted and changed over time but they still affect our relationships and influence if and how we are institutionalised. Truths of the normal child matter because we use them as we construct relationships and institutions around what we see as the normal child, the abnormal child and the delayed child. Developmental truths of the children matter because governments – such as the Canadian government – use them to inform their policies and to 'improve the community's capacity to use these data in monitoring child development and creating effective community-based responses' (KSI Research International, 2003 – Executive Summary: online).

Seeing power: from 'truth' to 'regimes of truth'

Truths about, for instance, normal gender development or normal sexuality resonate more powerfully in us and through us when they are institutionally produced and sanctioned. In Foucault's terms, institutionally produced and sanctioned truths govern and regulate us. They produce in us 'tact and discretion' (Foucault in Rabinow, 1984, p. 301) about where we talk, how we talk and what we talk. Each field of knowledge, such as early childhood studies, health care or social work, expands by developing officially sanctioned truths that govern normal and desirable ways to think, act and feel. For instance, the field of early childhood studies has grown through developing sets of truths about the normal and desirable way to be a child and an early childhood educator that are sanctioned and systematised by government, by professional associations and by the academy. The Canadian government's 'Understanding the Early Years' national initiative is a very clear example of the official sanction of developmental truths of the child. Teachers and parents were asked to assess children using a variety of child development measurement scales. If the scales produced results that matched what teachers in Montreal had learnt about normal development in their training, their influence in Montreal is likely to grow, as teachers use them to govern normal and desirable ways to think, act and feel as a child in their classrooms.

Foucault described a set of truths within a given field as a 'regime of truth' that generates an authoritative consensus about what needs to be done in that field and how it should be done (Gore, 1993). A regime of truth has both political and ethical substance: its truths establish power relations that imply ethical choices about how to engage with them. Feher described the relationship between the political and ethical substance of a regime of truth as follows:

> One the one hand, there is the political question of the body as a battlefield of power relations; on the other hand, there is the ethical question of one's relation to one's own body and how that relation shifts. So intertwined with the political regime of the body is an ethical typology defined by the relationship of people to their bodies.
>
> (Feher, 1987, p. 162)

The political substance of a regime of truth consists of the practices of power that bring a regime and its truth to life. The practices of power produce rules that organise and guide behaviour (Foucault, 1984b). In classroom research, Gore (1998) drew on Foucault to identify eight 'micropractices of power' that can be used to analyse how our daily practices bring to life a regime of truth in a specific field, such as early childhood studies. They are:

- *Surveillance*: being – or expecting to be – closely observed and supervised in and through reference to particular truths.

For instance, an early childhood educator who expects to be observed and supervised closely by people who believe that high quality early childhood pedagogy equals developmentally appropriate practice will act in developmentally appropriate ways. By doing so, they will bring to life a developmental regime of truth.

- *Normalisation*: comparing, invoking, requiring, or conforming to a standard that expresses particular truths about, for example, the developing child. For instance, observing children and comparing their behaviours with developmental norms.
- *Exclusion*: using truths to establish the boundaries of what is normal, to include or exclude particular ways of being as desirable or undesirable and, in doing so, to define pathology. For instance, an early childhood educator who uses developmental truths will see non-developmental truths as inappropriate or wrong and exclude them.
- *Classification*: using truths to differentiate between groups or individuals. For instance, an early childhood educator will talk about normal or delayed development by classifying children according to their stage of development.
- *Distribution*: using specific truths to decide how to arrange and rank people in space. For instance, an early childhood educator will use developmental truths to assign children to different groups according to their stage of development.
- *Individualisation*: using truths to separate individuals. For instance, an early childhood educator will use developmental truths to separate the individual children who are developing normally and those who are not.
- *Totalisation*: using truths to produce a will to conform. For instance, an early childhood educator will use developmental truths to guide decisions about what all children should be like or should do at a given point in their life – e.g. all children should leave kindergarten able to tie their shoelaces.
- *Regulation*: using specific truths to control ways of thinking and being by invoking rules and limiting behaviours – often through sanctions or rewards (Gore 1998). For instance, an early childhood educator will use developmental truths to decide the rules of behaviour that are appropriate for children at specific ages and stages of development, such as all children

eighteen months of age need to sleep during the day. A routine is then established to ensure this occurs.

The ethical substance of a regime of truth consists of the ways we use those micropractices of power to govern ourselves and discipline ourselves in and through the regime's truths. We will explore this idea further in a while, as it is important to the unmasking of regimes of truth.

In the next chapter, Miriam Giugni writes that she felt that she was a 'failed' early childhood educator during her first five years of work, because she couldn't do and think what was officially sanctioned in the field. In the following extract from Miriam's story, note how she engaged in surveillance of herself through the truths of child development and how she regulated her behaviour accordingly – she worked hard to 'do the right thing'. Through her self-surveillance and self-regulation, Miriam actively brought to life a regime of truth within which she saw herself as a 'failure':

> I spent the first five years in my identity as an early childhood educator failing at the 'regime of truth' (Foucault, 1977d) that early childhood asked me to deploy and produce. At the time I felt like I was never quite successful in everyday practice, particularly when other colleagues saw child development and assessment differently to me. So I thought I had to work harder at 'getting it right'
>
> (Miriam Giugni, early childhood educator
> and researcher, New South Wales)

Knowledge that is sanctioned institutionally can produce such an authoritative consensus about how to 'be' that it is difficult to imagine how to think, act and feel in any other way. In Foucault's terms, the officially sanctioned 'truths' discipline and regulate us, i.e. they govern us. Foucault viewed truth as an 'art of government' (Gore, 1993, p. 56); and he understood 'government' in the broad sense of 'techniques and procedures for directing human behaviour' (Foucault in translation in Rabinow, 1994/ 1997, p. 81). Officially sanctioned 'truths' are woven together into a regime (or system of management) that governs what is held to be normal and desirable ways to think, act and feel in, for instance, early childhood institutions. In doing so, they produce a system of morality (its ethical substance) with the authority of the 'official sanctioned', to say what is and isn't a 'good', 'true' way to be, for instance, an early childhood professional (Mac Naughton, 2000). During her first years as an early childhood educator, Miriam experienced the weight of the regime's morality (or ethical substance).

It has been argued that in the early childhood field, child development knowledge has become a regime of truth in that it regulates and governs what is the appropriate or correct way to understand and organise young children (e.g. Walkerdine, 1981; Cannella, 1997; Alloway, 1997; Mac Naughton, 2000). Early childhood educators certainly use developmental truths of the child to normalise, classify, distribute and regulate children. They place children of different ages and/or developmental abilities in different classrooms; they offer them different types of experiences based on perceived developmental needs; and they observe them closely, using developmental norms to categorise and judge their behaviour. Within this regime, developmentally appropriate education is the mark of a good early childhood educator and developmentally inappropriate education marks out a bad early childhood educator. This belief is sanctioned officially by peak early childhood associations (e.g. Association for Childhood Education International (ACEI), 2004; Early Childhood Australia – see www.aeca.org), by government regulations (e.g. Indiana Professional Licensing Board, US, 2004; National Child Care Accreditation Council, Australia, 2001), by early childhood centres (e.g. Oakton Early Childhood Education Centre, US, 2004) and by the academy (see National Research Council and Institute of Medicine, 2000). Specific illustrations include:

Professional association

> Child Development
> Teachers of young children should possess a broad synthesis of knowledge of child development principles derived from studying research in the social and behavioural sciences that influence learning (i.e., biology, physiology, psychology, sociology and anthropology). In addition to knowledge of child development theory and research, teachers should study children in a variety of situations to understand better the meaning

and degree of variation and exceptionality among individuals. Moreover, techniques for observing and recording such behaviour need to be developed in accordance with research and theory.

(ACEI (US). Online, accessed 2 February 2004)

Government regulations

Standard #2: Child Growth and Development
The early childhood education professional understands typical and atypical growth and development within each developmental domain and possesses the knowledge to facilitate healthy growth and development in all young children.

(Indiana Professional Licensing Board
'Licensing Rules for Early Childhood Teachers'
(US). Online, accessed 2 February 2004)

Early childhood centres

To work effectively with very young children, it is essential for teachers to have a strong knowledge of child development theory. A child-centered approach to teaching, coupled with an understanding of theory, is important to creating a nurturing classroom environment in which children can explore all kinds of ideas and relationships.

(Oakton Early Childhood Education Centre (US).
Online, accessed 2 February 2004)

Miriam encountered this developmental regime of truth during her first five years as an early childhood educator struggling to 'get it right'. Developmental truths became an instrument of discipline – indicating what is normal, abnormal or deviant development for children – by accumulating the institutional authority of the academy and the sanction of the scientific research community. They have effects on educators (e.g. Miriam) because of their long history as foundational knowledge in early childhood teacher training, with the result that they are rearticulated in conferences, professional journals and other publications and are used increasingly by policy makers. As developmental understandings of children circulate as a regime of truth in early childhood studies, they increase their ability to discipline and regulate those working within that regime. In the following extract, Miriam's readings of the child were reproduced and thus authorised by her colleague and by a tertiary educator:

> By chance, I came across some old observation notes I had kept for 13 years. Re-reading them, I was aghast at the way I described children's 'socially unacceptable behaviours' and planned for them to be 'dealt with'. As I read I noticed that another staff member and a tertiary educator, had both affirmed my claims to truth about behaviour and endorsed these notes. But, by re-reading with a poststructural eye, I now understand these claims to be methods of 'normalisation', 'insidious objectification' and perhaps white, middle class psychosocial expectations. I also fear that these claims have been attached to and have constructed this child for 13 years.
> (Miriam Giugni, early childhood educator and researcher, New South Wales)

Foucault believed that all modern societies and the institutions within them survive by requiring and produce 'regimes of truth' about how we should think, act and feel towards ourselves and others (Ball, 1990; Foucault, 1977a; Foucault, 1977b; McNay, 1992; Weedon, 1997). For instance, all early childhood institutions (e.g. early childhood services, departments of education or universities) survive by producing a set of officially sanctioned truths about how those working within them should think, act and feel towards children, parents and colleagues. The US-based ACEI *Position Paper on Preparation of Early Childhood Education Teachers* is a clear example of an officially sanctioned and widely held set of truths about how to think, act and feel towards children. It presents early childhood education as framed by developmentalism and driven by closely monitoring children to detect any developmental 'variation and exceptionality':

> Teachers of early childhood education should be well acquainted with the broad spectrum of child development, beginning with the prenatal period and including infant/ toddler, pre-primary, primary and elementary school age children. . . . In addition to knowledge of child development

theory and research, teachers should study children in a variety
of situations to understand better the meaning and degree of
variation and exceptionality among individuals. Moreover,
techniques for observing and recording such behaviour need
to be developed in accordance with research and theory.

(ACEI (US). Online, accessed 2 February 2004)

The ACEI statement is repeated throughout the international field
of early childhood studies. However, such officially sanctioned
truths – like all knowledge – represent not facts but ways of thinking that serve as social control (McNay, 1992; Haugaard, 2002).
Thus, despite the pervasiveness of developmentalism, Miriam chose
to act and think differently by placing herself outside of developmental discourses – a point to which we shall return in the next
chapter when we explore how to disrupt regimes of truth and their
effects. First, I will situate the tactics of disrupting a regime of truth
(e.g. developmentalism in early childhood) within the broader
project of being an activist educator.

Power effects: seeing the equity effects of developmentalism as a regime of truth

At the core of becoming an activist educator is identifying the
regimes of truth that govern us – the ideas that govern how we
think, act and feel as eductors – because it is within regimes of truth
that inequity is produced and reproduced. Regimes of truth have
equity effects because they themselves are the effects of domination
– the domination of one truth over another. As one truth accumu-
lates official sanction, others become marginalised and/or silenced.
Foucault (1977c) referred to this process as a 'violence' (p. 163) that
privileges homogeneity and marginalises diversity. For instance, in
early childhood studies, dominant developmental truths of the child
privilege Western/Minority views of the normal child and marginalise Majority views. Many developmental norms express specific
Western, white and middle-class values (Danesco, 1997; Harry,
1992; McDermott and Varenne, 1996). For example, age norms
associated with specific developmental domains (e.g. social, cognitive, emotional, physical domains of development) reflect white,
middle-class child-rearing norms, not universal norms of development (Valdivia, 1999; Lynch and Hanson, 1992; Mangione, 1995;
de Soto, 2001). Read, Gardner and Mahler (1993) believe that

'independence from adults' (a standard developmental measure) embodies a Western/Minority view that many families from 'non-Western'/Majority cultures would dispute. Early childhood educators who reproduce and act on these allegedly universal developmental norms are committing a form of violence that privileges cultural homogeneity and marginalises cultural diversity.

A consensus that rests on authoritative and officially sanctioned truth always silences alternative truths, marginalises diversity and reduces it to abnormality. Like all truths, developmental truths filter and order our knowledge towards an authoritative and officially sanctioned consensus on the 'normal developing child'. In early childhood education, 'developmental normality' has strategic implications for social justice and equity. 'Normality' – like inequality – is the production of inclusion and exclusion. Children from the Majority World, those living in poverty and those struggling to live among war and with violence, do not readily fit the norms of developmental psychology and are not considered in them. Their ways of being, thinking, acting and feeling are marginalised by those norms.

Developmental truths about the child operate as a regime of truth in different ways in different places, but many children and many adults have experienced their consistently inequitable and unjust effects (Smith, 2000; Campbell and Smith, 2001; Mac Naughton, 2000; Cannella, 1999; Johnson and Jipson, 2001; Viruru and Cannella, 2001). For instance, Valdivia (1999) discussed a series of developmental skills, the emergence of which depended on responses to tactile stimulation, verbal interaction, nonverbal interaction, and feeding routines. These ways of interacting are culturally specific and so it's no surprise that researchers in the US found different responses in children from African-American, Chinese-American, Mexican-American, Hopi and Navajo families. Nonetheless, when researchers found developmental differences in children from different cultures, they assessed them as developmental delay and placed these children in programmes to redress their delays. In this way, the researchers defined the 'normal' interactions of these children and their families as problematic and denied them the opportunity to grow 'normally' within their own culture. In this instance, developmentalism operated as a regime of truth in the early childhood field in the US to marginalise 'other' ways of being, thinking and interacting. This point is deeply important to those committed to a project of social justice, democracy and equity. It is in honouring our diversities of gender, 'race', class, ability, sexuality, age, geography and language that social justice, democracy and equity become possibilities (Derman-Sparks, 2001; de Soto, 2001; Rizvi, 1998; Hage, 1998; Gore, 1993).

Unmasking regimes of truth: knowing your will to truth

Valerie Walkerdine (1981; 1982) was one of the first feminist post-structuralist thinkers to scrutinise the developmental 'truths' of the child and their associated regimes through a Foucauldian lens. Walkerdine's extensive and highly influential body of work has examined relationships between truths about child development, pedagogical practices in the early years, and gender. Walkerdine (1990; 1992) argued that the child-centred pedagogies at the heart of early childhood education constitute its current 'regime of truth' and are based on an ethics of individualism and on the 'dream of democratic harmony' (Walkerdine, 1992, p. 22) based on fantasies rather than facts of who the child is (Walkerdine, 1988). She also argued that it 'permitted, sanctioned and celebrated' (Walkerdine and Lucey, 1989, p. 137) violence in boys as natural.

Walkerdine's work shattered my beliefs (built at that time over almost twenty years in the field) that child development offered a true and neutral picture of the child. Her work also shattered many of the truths of the child that were at the heart of my understanding of 'good' early childhood practice. In response, I struggled to produce new meanings of the child. This required me to unmask the uncritical truths about the child that had governed my work as an educator and to know my 'will to truth' – my desire to know the difference between truth and fiction and, in doing so, to establish particular truths as fact. The following questions took me to my will to truth as an early childhood educator and researcher:

- What is the right/true way to understand and practise my work as an early childhood educator?
- What are the origins of these understandings and practices?
- What is the authority of these understandings and practices?
- Who will sanction me if I don't conform to these understandings and practices?

As I sought to answer these questions, I sought 'the truth'. The answers to these questions expressed the discourses of pedagogy and of the child in particular regimes of truth that had governed my work as an early childhood educator; and they expressed the politics that wills these truths to exist. We are able to unmask the regimes of truth that govern us precisely because it is we who hold them in place and reproduce them – what Foucault referred to as a regime's 'ethical substance'. To unmask a regime of truth, we seek its ethical substance in ourselves by asking, 'How should we think, act and feel to be "true" to ourselves and to prove to ourselves and others that we are "true believers"?'. For instance, early childhood educators, like Miriam, wishing to unmask a regime of truth by seeking its ethical substance in themselves can ask, 'How should we think, act and feel to be "true" early childhood educators and to prove to ourselves and others that we are "true believers" in early childhood? What must I do to myself to hold developmentalism in place?'. Through these questions, we can analyse the micropractices of power in what Foucault referred to as the 'care of the self' (Foucault, 1984b) that is both produced by a regime of truth and helps to reproduce it. The care of the self is what we do to ourselves to be 'true' to our truths. Through care of the self, we remind ourselves how to act and think if we are normal (e.g. a normal early childhood educator). Care of the self is our choice – time and time again in our daily thoughts and actions – to act within the regime of truth that holds the care of the self in place.

Early childhood educators working within developmentalism as a regime of truth need to know how to think, act and feel as normal early childhood educators. This knowledge comes partly from their initial training and partly from the texts that are institutionally articulated and circulated by their colleagues, by professional associations, by governments and by the academy. They know that they must frame their work developmentally if they are to be considered a good/appropriate early childhood educator, but they *could* discard the truths of children development in favour of other truths through which to assess and work with young children. Foucault (1980a; 1988) argued that we can choose the truths we privilege and that the possibility of choice implies the possibility of disrupting a regime of truth and its inequitable effects. Choice enables us to choose our truths with political intent and with this choice comes the possibility to disrupt regimes of truth whose effects are inequitable and unjust. (That choice might be constrained in an institution where evidence of developmentalism is a requirement of teacher registration or of other formal accreditation processes. In these instances, choosing 'non-developmental' truths of the child could lose someone their job!)

Towards disruptions in the developmental regime of truth

Troubling the developmental truths of the child has produced considerable debate within the early childhood field (see Lubeck, 1994; Lubeck, 1998) as people have assessed the political effects of the accuracy and authority of developmental knowledge of the child and of the pedagogies it engenders. As Sally Barnes wrote on p. 16 of the Introduction to this book, it can be 'shocking and unsettling', to look at children and work with children through a poststructuralist lens, because it highlights questions of power, privilege and desire and marginalises judgements about developmental norms.

Producing non-developmental, often politicised, truths of the child and childhood can be troubling for early childhood pedagogies that have for so long drawn heavily on depoliticised, developmental truths of the child. What can early childhood pedagogies draw on if not the developmental truths of the child? What can early childhood educators do when confronted with the idea that the accurate, factual and therefore correct understandings of the child produced in the discourses of developmental psychology are but one view of the child? What happens when they encounter the view that there are omissions and oppressions in developmental truths of the child? How is it helpful pedagogically to encounter such ideas? Can an early childhood educator act meaningfully without truth?

The next chapter explores the work of early childhood educators, including Miriam Giugni and Kylie Smith, who have chosen to disrupt the discourses within a developmental regime of truth that governs their work in early childhood. To take this choice, you need to understand your own will to truth – a powerful force that brings certainty (there is a right way to assess a child, to know a child and to be an early childhood educator) and acceptance by those in the field who hold the regime of truth in place. The desire for this acceptance can be powerful. Remember Miriam's hard work to 'get it right'. To understand our desire for certainty and acceptance and to understand the politics of the truths that we will into being is to begin to become poststructurally reflective. The following questions may help you to reflect on your own will to truth in early childhood studies and on how it supports or disrupts a developmental regime of truth in the field.

For reflection

- What do you see as the main ideas within a developmental approach to early childhood pedagogies?
- What is the right/true way to understand and practise your work in early childhood?
- What are the origins of these understandings and practices?
- What authority do these understandings and practices have?
- Who will sanction you if you don't conform to these understandings and practices?
- How much do your understandings of children rely on developmental truths?
- To what extent do your understandings of the child reinforce a developmental regime of truth in early childhood studies?

Chapter 2

Confronting a 'will to truth'

Troubling truths of the child poststructurally

> Searches for truth about something about the proper way, best, right way to do this. We are used to there being right and wrong answers. If we focus on truth or the right way we come to a dead end. Why do anything else? . . . We don't ask any more questions. We stop being seekers of new knowledge.
>
> (Minerva's journal, 11 April 2004, Trembarth Project)

> We escaped a domination of truth, not by playing a game that was a complete stranger to the game of truth, but in playing it otherwise or in playing another game, another set, other trumps in the game of truth.
>
> (Foucault, 1988, p. 15)

Disrupting regimes of truth: using power/ knowledge tactically

This chapter presents ways for activist early childhood educators to use knowledge tactically. Specifically it:

- outlines strategies for the practice of free speech (Foucault, 1989) and the deliberate practice for liberty (Keohane, 2002) to disrupt regimes of truth;
- focuses on how activist educators can seek multiple and marginalised truths of the child to guide actions for equity and social justice;
- shares vignettes from early childhood educators who are deliberately practising for liberty and disrupting the regimes of truth that govern their work by knowing their will to truth, reading for equity and acting for justice.

Foucault contended that our efforts to produce truths that govern us – our will to truth – produce inequalities because it is a violence to be 'enslaved' within a regime of truth:

> Knowledge does not slowly detach itself from its empirical roots, the initial needs from which it arose, to become pure speculation subject only to the demands of reason. . . . Rather, it creates a progressive enslavement to its instinctive violence.
> (Foucault, 1977d, p. 163)

However, we can contest enslavement. Recall how Sally and Miriam came to contest developmental discourses in their work with children. We can use knowledge tactically (Foucault, 1980a, p. 83) by destabilising officially sanctioned truth with its inequitable effects. Tactical use of knowledge produces spaces for progressive social and political change in our truths and, thus, in our relationships; and it can shift knowledge/power relationships embedded in specific regimes of truth.

Tactical use of knowledge in early childhood studies produces spaces for 'other' ways of knowing and acting with children for social justice. Consider Walkerdine's (1989) tactical use of knowledge in the statement below to produce spaces for feminist ways of knowing about how mathematical meanings are produced in the lives of young UK preschool girls. She analysed mathematical meanings in transcripts of mother–daughter interactions in the home. As a feminist she focused on how these meanings expressed gender relations and she argued that the girls' meanings for mathematical concepts such as 'more' and 'less' were intimately linked to 'the specificities of women's domestic labour' (p. 54) not their natural cognitive development:

> Mathematical meanings – indeed, the development of language and word meanings in gender – cannot be separated from the practices in which the girls grow up. . . . All meanings at home are produced in aspects of domestic regulation. For example, taking the pair *more/less*, all instances of *more* in these transcripts come from the mother's regulation of the child's consumption of commodities and are therefore part of her regulation of the domestic economy. . . . In every case initiated by the child, she either wants more precious commodities on which the mother sees it as her duty to limit consumption,

or does not want to finish food that the mother sees it as her
duty to make her eat.

(Walkerdine, 1989, p. 53)

Foucault did not regard power and its effects as always negative and he didn't believe that power relations of domination are
fixed for all time. Power can be productive – producing forms of
resistance to domination – and it can be positive in producing new
truths that make relations of domination and inequity reversible
(Alvesson, 2002). Walkerdine's production of feminist knowledge
about the mathematical 'development' of preschool girls is an
example of this. Power's productivity implies the possibility of
freedom and so we can, for example, contest inequity in our daily
work with children. As Foucault explained:

> if there are relations of power in every social field, this is
> because there is freedom everywhere. Of course, states of dom-
> ination do indeed exist. In a great many cases, power relations
> are fixed in such a way that they are perpetually asymmetrical
> and allow an extremely limed margin of freedom.
>
> (Foucault in Rabinow, 1997, p. 293)

Walkerdine (e.g. 1981; 1982; 1989) has persistently contested ways
of seeing children that ignore the impact of living in patriarchal
cultures on young children, inspiring others to do the same (e.g
Mac Naughton, 2000; Campbell and Smith, 2001).

Invoking the tactics of 'parrhesia': deliberating practising for liberty

Foucault said that 'Power is everywhere; not because it embraces
everything, but because it comes from everywhere' (Foucault cited
in Dreyfus and Rabinow, 1982, p. 231), including from us. Thus,
to free ourselves from asymmetrical relations of power and their
effects within specific regimes of truth, we must tackle our will to
truth within the very regimes of truth that govern us – we must
play 'other trumps in the game of truth' (Foucault, 1988, p. 15).
We can do that by deploying what Foucault called 'parrhesia'
(Foucault 1989). Parrhesia is the practice of 'free speech' to
generate alternative truths that are generally 'denied official status'
(McNay, 1992, p. 136). To challenge our governance by a regime

of truth that delivers asymmetrical relations of power is a political act (Foucault 1989) requiring 'the deliberate practice of liberty' (Keohane, 2002, p. 74). For example, to resist the uneven power effects of domination by discourses of developmentalism or child-centred pedagogy acting as a regime of truth, early childhood educators must deliberately free themselves from it by disrupting it. Walkerdine's work in the 1980s offers feminist discourses that can support such efforts. More recently, other early childhood scholars, often referred to as reconceptualists, have expanded the possible discourses through which early childhood educators can act (see for example, Dahlberg, Moss and Pence, 1999; Cannella, 1997; Cannella and Grieshaber, 2001; de Soto, 2001; Mac Naughton, 2000; Kessler and Swadner, 1994; Jipson, 1998; Goldstein, 1997; Silin, 1995).

We can also find challenges to the officially sanctioned truths that hold in place uneven relations of power and their effects within specific regimes of truth in the often partially articulated truth of those marginalised by the official truths. These marginalised or subjugated truths are no more factual or genuine than officially sanctioned truths but they can be politically progressive, 'in so far as they hinder the domination of truth by those who govern' (McNay, 1992, p. 137). Examples of subjugated truths in early childhood include the unofficial 'truths' of parents or of children themselves. More especially, they would include the truths of parents who do not fit the norms of the dominant groups within society – for example, single parents, lesbian and gay parents, parents with a disability, indigenous parents, and so on. In the truths of these groups of parents come challenges to ideas such as:

• for healthy development a child needs two parents;
• to be normal a child needs a mother and a father;
• to learn effectively a child needs a 'normal' parent;
• to be successful a child needs to know 'Western' ways.

Reflect on how one single parent in an Australian early childhood service expressed her frustration in a research interview of how her family norms were marginalised in the daily 'truths' of a predominantly two-parent family service. Sally lived with regularly feeling that the newsletters, noticeboards and notes that represented much of staff communication marginalised her ways of understanding her child:

I'd like to communicate with them and I do when it comes to Father's Day and stuff like that when they are making cards. I make a point of saying you can make a card for Poppy, like a Poppy's Day card. I have had to force myself with things like that to protect him because I think you have to. Not that you can wrap them up in cotton wool but I don't think Ben needs to be making a Father's Day card when he doesn't have one. . . . I think they've done what they can but I think there are certain situations where perhaps they haven't taken that into account.

> (Sally, a single parent, interview transcript, Parent
> Research Project, Mac Naughton, 2004, p. 1)

In contrast, Jana, a mother living in a two-parent family, enjoyed how her culture was represented in the same centre. For her, the truths of the newsletters, notes and noticeboards worked because they matched her truths. Another mother (Debbie) in the same centre described it as a 'typical Aussie centre' that she chose because staff 'shared her values'. For Jana and Debbie, Father's Day is just a normal part of being a 'typical Aussie'. When there is an obvious and easy consensus between the views and values of staff and parents, the normal, formal written forms of communication can produce 'officially sanctioned' local truths about how to be a normal family (Mac Naughton, 2004). In these circumstances, speaking out to place your 'truths' on the agenda is tricky. How do you as a parent establish your truths as 'normal' when your language is different from that of the staff? How do you as a parent establish your truths as 'normal' when your cultural values are in the minority? Yet, Sally 'forced' herself to find ways to speak her truths. Speaking 'freely' is possible but difficult. It is especially difficult when your knowledge is persistently subjugated by those around you.

In early childhood texts and practices parental knowledge is persistently marginalised and subjugated by statements that officially sanction truths of the Minority World developing child (Hughes and Mac Naughton, 1999). Berger offers a simple illustration of this at work:

> The style recommended by parent educators is the authoritative, democratic style, because it is through that children raised

under that style will achieve, be dependable and responsible, and feel good about themselves.

(Berger, 1995, p. 83)

In these circumstances, finding spaces in which to 'speak your truth' as a parent can be a struggle. Yet, some parents, like Sally, do find that space. Activist early childhood educators face similar struggles and similar possibilities that you will read about later in this chapter.

Tactics and strategies for seeing 'regimes of truth' in daily life: deliberately practising for liberty

The deliberate practice of liberty attempts to disrupt regimes of truth in daily life to resist their power effects. This chapter offers two strategies with which educators can deliberately practise for liberty. They are ways to explore how to become a poststructurally reflective activist, not guides to a certain way. They offer inspiration and provocation, not certainty:

• seek multiple perspectives on your work that challenge your governance by truth and its associated regimes;
• overlay your own truths with marginalised meanings as a way to develop meanings and actions that are more equitable and just.

Being strategically multiple: challenging truth and its regimes

A regime of truth can 'eclipse' (Davies, 2001) meanings because a fact that is seen as indisputable closes off the possibility of other meanings. To seek meanings that are not always apparent immediately to us requires us to 'play' with what we know and with other ways to make sense of a particular situation. One way to do this is to deliberately seek alternative perspectives on a situation, especially from groups and individuals who experience discrimination and/or marginalisation in a specific regime of truth. Kylie felt that she had opened up new meanings for her observational work in early childhood by moving beyond her usual developmental truths about how to observe young children. To move beyond our usual perspectives we can ask:

- How do I currently understand this situation (or child, or pedagogy, etc.)?
- How else might I understand it?
- What other meanings can I overlay on the situation?

Minerva (an early childhood educator in the Trembarth Project) likened this process to 'creating different lenses to think about what you are doing, opening yourself up to multiple perspectives' (final session). Kylie Smith sought perspectives on observation of the child that were beyond her usual developmental meanings. Her search led her to Foucault:

> Using Foucault's challenging idea that 'observation is a disciplinary apparatus' I began to question my right to know the child. There are thoughts, questions, dreams and imaginings that I keep within myself that I have never shared with even the closest people in my life. Yet, I turn my gaze on the child expecting to know all of her. These reflections upon Foucault's arguments about the place of observation in institutional life produced the moment in which I began to consider how I might see my practice differently by turning the gaze within to illuminate my subjectivities and their effects for children, parents and colleagues.
>
> (Kylie Smith, early childhood educator
> and researcher, Victoria)

To understand our lives with children from multiple perspectives expresses and honours the view that truths are partial and, therefore, biased; and that they can be involved in asymmetrical power relations (e.g. between genders, between 'racial' groups, between people of differing abilities or people of different ages). By using multiple perspectives, we can produce new truths of resistance or 'other trumps in the truth game' (Foucault, 1988) to those that dominate a particular social field, such as early childhood studies.

Again, Walkerdine (1989) is useful. She highlights how, if we can multiply perspectives on the child using feminisms, we learn the partialities and biases of the Minority World discourses of the naturally developing child. She uses feminisms to point to the naturally developing child as a fiction painting pictures instead of socially produced gendered 'children' whose class and 'race' is ever present in what develops. The child is multiple, with many stories to tell of herselves. For Walkerdine (1989) there is not a single developmental story of the universal child to be told. Furthermore, Walkerdine (1989) argued that girls will always struggle to achieve 'normal development' in patriarchical discourses which establish the masculine as the standard of what is normal. In particular, they establish rationality (reason) and reasoners as normal and silence its role in power. She writes:

> Nothing could seem more apolitical, more cognitive, perhaps more boring, than analysing children's learning of mathematics. But, as I have tried to demonstrate, the calculating mind and the calculating child are as one. It is my contention that the modern order is founded upon a rational, scientific, and calculating form of government. . . . Mathematics became reason.
>
> (Walkerdine, 1989, pp. 211–212)

Children have to struggle to become reasonable and it is not accomplished without the play of power between children and between children and adults (including teachers). In recent years many early childhood researchers (e.g. Cannella and Grieshaber, 2001; Mac Naughton, 2000; Campbell and Smith, 2001) have built detailed pictures of what this play of power looks like and does in specific early childhood centres at specific points in time. Their work highlights the 'ever-presence' of gender in young children's lives and its effects on how children build relationships, rituals and routines in the everyday life of early childhood services.

Being tactically marginal: provisionally reading for equity

To 'read for equity' is to explicitly insert issues of power and inequity into our understandings of the world. There are many strategies and tactics through which to read for equity but most insist that we ask these questions of what we feel, know, do and say:

- Whose voice is heard in my work? Whose is silenced?
- To what extent do multiple readings highlight the voices of those groups who have traditionally been marginalised?

- How have gender, 'race', ethnicity, ability, sexuality and class influenced my actions and understandings, and those of other people?
- Who has exercised power in my work and how? How has their exercise of power affected them and affected others? Do those effects reinforce or challenge the unjust power dynamics in this regime of truth?

These questions offer provisional grounds for 'playing other trumps' (Foucault, 1988, p. 15) in a regime of truth, thus disrupting it. Provisional grounds are 'claims, beliefs and theories that we find useful and reliable, but whose obsolescence we can always imagine . . . opening up new paths of discourse, and revealing new ways to deal with situations, and new connections with the world' (Heldke, 1989 cited in Berge and Ve, 2000, p. 34).

Activist educators wishing to deliberately practise for liberty can use these questions to constantly challenge a 'will to truth' and push them towards a more deeply and critically informed 'will to know differently, will to know justly', as I have called it.

Deliberately practising for liberty: beyond a will to truth

In what follows, early childhood educators and researchers Miriam Giugni, Kylie Smith and Sheralyn Campbell share their deliberate practices of liberty. Each uses poststructuralist insights on the politics of truth to be 'strategically multiple and tactically marginal' as she strives to move beyond a will to (developmental) truth by:

- seeking critically informed *knowledge* about children, rather than *the truth* about them;
- embracing the possibility of many ways forward in their efforts to live more justly with children;
- seeking meanings not always apparent to them;
- beginning again always in deeper and often more hopeful ways.

However, Miriam, Kylie and Sheralyn use different tactics to be 'strategically multiple and tactically marginal'. This reminds us there is not a simple recipe with which to produce an activist educator who is poststructurally reflective. Instead, there are possibilities to be shared and explored that might inspire and sustain others who are becoming poststructurally reflective.

I start with Miriam, who has recently finished an honours thesis in which she researched with young children what she called 'secret children's business'. She writes here as a researcher and as the director of a children's service in New South Wales, Australia about the place of being poststructurally reflective in her daily life with children and in her ways of understanding herself as an early childhood educator. Miriam describes the struggles she experienced while working as an early childhood educator within a developmental regime of truth, the doubts it produced within her and her move to become poststructurally reflective. She shares the questions she crafted to help her to see and to know beyond the politics of truth in her everyday work. Such questions are tactics with which to contest the uneven power relations embedded in seeking a singular truth of the child.

MIRIAM GIUGNI
'I contest, I theorise and I critically reflect': becoming poststructurally reflective about truth

To articulate how critical reflection is integral to my daily living as the director of a children's centre and an early childhood researcher, I first delve into my past to describe a less critical and non-reflective me. I realise that I spent the first five years in my identity as an early childhood educator failing at the 'regime of truth' (Foucault, 1977d) that early childhood asked me to deploy and produce. At the time I felt like I was never quite successful in everyday practice, particularly when other colleagues saw child development and assessment differently to me. I thought I had to work harder at 'getting it right'. In hindsight, and with a more critical way of reading the situation, it seems that by not 'getting it right' I was in search of t he 'truth'.

Consequently, through this 'truth of the teacher regime' I sought 'the truth of the child'. I found neither. Ten years on I can reflect on why this was and what it means for me in my current position. I can describe the usefulness of critical reflection and come to know myself in vastly different ways. What happened was that I began to ask myself different questions.

In the early stages of working in early childhood education, I asked questions like, 'What am I doing wrong?' and 'Why is this not working?' and 'What is wrong with all these children?' and 'Why don't we fit?'. These kinds of questions led me to doubt my ability as an educator.

My questioning changed when I was introduced as a mature age student to the work of Foucault among a series of other postmodern, poststructural and critical theorists. My first response after an encounter with Foucault's *Discipline and Punish* (1977d) was that all this time I had been discursively practised/locked into a regime of truth about my identity: an early childhood educator with a singular pursuit to seek and produce the truth of the child through the truth of herself. I colluded with the power networks created by these truths, positioning children and adults in their 'rightful' places. Foucault (1977d) inspired me to think differently about this situation:

> to substitute for a power that is manifest through the brilliance of those who exercise is a power that insidiously objectifies those on whom it is applied; to form a body of knowledge about these individuals, rather than to deploy the ostentatious signs of sovereignty.
>
> (p. 220)

I began to explore what power and control were in the context of early childhood education. I began to investigate how power works in the institutions that we call early childhood settings and I was astonished. I realised I needed to look back and rethink, retheorise and contest my past *knowing* of what it meant to be an early childhood educator. I found myself developing several ways to look back and rethink. For example, by chance I came across some old observation notes I had kept for 13 years. Rereading them, I was aghast at the way I described children's 'socially unacceptable behaviours' and planned for them to be 'dealt with'. As I read, I saw that another staff member and a tertiary educator had each affirmed my claims to truth about behaviour and had endorsed these notes. But, by rereading with a poststructural eye, I now understand these claims to be methods of 'normalisation', 'insidious objectification' and perhaps white, middle-class psychosocial expectations. I also fear that these claims that have been attached to and have constructed this child for 13 years.

Importantly, I realised that I needed to differentiate between 'reflection' and 'critical reflection'. Reflection is a process of looking back, looking at the past and questioning. This process enables one to grow from past experience and think differently about things. Critical reflection, however, is the process of looking back and questioning with an agenda. My agenda is one of social justice and equity. So, critical reflection is taking risks to look back with a critical and political eye. The critical reflector risks fragmenting her *knowings* of what she does and who she *'is'*. She risks the perils of uncertainty. But, she has the capacity to establish her position in things and consider what that means in the context and lives of those she works and lives with. Here, poststructural discourses can help to start the process of questioning the operations of power.

Poststructural discourses enable the thinker to be creative and flexible in how meanings are constructed rather than constrained by the fixed and static meanings some psychological ways of thinking would have her believe. So, a poststructural thinker might choose to ask questions about how people access and exercise power in relationships, demonstrating the ways people are both emancipated and marginalised.

Subjectivity, agency, discourse, choice, normalisation and power become key terms for making sense of what was, and how things could look different in future experiences. Of course, things can only be different if one is willing to take action. Critical reflection means taking risks and taking action in the everyday experience of living and working in early childhood. Critical reflection means taking the risk of questioning yourself and your practices in fair and equitable ways.

There is not one particular way to 'critically reflect', rather one has the capacity to develop many or their own ways to explore risk taking and questioning. What follows is a series of questions I find useful to critique my own practice and consider my actions in relation to others. I do not use these questions in a particular order, but remind myself to delve in deeply to examine possibilities for my future decision-making and practice. Sometimes my choices are contradictory, reflecting the fluid nature of time and circumstance. Additionally, this is one of the ways I 'theorise' my practice in order to make links between the theories that have inspired me to critically reflect and the practice that drives me to strive for equity and social justice. Here I choose a poststructural discourse because it allows me to formulate questions for critical reflection. I rethink in a way that enables me to consider the unstable manner in which I seek understanding. Rather than seeking the truth about a situation, I recognise the contextual specificity of it and imagine how it could 'look different' in a different time and place. To do this I use a process in which the crux is questioning:

- Think of an interaction, event or episode you experienced.
- Describe what happened – this might include the context, space, time, people, conversations, nonverbal interactions, etc. It is important to specify what you did in the situation.
- How did you feel?
- How did you come to be in this situation?
- What kind of choices did you make to be in this situation?
- Why did you choose to act or approach the situation in this way?
- What do you think this might mean for you, others and the context?
- What if you were to explain this situation to someone else (colleague, parent, child, manager, bus driver, etc.)? What would you say? How would you say it?
- Why did you choose these ways? What might that mean for you, them, others and the context? – Use many perspectives and theories, and consider the ways some perspectives and choices can privilege, silence and marginalise social and cultural groups.
- Who is it about? What is it for?
- Share these reflections with others.
- Develop some possibilities for social action!

Questioning is one of many possibilities that I engage to be critically reflective. My strategies have changed across time and they will continue to change as I come to embrace the complexity of uncertainty. It can be described as one tool from a theoretical toolbox full of useful bits and pieces. By using a process of questioning informed by poststructuralist thinking I have come to see my daily experiences in a critical way. Reflection is ongoing. I have the opportunity to remove myself from the limiting right/wrong binary I had known so well in the early parts of my work as an early childhood educator and continue to create opportunities for myself to question my 'self' and my work for social justice and equity. Therefore, poststructuralist theories have changed the ways I 'do' every day practice because I contest, I theorise and I critically reflect.

The poststructuralist mix in Miriam's journey

Miriam's vignette shows how exposing prejudice in our truths is profoundly entwined with her 'agenda of social justice' and with questioning what you have believed is certain, sound and right. It also shows the need to keep asking questions that push you to see cultural prejudices in your professional and personal ways of being and thinking. For Miriam, those questions persistently push her to contest whatever she considers certain and to 'embrace' complexity and it puts her 'agenda of social justice' to the fore in her work with young children. An 'agenda of social justice' often leads early childhood educators towards Foucault and the feminist poststructural. In his work, as Miriam has found, there are many 'tools' for deepening our understandings of what needs to change to achieve greater social justice and equity in work with young children.

Using Foucault to generate a will to know differently

Different people meet Foucault's ideas in different ways. Miriam met them through her honours research. I first stumbled across his work in the early 1990s when I was struggling to rethink approaches to gender equity in early childhood studies (Mac Naughton, 2000). Frustrated and disappointed by the tokenistic, simplistic and ineffective approaches to gender equity in early childhood studies, I turned to feminist theory for insight and support. In the work of feminist poststructuralist theorists such as Valerie Walkerdine and Bronwyn Davies (e.g. Davies, 1989) I met Foucault. Davies and Walkerdine drew on his radical and unsettling ideas about the relationships between individuals and their social world and about knowledge and power to rethink why centring radical practices for gender equity in early childhood pedagogies had remained so elusive for so long.

Below, Kylie Smith tells of reading Foucault's 1977 text, *Discipline and punish: the birth of the prison*. At that time, Kylie was the director of an Australian long day care centre where she was also engaged in collaborative action research initiated by an early childhood researcher, Sheralyn Campbell. Kylie and her fellow teacher–researchers were exploring how social justice was enacted and experienced by children, staff and parents, and how to create classrooms that are socially just for all. At the same time, Kylie had begun a second critical collaborative action research project in the centre that focused on how child observation practices might be reconceptualised in their broader interests of working towards a more socially just community.

As discussed in the Introduction, theoretically and politically informed critical reflection drives change in collaborative action research. For Kylie and Sheralyn, this meant searching for theory that could support their efforts to reflect critically on social justice in their classrooms. While their search for texts to support their critical reflection began with early childhood texts on anti-bias curriculum (e.g. Derman-Sparks and the Anti-Bias Task Force, 1989: Dau, 2001) and on equity in early childhood (e.g. Davies, 1989), it also led them to the texts of Michel Foucault and to questions about the extent to which the knowledge that informed their efforts at social justice were 'culturally prejudiced'. The texts of Foucault and other poststructuralist theorists supported Kylie, drove her as a teacher–researcher to challenge her truths about how she observed children and drove her ever more surely towards a will to know differently how to observe children. It pushed her to understand her own subjective investments in the truth of the child. She confronted her own subjectivity (ways of seeing herself) and how it was formed in and through her position as a white, middle-class, female, Anglo-Australian.

In confronting the intersection of her own desires with truths about the knowable child, Kylie exposed what Foucault referred to as the ethical substance of the regime of truth, which holds truths in place because we invest in them emotionally and politically. Kylie now has an emotional and political investment in multiple truths and in negotiating the uncertainties that accompany a move beyond a will to a developmental truth of the child. Her care of the self has shifted. Kylie uses questions as tactics in this work. She shares the questions she uses to know children differently rather than to discover truths about them. Like Miriam, Kylie's questions are tactics through which to contest the uneven power relations embedded in seeking a singular truth of the child.

KYLIE SMITH
'I began to question my right to know the child': becoming poststructurally reflective about truths

Critical reflection for me is about being ever vigilant in examining and making visible my subjectivities. I bring my unconscious to the conscious by asking myself why I speak and act in the ways I do and what are the effects for the people around me. The question I continually ask myself is: 'In whose best interests am I speaking and acting?' Critical reflection for me is about taking time to locate and recognise the political, social and historical construction of the discourses I circulate. It is about recognising the discourses that I am drawn to and what is seductive about those discourses while I resist or silence other discourses.

Some of the key postmodern/poststructural theorists that have supported my processes of critical reflection include Michel Foucault (1984a and b, 1982, 1980a and b, 1978, 1977d, 1972), Jennifer Gore (1998, 1995, 1993), Gilles Deleuze (1986) and Bronwyn Davies (2000, 1994, 1993, 1989). These writers provide me with information about the construction of knowledge and with understandings of where that knowledge came from and why. This helps me to explore the political, historical and social construction of knowledge. Each time I read or reread a piece of theory it supports my critical reflection on whose knowledge informs my work and what the effects of different ways of understanding my work are for parents, colleagues and children. Further, their theory draws me to consider the effects of my practice for children and parents and It supports me to be political by exploring these effects in order to critique my taken-for-granted truths that emerge within my taken-for-granted practices.

Reading Foucault's (1977d) *Discipline and punish: the birth of the prison* was a catalytic moment in bringing the critical to my reflection. This was when I began to weave theory and practice together to illuminate my subjectivities and consider what I bring to bear on my gaze of others. Further, this was the point when I began to turn my gaze on myself when I began to read how Foucault (1977d) believed that institutions used observation as a disciplinary apparatus:

> A central point would be both the source of light illuminating everything, and a locus of convergence for everything that must

be known: a perfect eye that nothing would escape and a centre
towards which all gazes would be turned.

(Foucault, 1977d, p. 73)

After reading this, I thought about how I turn my gaze on the child
and how I turn parents' and other early childhood professionals'
gazes on the child. I reflected that I do this so I can use their comments and my own knowledge to *know* the child. Using Foucault's
challenging idea that 'observation is a disciplinary apparatus' I began
to question my right to know the child. There are thoughts, questions, dreams and imaginings that I keep within myself that I have
never shared with even the closest people in my life. Yet, I turn my
gaze on the child expecting to know all of her. These reflections
upon Foucault's arguments about the place of observation in institutional life produced the moment in which I began to consider how
I might see my practice differently by turning the gaze within to
illuminate my subjectivities and their effects for children, parents and
colleagues.

I can pinpoint the exact moment I began to critically reflect drawing on these ideas. I was outside in the playground at the centre
talking with Sheralyn Campbell (a colleague and author in this book)
about the collection of data in her action research project that
day. I had begun to read *Discipline and punish: the birth of the prison*
and was engaging with Foucault's idea of 'regimes of truth'. I had
begun to consider how he used concepts of normalisation, surveillance, regulation, categorisation and totalisation to explore how
truth and power operate to limit and to govern what we do and say
and I began to see links between these ideas and the practices of
observing children. While talking about these ideas and the issues
emerging from the classroom with Sheralyn I suddenly thought that
if the 'regimes of truth' circulate within my observation of the child
what does that mean for parents?

I began to critically reflect on what observation means for parents
by asking the question: 'How do I normalise and regulate parents'
knowledge and practice?' Using this question I began to cast a shadow
over my relationships with parents. I had always believed that I
worked collaboratively with parents yet I now began to recognise
that I worked collaboratively with the parents who fit in my white
middle-class understandings of the world. For the parents that didn't
fit into this framework I worked to teach them what they needed

to do to support their child, the teacher and the service so that they were seen as 'the good parent' rather than the 'difficult parent' or the 'parent who didn't understand'.

Poststructuralist theories have provided space for me to consider multiple truths. Poststructuralist theories provide information to explore how power, knowledge and truth circulate in and through discourses. The effects of using these theorists to critically reflect are many. My relationships with parents and children have changed. I have less certainty that there is one correct answer. I no longer enter into a conversation with answers. In the past my answers meant that I often did not listen to the knowledge of others, rather I made a statement and the effects were that parents and children were silent. Conversations now are about dialogue between people. This community of dialogue is about sharing questions, ideas, dilemmas and desires. It is about sharing my critical reflections with others and collaborating with them for change. Action research is the vehicle I have used to drive this process.

One of the key effects for me of using poststructuralist theories is that it has created uncertainty for me as a teacher as I no longer have the truth about the child, the parent or my own pedagogy. The effects of this uncertainty shift everyday. On some days, the uncertainty is liberating as I can explore possibilities rather than conform to the image of the good teacher. I learn about ideas, interests, beliefs and lived experiences that I knew nothing about. Uncertainty can provide space to move through different terrains where more equitable moments might be available to others. For example, when I'm working in the classroom and I observe the children interacting I no longer presume to know exactly what is occurring within the group. Instead, I ask questions rather than make knowing assessments and statements about the children and their actions. Some of these questions include:

- What are the discourses in circulation?
- How are children's actions and language politically and strategically being used within the group?
- What are the storylines?
- Who is included and excluded in the play and what are the effects for social justice?
- How do my subjectivities reflect how I see the play and intervene?

These questions become a basis for reflection and for action in my ongoing work as an action researcher. However, some days uncertainty is problematic and frustrating. These days are usually the days when I'm feeling tired. I juggle the role of director, teacher and researcher. Working in a long day care service means that I work an eight-hour day and that I have little opportunity or space to stop and think. Jeni, my co-worker, and I usually only get space to ponder dilemmas and share ideas while we are in the middle of teaching. On these days I try to create space to write in my journal where I critically reflect. I can usually bring focus to my thoughts by pondering the idea that there are always multiple truths but what are my bottom lines. My bottom lines are that people are treated in safe and respectful ways and that social justice is the platform from where I begin. For instance, I will never support guns and war. My subjectivities as a white working-class catholic female means that unconsciously I do not always speak and act in fair and equitable ways but it is in these moments that I must make these contradictions visible. Further, I need to make space for different knowledge to be heard and privileged. When I critically reflect on this my uncertainties change because I am always certain that while there are multiple truths I will always attempt to create space for the truths that support social justice. I continue to remind myself that it is with political intent that I should choose my truths.

There is danger in uncertainty because I feel like my uncertainties often marginalise me and place me on the fringes of being a good teacher. However, Foucault (1983) said: 'If everything is dangerous then we always have something to do' (pp. 231–232) and this certainly reflects my work. I have been at my current job for eight years. Previously I would have chosen to move jobs every three years. In my current position the uncertainty, shifting, changing and contingent nature of my teaching due to critical reflection combined with action research means that every day is exciting and challenging. Every day there are new dangers and possibilities to explore, challenge and discuss – so every day there is something to do.

The poststructural mix in Kylie's journey

In her daily work, Kylie engages deeply with the poststructuralist interest in the politics of knowledge, as is evident in the questions that guide her critical reflection. Her questions focus on inclusion and exclusion, the implications for children of her ways of seeing (her subjectivities) and how children and adults exercise and experience power. Kylie's questions intentionally focus on power, reflecting her concern to understand who is silenced and who is marginalised by her accounts of her teaching. Her poststructuralist scepticism about the possibility of finding one true account of her work with young children leads her to embrace the idea that there are multiple truths about parents, about children and childhood and about her work as an early childhood educator to be explored and discovered. Her critical reflection aims not just to explore and discover these truths, but also to privilege truths that produce greater social justice. However, as Kylie discovered, becoming a poststructurally reflective educator and resisting the will to a developmental truth of the child is not without its uncertainties, dangers and challenges.

The dangers of confronting a will to truth

Kylie is not alone in finding moving beyond a will to truth dangerous and challenging. In the CRIUT project (refer to the Appendix) moving beyond singular truths about pedagogies produced shifting ideas about teaching rather than a secure basis for action. What was once certain became not just uncertain but potentially dangerous. Lily was in both the CRIUT and Trembarth Project. The dangers of becoming poststructurally reflective surfaced for her in a conversation with a colleague with whom her relationship had become difficult. Lily had been reflecting critically on what lay behind their difficulties and had shared her thoughts with her colleague. This led to the following exchange:

> She actually said reflective practice could be quite dangerous. I actually spoke to her about that again. She said yeah, I think you're right, it can be quite dangerous. But I think we were thinking of it in different ways. She was thinking of it as being that you can reflect too much. You have to worry about it over the weekend and things like that, and people haven't got time, and that type of thing. I think it can be quite dangerous because I think it actually disrupts practices that people believe. Okay, we've been taught this in college or at university and by critically reflecting it actually disrupts that knowledge. It then takes away the safety net that I actually

think is a good thing, even though it's difficult at times – there's tears and there's tantrums, and there's laughter and good things. I actually think taking away that safety net and saying, okay, what we did when we were at college or in the years following, was it okay, and that's what we were taught, not that it was wrong, but there are different ways, and change keeps occurring and we need to move with those changes, to actually make changes, in the early childhood field.

(Lily, early childhood educator, journal
entry, CRIUT project)

Lily and her colleague understood the demands and dangers of critical reflection about truth differently. It demands the very conditions that many early childhood services lack, i.e. sufficient time for dialogue that allows a climate of reflection to grow. It also brought with it new questions and its effects were destablising. So why would early childhood educators engage in it? What can and does it offer early childhood educators who seek to innovate and to develop their understandings and practices? How can educators who chose to become critically reflective withstand its demands and dangers?

Miriam, Kylie and Lily have each provided some answers. They wrote about engaging with the uncertainties associated with becoming poststructurally reflective and how this motivated them to change their practices. To change the effects of a regime of truth in practice requires an ethical commitment to change that they each demonstrated. In making this commitment, they began to unsettle the ethical substance of the regime that governs their understanding of what is a 'good' early childhood educator. Each has begun to carve out a position that says that a good early childhood educator is a non-developmental educator committed to a will to know differently and justly. Each is disrupting a 'local' regime of truth.

Disrupting local regimes of truth: practising the will to know differently and justly

Gore (1993) suggested that seeing local pedagogical practices as regimes of truth can help us to 'do' pedagogies differently and to strengthen the wider project of social transformation through education. Seeing local pedagogical practices as regimes of truth can generate closer, more finely grained understandings of how power relations, especially asymmetric ones, are brought into being in educators' daily lives. This, in turn, highlights possibilities of using eight of Gore's (1995) nine 'micropractices of power' (Surveillance, Normalisation, Exclusion, Classification, Distribution, Individualisation, Totalisation, Regulation) to shift and remake pedagogical practices.

In the following story, Sheralyn Campbell recounts how she used Gore's nine 'micropractices of power' to analyse her daily pedagogical practices as regimes of truth as she searched for a will to know differently and justly; to find new meanings that might disrupt the gendered and racialised relations of power/knowledge and its regimes of truth in her early childhood community, Sheralyn overlaid questions of equity and power on her own meanings. In this way, she sought to practise the will to know differently and justly. In this work she met 'puddles' and 'snakes'.

SHERALYN CAMPBELL
Practising liberty: risky business in the bush – watch out for puddles/watch out for snakes

It has been just over 12 months since I made the post-doctoral decision to go back into a community-based childcare centre. Let me take you into the world that I am part of – our centre is a 39-place centre located in a beautiful Australian coastal town. Our resident population is around 3,500 and this swells in school holidays, particularly at Christmas. However, even then it is not unusual to find yourself on a beach with only one or two other families in sight. We are surrounded by national parks and the wildlife that goes with them, including snakes. There is a supermarket, a licensed grocer, a fishing tackle shop, two bakeries, two hardware stores, a $2 shop, a newsagent, two pubs and several small clothing shops.

Just over three years ago, the town was decimated by several global and national events in close succession. These events resulted in the closure or reduction of three major industries: fishing, woodchipping and dairy farming. In almost every family, someone lost their job or went from full-time to part-time work, and part-time and seasonal work continues to be many families' main source of employment. In some families, a person works three part-time jobs to earn a full-time income. The people who visit the town in school holidays see a beautiful and idyllic retreat. Their vision excludes the underlying issues that the community faces on a daily basis. These issues include:

- high unemployment;
- drug and alcohol abuse;
- poverty;
- drought;
- diverse family configurations and relationships (and disputes) that come with a small community that has had children, married and intermarried over generations, and the struggles associated with teen pregnancy, single parenthood and family violence;
- reconciliation with our indigenous community;
- lack of local support services, people and agencies that can provide specialised medical and social support.

Ninety-five families use our centre each week. They use us because their children know each other, are related to each other, live next door to each other and we provide a place where they can play and learn with each other.

When I came to this community I resolved to keep a journal and I began by saying what I wanted my work to bring:

> *Equity:* that children, families and co-teachers will share my passion for fairness; and experience a respect for each other that opens doors for and to everyone.
> *Community:* a place where people are joined in pleasure, sorrow and life.
> *Peace:* a time and space for pleasure in life, reflection and wisdom.

I also wrote (almost as a prayer!): give me strength to remember my questions:

- How is power able to operate?
- What sources of knowledge does it authorise and what sources are authorised by how it operates?
- Who benefits and who is silent or marginalised by these relations of power/knowledge?
- How can I effect change and what are the implications of change for each person in my community?

So this is where I am. I spend three days a week as the preschool teacher in the 3–5 years room, and two days a week as the Centre Director, undertaking management and administration. I am reminded constantly that the community that I am part of has a different social and cultural history to my own and to that of the other communities of which I've been part.

My first real sense of the risks associated with being in the bush (an Australian term for a rural forested area) came from the children. I was walking along the bush track next to the centre's lower playground on my way to meet the preschool teacher at the local preschool for the first time. Two boys saw me through the fence and called out, 'Hey Sheralyn. Where you goin'?'. I said, 'Down to the preschool. I'll be back soon'. They called out 'OK'. Then one offered me some helpful advice, 'But watch out for puddles'. It had rained a little in the first week that I had started. I smiled to myself as I waved and walked on. I knew about puddles. Then the other boy called out, 'Yeah – and watch out for snakes!' The smile left my face, I hastened my stride and made lots of noise as I walked. Snakes were a whole different ball game.

The boys' advice has stayed with me and I think about it as I negotiate the risky business of doing equity work with children, staff and families in our community. I think of puddles as a sign that we have had some rain. While they are familiar they are also uncertain terrain. They sit on the surface of the ground and can be deceptive – shallow or deep. They reappear unexpectedly. I think of snakes that lie quietly – openly sunning themselves or hiding in the long grass that surrounds us. They are dangerous and can be aggressive when threatened, or timid and slither away.

Puddles and snakes represent different risks. Let me share one of the puddles in the classroom. In my first three months at the centre, I observed two four-year-old girls using racist remarks to exclude another girl from their play. These three girls had lived all their lives together in the community and I thought they knew each other well and cared about each other.

Ruby and Imogen were seated on a seesaw. As I watched I could see the pleasure that they were sharing. Their laughter echoed across the playground as they went up and down. Alissa (a Koori girl) joined them and sat in the middle seat. Ruby immediately shouted at her to 'Get Off!'. Alissa sat very still, but made no move to leave. Ruby and Imogen used a range of threats and strategies to force her to leave. These included:

- hitting her;
- yelling at her to get off;
- calling her a 'dickhead';
- telling her that they would get Ruby's brothers to bash her up when they arrived for after-school care.

Despite my interventions on Alissa's behalf Ruby and Imogen continued to threaten Alissa. Their final words were 'We don't like people with black skin'. I challenged them, telling them that their words and actions were unacceptable. Ruby and Imogen ran off leaving Alissa sitting alone on the seesaw. The two girls were able to 'resist' me, and continue to exclude Alissa.

Ruby's and Imogen's open invocation of racist and sexist relations of power/knowledge to abuse Alissa gave my teaching a clear focus over the next few weeks. The seesaw 'puddle' sat there as evidence of past and present racisms in our community, but was also a 'challenge'. I decided to revisit the incident through a persona doll story. Suzannah is my persona doll. She has 'Asian' features and a calliper on her leg. I retold the seesaw incident placing Suzannah in Alissa's shoes. I used the two girls' dialogue as accurately as I could remember it. The girls involved reacted differently to the story. One smiled at me in what seemed like recognition and pleasure; one refused to make eye contact; and Alissa sat quietly, looking at Suzannah intently.

I had put my foot in this puddle and it splashed all of us. I'll share the children's reactions in a moment. However, first one of the really interesting outcomes of this story was the effect on my co-teachers. They were confronted, affronted and disturbed by the story. Their comments included:

- 'I haven't heard children say those things before.'
- 'Everybody plays together here – race has never been an issue.'
- 'I'm not racist, but Sheralyn there are some Kooris that are a real problem in this town. You have to grow up here to know.'
- 'Did you see Ruby's face when she smiled? I can't believe it!'

Underneath these comments was an implication that I had somehow 'caused' the issue by making it visible. I knew that I was on risky ground – the newcomer bringing trouble to previously happy relationships. I retold the story several times to different groups of children. Each time, the non-Koori children said things like:

- 'It doesn't matter what colour your skin is.'
- 'You could tell a teacher.'
- 'You could just say, "Everyone can play".'

The Koori children sat quietly. I hear echoes of the story that Glenda tells in Chapter 4 about a child of Asian appearance who blushed as she chose the 'white' persona doll when asked which most looked like her. The non-Koori children knew that there were other discourses that reconfigured and displaced racist relations of power-knowledge. The Koori children made no comment.

These contradictions between what had happened and what the children said in group-time inspired me to begin a conversation with my co-teachers about what we could do. One of the ways I began this conversation was to admit to my co-teachers that I really didn't know how to respond to the whiteness that dominated our classroom. I took a step that my co-teachers felt was risky – I spoke with a Koori mother about how little I knew about what to do and asked how she thought I could begin to teach with her children. My co-teachers were concerned that I would, for example:

- create more problems between children;
- create divisions between families;
- make an issue of something that was about one or two children who were always going to have 'racist' attitudes because their families would feel the same way.

I have to acknowledge the courage and support of my co-teachers who allowed me to take the risky step, despite their misgivings. When I spoke to the Koori mother, her first reaction was to look closely at me. She was quiet for some time. Then she offered to give me some books to read and asked if she could come into the centre one day and spend some time with the children and teachers. She began coming on Fridays and spending some time with us. There seemed to be a shift in our relationship with this Koori family and, slowly, with others. The children seemed to look forward to her visits and they talked about the things that she did with them – things that were different to what I did. However, I also know that although the racist puddle dried up a little with her help at that time, it refills with the next rain. It is still there in all of us.

Watching out for snakes in our classroom

Snakes are the dangers that lie quietly in the open or hidden away, obscured from view. They wait to bite or to slither out of reach. I also see snakes all the time in my teaching. For example Tina and Luke were blowing bubbles together. For some time, I had been hoping that Tina would step outside of her good-girl persona and take a 'ride on the wild side' with other children. I had been structuring some opportunities for Tina to 'break out' with boys like Luke. Luke was able at times to cross traditional gender boundaries, so he offered interesting ways to entice Tina to explore other girlhoods.

It was late afternoon. Luke and Tina giggled loudly as the bubbles overflowed their containers and threatened to drip onto the floor. Suddenly, they were surrounded by a small group of children who variously watched and gave advice. Later, I used eight of Jennifer Gore's nine micropractices of power (surveillance, normalisation, exclusion, classification, distribution, individualisation, totalisation and regulation) to reflect on what had happened. It was then that I met the snake that lay in the grass:

George: Sheralyn, the bubbles are spilling on the floor! *[Surveillance, Regulation]*

Annie (scornfully): Tina, that's not how you do it. You have to keep them in. *[Normalisation]*

Sabina: You've got paint on your dress now [Tina]! *[Regulation, Exclusion]*

Pauli: Lukie you made a big one. It's the biggest one I ever seen. It's bigger than the whole world. [Laughing] It's gunna go right over the edge. [Tina] You can't do big ones like Lukie. Yours are just on the table. *[Classification, Distribution]*

Finally, I intervened. I had been helping children who had rested to tie their shoe laces, but I glanced up in response to George's warning to me that the bubbles were spilling onto the floor. I reminded Tina to keep the bubbles on the table and told her that if they went on the floor they would make it slippery *[Surveillance, Regulation]*. George's warning to me had made me first 'watch' Tina and then 'tell' her that she needed to do 'it' differently *[Surveillance, Regulation]*. I saw that Annie and Sabina had used words that told Tina she was getting 'it' wrong and then instructed her how to get 'it' right *[Normalisation]*. I saw that Pauli made sure that Tina and

Luke knew there were important contrasts in how they were doing 'it' *[Individualisation]*. So what was the 'it' that they were doing? Was 'it' bubble blowing or something else?

Overlaying stories of gender, 'race' and class

My reflections on the snake at the bubble blowing became another example of how power regulates and sustains a regime of truth. In this incident, the regime of truth concerned a gendered social order; the seesaw story shows that there are racisms that are part of that social order. I overlaid my story of how children should use bubbles safely with the snakes that lie hidden in other stories. I asked how the categories that the children had used with Luke and Tina had invoked gender, 'race' and class. For example:

- Were there stories that could be told of classism when Annie said to Tina 'That's not how you do it. You have to keep them in'? Annie was proud of her knowledge of many Western commodities that Tina's family could not afford.
- Were there stories of sexism in Pauli's claims that Luke could blow bigger and better bubbles than Tina? Pauli rarely played with girls but often attempted to join play with other boys by demonstrating his physical prowess.
- Were there stories of gender and 'race' in Sabina's concern that Tina was getting paint on her dress? Sabina often noticed and commented on how girls with different cultural and social histories to her own dressed.

I returned to my reflections in a discussion with my co-teachers. Specifically, I asked why I had cautioned Tina and not Luke about getting the bubble mix onto the floor. I asked whether my concerns about 'safety' could be displaced and reconfigured with a discourse in which girls were feminised in ways that meant:

- they should play gently and be good (George and Sheralyn);
- they should perform their femininity in some ways and not others (Annie and Sabina);
- they were less skilful in the traditional domains of masculine play (Pauli);
- their relationships with boys were based on gendered differences (Pauli and Sheralyn).

The teachers and I then reflected on examples from our lives and from our teaching of a social order that depended on gendered differences like these. We found examples such as:

> Christine (teacher): I grew up on a farm. I remember when I was screen cementing and a customer mistook me for a man. He was horrified with my father when he realised I was a woman. It wasn't women's work.

> Allan (4): [Boys] can play with Power Rangers and shooting games on the computer. Boys can play with girls. You play nicely when you play with girls.

> Anna (4, white Australian) to a Koori girl: If you don't get off the seesaw, I'll get my brothers to bash you up when they come in.

The grass parted to show us the snake lying quietly and waiting to bite in our words and in our relationships in the classroom. In our classroom, gender *did* make differences and it mattered.

Returning to the children about the snake

We went back to the children and asked questions about the issues that our overlay of stories had provoked. These are two examples of how we did so:

EXAMPLE I

I read the story of *The Paper Bag Princess* to the children. In the story, a dragon destroys Princess Elizabeth's castle and abducts her prince. She outwits the dragon and rescues her prince dressed only in a paper bag. However, she chooses not to marry the prince when, despite her bravery, cleverness and resourcefulness in overcoming the dragon he rejects her because she no longer looks like a real princess.

When the children discussed the story with me, they drew on classist and sexist 'rules' about relationships between men and women. They said that Elizabeth was wrong to choose not to dress like a princess. They said she needed beautiful clothes and that Prince Ronald should have a real princess. They assured me that how you dress affects whether you're included in play.

EXAMPLE 2

I used my persona doll called Suzannah to recreate a story of one girl's exclusion from play. In the incident and the story, the boys excluded Suzannah from their play because she was a girl. The children said Suzannah could say she didn't like what had been said. They told me that Suzannah could ask a teacher for help. They told me that everyone could just be friends.

The children's responses showed me that they know there are different ways for men and women, boys and girls to work together in the social world. However, I believe that this shows how gender work is like the snake that can slither away timidly, only to reappear in the sun. The children tell me what they think I want them to say, or what they would like to say if it didn't mean being excluded too.

I believe that I'm finding in my community that the puddles and snakes that I see are produced in and by my own teaching within the early childhood classroom. I find it helpful to continue to engage with these issues by sharing with my co-teachers a process where we:

- seek the children's strategies and tactics with which to include and exclude each other from play;
- overlay these inclusions and exclusions with the different and political stories that they produce for us;
- reflect with each other about how we see these strategies, tactics and stories in our own lives and in our teaching;
- return to the children with questions about the stories that our conversations and shared reflections produce.

There are always puddles and snakes to watch out for and even when we recognise them, we must decide whether to stride ahead making lots of noise or to turn and walk away. For example, on one occasion when I told the story of The Paper Bag Princess, as I came to the last page, I saw that one of the fathers had come in and was listening to the story. I have a complex relationship with him, because he has had several conflicts with the centre. He also holds many traditional patriarchal beliefs and practices. On the last page of the story Elizabeth says:

'Ronald ... your clothes are really pretty and your hair is very neat. You look like a real prince but you are a toad.' They didn't get married after all.

(Munsch, 1980, p. x)

As this father stood there, I paused mentally before reading this line. I could see the risks involved in placing my gender politics in front of a person that I wanted to include in the service, even as I wanted to take the step into the dangerous long grass. Should I read it? If I return to the questions that I say drive my work I should ask:

- What relations of power/knowledge would the words in the story authorise?
- Who would benefit and who would be silent or marginalised by these relations of power/knowledge?
- How would my words effect change in my community and what are the implications of change for each person in my community?

I didn't make the decision. The pause enabled this father to greet his daughter, smile at me and say goodbye. The snake and the puddle were left to lie quietly this time.

Reflecting on this moment makes me return to an issue that a trusted friend and colleague has raised with me many times. We ask children to do things that we find difficult to do. This is one of my current challenges; how do I continue to take the dangerous decisions that can disrupt a regime of truth? What are the risks for teachers, for families and for children? These decisions are part of the puddles and snakes of teaching in a rural setting.

The poststructural mix in Sherlayn's story

Sheralyn's struggle to disrupt truths in her daily work with children and their families is risky and uncertain. She analyses the micropractices of power that hold a gendered and racialised regime of truth in place in her local community in order to play it 'otherwise' (Foucault, 1988, p. 15). But Sheralyn cannot guarantee the effects or outcomes of 'playing it otherwise' or in attempting to play 'another game' (ibid.). She can contest the uneven effects of racialised and gendered regimes of truth by doing the 'undefined work of freedom' (Foucault, 1984b, p. 46) and by 'participate(ing) in the formation of a political will' (Foucault, 1988, p. 265). Puddles and snakes will continue to challenge this work.

Beginning again: knowing your will to truth, reading for equity, acting for justice

Becoming poststructurally reflective disrupts truth and the certainties it brings and it often creates a journey, to borrow from Sheralyn, that is full of puddles and snakes. This can be unsettling and troubling. The field of early childhood studies has a strong need to have the right answer and a certain way forward. We all want to be certain that we are acting in the best way – from the early childhood student who says, 'Just tell me the answer' to the researcher who maps children's learning outcomes. Consider this statement by Professor Lillian Katz, a leading early childhood scholar in the US who is widely known internationally:

> It seems reasonable to assume that effective teaching requires us to act with *optimal* (rather than maximal or minimal) certainty in the rightness of our actions; that is, to act with optimal intentionality, clarity, and decisiveness. . . . The issues of teachers' confidence in their own curriculum and pedagogical decisions is a serious one, and has significant practical implications. . . . I continue to believe that in order to be effective, practitioners must have optimal confidence in their own actions and the underlying assumptions on which they are based.
>
> (Katz, 1996, p. 145)

In contrast, Miriam, Kylie, Lily and Sheralyn have learned to use the process of questioning truth and the doubt it brings to practise for liberty, as have many people who have become poststructurally reflective activists. However, Miriam, Kylie, Lilly and Sheralyn are not what Parker (1997) calls 'semantically and metaphysically stranded' teachers who are 'unable to give meaning' (p. 123) to their work. Instead, they are semantically and metaphysically engaged educators deepening the meaning in their work and their commitment to it. Becoming poststructurally reflective activists has enabled them to refuse to naturalise the existing relations of power – an ability that McLaren (1995) sees as a hallmark of a postmodern teacher.

Sheralyn risks a lot as she 'reads' for equity to disrupt uneven power relations, but reading for equity can also enable us to imagine a different world. Miriam, Kylie and Sheralyn have each come to know their will to truth in their work with young children and have tried in their practices for liberty to disrupt the regimes of truth that govern them and to uncover subjugated knowledges. Each has used particular strategies and tactics to disrupt the truth, but all have done so in the pursuit of equity and social justice. Poststructurally reflective activists like Miram, Kylie and Sheralyn seek ways of knowing that reorientate, refocus and re-energise their efforts to transform asymmetrical power relations in their daily lives. As Shana says:

> I try not to be fearful of the unknown. I keep thinking about the explorer who doesn't know what's ahead. The explorer is willing to fail but we'll never know if we don't try and even if we do fail, children will learn something surely through our efforts to make a difference.
>
> (Shana, early childhood teacher, research interview, CRIUT project)

Each of the following three chapters introduces specific tactics with which to expose how uneven power relations operate in specific regimes of truth through specific discourses. Those tactics are:

- deconstructing texts
- rhizoanalysis
- seeking the 'otherwise'.

For reflection

The following questions may help you to reflect on the poststructurally reflective will to know differently and justly in the early childhood studies and in the daily lives of children, colleagues and parents:

- What did the early childhood educators in this chapter believe were the benefits of being poststructurally reflective activists?
- What led them to poststructural reflection?
- What challenges did poststructural reflection pose for them?
- What possibilities did poststructural reflection offer them?
- What possibilities do you think that poststructural reflection offers you in your daily lives with children?

Chapter 3

Mapping classroom meanings

Engaging the tactics of deconstruction locally

> Well why would you want to look at the word curriculum? A curriculum is a curriculum why pull it apart? Just leave it alone and go with the flow.
>
> (Angela, early childhood educator, CTP project, research interview)

> Deconstruction: A postmodern approach to analysis, which aims to show the fragility of all positive statements. Deconstruction points at the contradictions and cracks in any text and the assumptions it builds upon.
>
> (Alvesson, 2002, p. 178)

Local truths: classroom meanings and classroom texts

This chapter presents tactics for deconstructing (pulling apart) specific texts within a regime of truth to reveal their 'contradictions and cracks' (Alvesson, 2002, p. 178) and their relationships with power. Specifically, it:

- provides an overview of the origins of deconstruction in the work of Jacques Derrida;
- shows how Derrida goes beyond structuralist understandings of language and meaning to challenge the politics of binary and hierarchical thinking in language;
- offers deconstructive tactics including binary analysis, erasure and metaphor that ethically and politically affirms and attends to the other (Derrida, 1992) using illustrations from within early childhood texts;

- shares vignettes of early childhood educators mapping and deconstructing classroom meanings as an effort to deliberately practise for liberty.

Texts convey meanings and they are widely understood to mean 'books' and 'writing'. We 'read' texts to understand and interpret their meaning. Cultural theorists have expanded the meaning of texts to cover anything in the social world that conveys meaning and can be 'read' (understood and interpreted) as if it were a book. They use 'text' to refer to speech (talk), writing (including books), images, audio-visual media (e.g. film, video, TV, DVD, cartoon), symbols (e.g. brand names), fashion, rituals, routines and bodies. For instance, cartoons convey meanings about 'good' and 'evil', 'right' and 'wrong', 'funny' and 'sad', etc. and it is possible for us to 'read' (understand and interpret) these meanings within a cartoon. Cultural theorists argue that all texts can be 'read' for meanings.

Classrooms are replete with texts and their meanings. From the books and posters used, the classroom routines in place, the daily talk of the classroom, through to the fashion worn by educators and children, meanings fill classroom life. Different forms of text enter classroom life in different ways but as they enter it they each contribute to the equity meanings that are produced, lived and experienced by children and adults in the early childhood classroom.

Curriculum texts include the books, songs or images used in daily work with children. They also include the curriculum documents or professional books and journals that educators use in constructing the early childhood curriculum. 'Teacher talk' includes the words and concepts that educators use to describe their work to others (for instance, parents or colleagues) or to interpret their interactions with children. Curriculum texts also include the 'scripts' that children use in their play with each other, the images they produce through their art, their daily 'talk' and the rituals and routines of classroom life. For instance, children's talk about gender, play using superhero scripts and rituals of celebrating birthdays are each classroom texts.

This chapter offers tactics for deconstructing (pulling apart meanings of) classroom texts, including everyday 'teacher talk' within a local regime of truth, that point to their cracks, contradictions and relationships with power. This work offers educators important insights into how equity 'works' in their classrooms. It can focus them on the daily 'play' of equity and the daily 'im/possibilities' of it in their specific classroom. In doing so, it deepens learning about the relationships between truth, power and language and it can be used tactically to disrupt uneven power relations at the local level of, for instance, the early childhood classroom, within specific regimes of truth. Understanding how a specific text (e.g. a birthday ritual or a moment of dramatic play) works to produce equity meanings (e.g. gender meanings) and how to 'pull apart' these meanings can be used tactically to disrupt uneven gendered relations in the classroom.

Disrupting local truths and the tactics of deconstruction

Deconstruction is a specialist term not commonly used in everyday conversations. We can glimpse its meaning by looking at its two parts: 'de' (implies reversal or removal) and 'construct' (meaning to put something together). To *de*construct something is to take it apart, to 'unconstruct' it. In poststructuralist theory deconstruction refers to taking apart concepts and meanings in texts to show the politics of meaning within them.

Derrida and the origins of deconstruction

> The very meaning and mission of deconstruction is to show that things – texts, institutions, traditions, societies, beliefs, and practices of whatever size and sort you need – do not have definable meanings and determinable missions, that they are always more than any mission would impose, that they exceed the boundaries they currently occupy. What is really going on in things, what is really happening, is always to come. Every time you try to stabilize the meaning of a thing, to fix it in its missionary position, the thing itself, if there is anything at all to it, slips away.
>
> (Derrida, 1997, p. 31)

The tactics of deconstruction stems from the work of a French poststructuralist language theorist called Jacques Derrida (1930–). Derrida explores the philosophy and politics of language. He is interested in how truth and logic are constructed in Western European philosophy by fixing meaning to specific signs (words and images). In particular, he is interested in how words and images are used to prove something and to fix how we understand it. For instance, the word 'child' is used to prove a young person is a child and to fix how we understand the differences between younger and older people. How did this social convention come to be? This question matters because we live our lives through the social conventions embedded in our language. There are social conventions in Western Minority World cultures that mean we act differently towards a child than we do towards an adult. As we fix meanings in a particular sign (e.g. child or adult) we also fix ways of acting (Belsey, 2002).

For this reason, deconstruction does not just explore how we fix meaning, it also explores our political and ethical responsibilities in this process:

> Because deconstruction has never been concerned with contents of meaning alone, it must not be inseparable from this politico-institutional problematic, it has to require a new questioning about responsibility, an inquiry that should no longer necessarily rely on codes inherited from politics and ethics.
>
> (Derrida, 1992b, p. 23)

So, borrowing from Derrida, deconstruction is a means to critically reflect on our responsibilities at a micro-level in the politics of truth. Deconstruction questions the meanings of words or concepts (ideologies, practices, texts) that are normally unquestioned using '. . . a form of analysis which exposes the multiplicity of possible meanings, contradictions and assumptions underlying our understandings and ways of knowing' Alloway (1995, p. 106). It exposes the internal contradictions in particular systems of thought (Weiner, 1994) to question who benefits and how from the assumptions about our social world embedded in those systems of thought. As such, it helps us to scrutinise how our language choices fix power relations in specific regimes of truth.

The local and tactical use of deconstruction

Deconstruction can be a tactic to examine how our language choices in early childhood studies can fix and/or disrupt power relations. It can localise efforts for social justice and equity by focusing reflection on the use of language in the texts (written, visual and spoken) used in specific local sites (e.g. a childcare centre, nursery classroom or tertiary institution) in early childhood studies.

Beyond truths: language and meaning

Deconstruction is based on poststructuralist assumptions about language and meaning that assume that meaning is arbitrary, shifting and contradictory rather than fixed. This contrasts to understandings of meaning in which there is an effort to make our definitions 'stick' (Ghandi, 1998, p. 40) to a particular word. In particular, poststructuralists draw on but go beyond (hence 'post') what became known as structuralist accounts of meaning and language. Some basic understandings of structuralism are therefore important to making sense of 'post' structuralism.

Structuralist accounts of meaning and language build from the innovative work of Swiss linguist Ferdinand de Saussure. In the first part of the twentieth century he argued that language was a social convention not an objective logical representation of reality. So the fact that the word 'baby' (or what Saussure called the sign for 'baby') in the English language means a recently born person is a result of social convention rather than any objective relationship between the two. To grasp his point we only need to think about the 'sign' for 'baby' in another language. For instance, a recently born person in Balinese is linked to the sign (or word) – 'bebe'. This being so there is no objective logical link between the sign 'baby' and the reality of being a recently born person. Instead, the link is a social convention established in the English language. A sign in a specific language comes to 'signify' particular meanings through social convention. As Saussure said, 'If words stood for pre-existing concepts, they would all have exact equivalents in meaning from one language to the next; but this is not true . . .' (Saussure, 1959, p. 116). Instead, Saussure talked of signs as arbitrary social facts rather than objective facts representing the real world. Saussure called the study of the signs and their meanings 'semiology' – or the science of signs.

Saussure's study of signs highlighted the part that difference plays in how we produce meaning in a particular language. All meaning relies on differences between signs. For instance, we rely on the fact that the sign for 'baby' looks physically different to the sign for 'adult' to know what the sign 'baby' means in English.

It also relies on socially fixing what a sign signifies. In each language social conventions fix meaning through fixing the relationship between a sign and what it signifies. Learning this relationship is essential to making sense of the world through language. As we learn a new language we have to learn the differences between signs (individual words) and the relationships between a sign and what it signifies. Language therefore structures the meanings we give to the world. If we don't know that a relationship exists between 'bebe' (a signifier) and a recently born person (what it signifies) in the Balinese language we can't give any meaning to the word – it is just a set of letters without mean-ing. But, its meaning is fixed in the Balinese language. Meaning is culturally constructed but fixed in language through a system of signs specific to that language that build our worldviews. It is our shared understandings of what a particular sign signifies in a language that makes language work for us. As Mansfield so clearly explained:

> In sum, to Saussure, language is not a set of tools haphaz-ardly connected, but a concrete system of conventions built around two relationships: the difference between one signifier and another and the arbitrary relationship between signifier and signified. Language is thus a complex cultural order.
>
> (Mansfield, 2000, p. 40)

Saussure's views were considered radical in his time as they suggested that individuals do not create meaning. Instead, lan-guage systems and cultural conventions create meaning. Meaning is not within us, but without us in the systems of language we use. In particular, for Saussure, meaning was contained in the cultur-ally set relationship between a signifier and what it signifies. So the sign only makes sense in relation to what it means, and vice versa (Chandler, 2002).

Poststructuralists drew on this structuralist view that meanings arise from social conventions and rely on a relationship between a sign and what it means and on differences between signs, but they went beyond (post) them in important ways. Poststructuralists, such as Derrida, argued that the conventions that link a sign with its meaning are not fixed within a language system. The conventions can be disrupted and remade because they are contra-dictory, shifting and incomplete. Meaning was not contained in the relationship between one sign and what it means, its meaning was produced in how that sign required (referred to) other signs and what they mean. This is a difficult point to grasp and we shall return to it shortly. As Cherryholmes explains, the difference between structuralists and poststructuralists rests on understanding where meanings come from:

> If we attempt to trace central ideas back to their origins, we find either that they continually lead to prior ideas or contradict themselves. ... Structuralism shows meanings to be decentred and external to the individual. Poststructuralism shows meanings to be shifting, receding, fractured, incomplete, dispersed, and deferred.
>
> (Cherryholmes, 1988, p. 61)

Understanding why poststructuralists see meaning as 'shifting, receding, fractured, incomplete, dispersed and deferred' is an important backdrop to using deconstruction tactically and locally to scrutinise the politics of language. A good starting point is the role of dichotomies (divisions into two) and binaries (pairs) in meaning making.

Language and our efforts to fix meaning: the role of dichotomies and binaries

Derrida (1976, 1978) argued that a majority of Western language relies on dichotomies (sharp divisions into two) and binary (paired) oppositions to produce meanings. To illustrate, gender relies on dichotomies such as masculine and feminine, male and female, or boy and girl to help us grasp gender and its meanings. In addition, gender meanings rely on pairing girl and boy and seeing them as opposite to each other. They form a binary opposition in which we are offered two mutually exclusive meanings. Boy is the opposite of girl and the meanings for 'boy' and for 'girl' are each mutually exclusive. A 'boy' is a young male and a 'girl' is a young female. Females are defined in the *Concise Oxford English Dictionary* (Fowler and Fowler, 1990) through their capacity to bear children, and males are defined through their capacity to 'beget' children through insemination.

'Binary opposites' are 'binary intimates': without 'female', 'male' has no meaning, and the same is the case for 'majority' and 'minority', 'active' and 'passive', 'good' and 'bad', 'rich' and 'poor'. Western languages tend to seek final, fixed meanings for words (spoken and written) through these oppositions. We can finally fix the meaning of male (begetting children through insemination) because it is paired with female (bearing children after insemination). Male is the opposite of female as there are clearly known sharp divisions between them, for instance in their role in childbearing. In each binary opposition (e.g. male and female) we know what one word means because it is opposite the other. Think of the following pairs of words:

- adult/child
- developed/underdeveloped
- normal/abnormal
- work/play
- slim/fat
- white/black
- straight/gay
- western/eastern
- rich/poor
- employed/unemployed.

Slim is the opposite of fat so we know that slim people are not fat. Each word in a binary opposition relies for its meaning on the other. We need the word fat to define slim. The same is so for straight and gay, black and white, etc. A pair always has two. One part of the pair is always the opposite of the other part. You cannot have meaning without having the opposite, or what Derrida describe as the 'other' (e.g. Derrida, 1976).

Contemplate the binaries implicit in the following statement about difficult behaviour and young children:

> Predictable environments and routine will help lesson anxiety. Help the child learn ways to manage stress and better express feelings.
>
> (Roe, 2001, p. 13)

'Predictable' relies on its opposite of 'surprising' or 'unpredictable' to tell us what an appropriate environment might be for relaxed (binary of 'anxious') children. Routine relies on its opposite of unusual. Unusual and surprising environments produce 'worse' (binary of 'better'), and 'uncontrolled' (binary of 'managed') feelings.

Hierarchies and the role of the 'other' in the politics of language

The significance of binary oppositions and their 'other' is that the 'other' is not equal to the main part of the pair. There is a hierarchy of value, set culturally in binaries and dichotomies (Ghandi, 1998). The pairs are always ranked, so one part of the pair always has higher value in the ranking and is privileged over the 'other'. So, using binary oppositions places some meanings in a secondary, subordinate position and often an aberrant position.

The term that is privileged establishes the cultural standard of normality (Biesta, 2001). Think of the following pairs of words:

- civilised/primitive
- man/woman
- white/black
- straight/gay
- slim/fat.

In each of these pairs the first word is often given more status or advantage in many societies. It is seen as normal, original, authentic and/or superior. The 'other' word is seen as abnormal, derivative and/or inferior.

If we revisit the statement about difficult behaviour and young children we can see this process at work. The 'other' words are:

- 'surprising' or 'unpredictable' which are each inferior to 'predictable';
- 'unusual' which is inferior to 'routine';
- 'uncontrolled' feelings that are abnormal compared to 'managed' feelings.

In this small excerpt of text from Roe (2001, p. 13), a cultural standard is established of what normal expressions of feelings look like and what a normal environment for a child is. The normal environment should be predictable and routine and a normal child has managed feelings. What does this mean for how the following would be 'read' and 'ranked' within this cultural standard?

- a Palestinian child wailing uncontrollably with her parents at the death of close relative;

- a traveller's child or the child of a 'nomadic' group who is constantly meeting the 'unusual' and 'surprising' in their daily environment;
- a child living in poverty who uncontrollably sobs because their favourite toy has just been taken by another child;
- a 'black' child's uncontrollable anger at having been teased about the colour of her skin.

Early childhood texts, like other texts, rely on establishing hierarchies of meaning through binaries to establish cultural standards of normality (Biesta, 2001) and, therefore, produce and express cultural standards of normality. In the following excerpts from early childhood texts, this process is readily identified by looking for the implicit/explicit 'other'.

> ... parents could also draw on upon the independent advice of staff about the progress of their child.
>
> (Foot *et al.*, 2002, p. 13)
>
> *[Binary – independent/dependent. Privileged position – independent. Cultural standards of superiority/normality – independence over dependence, e.g. over advice based on dependent relationships. Cultural groups who privilege dependence over independence in relationships, especially where advice is given, are inferior/abormal.]*

> As educators and future educators, we all recognise how important it is for each of us to meet the unique needs of all our students.
>
> (Penney, 2003, p. 28–I)
>
> *[Binary – unique/shared. Privileged position – unique. Cultural standards of superiority/normality – unique over shared needs, e.g. over needs shared by cultural or family groups. Cultural groups who privilege shared needs over 'individual/unique' needs are inferior/abnormal.]*

> At one time, children communicated with friends through paper cups connected by a string. They could not begin to imagine advanced communications.
>
> (Szente, 2003, p. 299)
>
> *[Binary – advanced/basic. Privileged position – advanced. Cultural standards of superiority/normality – advanced communication over basic, e.g. over ways of communicating without technology. Cultural groups who do not communicate without technology are inferior/abnormal.]*

Classroom educators might find it helpful at this point to practise 'reading' the texts they use to share ideas with parents, gain insights into children or to share with children for binaries and the cultural standards they establish.

Deconstructing to reveal the 'other' and its politics

The hierarchy within a binary is not inherent in the words and so is not inevitable or accidental; it is socially produced. For example, in the excerpts above the binary opposite of 'independence' was 'dependence'. It was given the secondary and subordinate position. 'Dependence' is not inherently secondary and subordinate to independence. For instance, in many groups 'dependence' of one member on another is valued and/or it is necessary. Advice that is 'dependent' upon knowing a child may be more valuable than advice based on in/dependence – a state of separation from the child. Similarly, communication without technology is not necessarily secondary and subordinate to other forms of communication. The writer of the text produced it this way. 'Basic' communication – communication without technology – can be more valuable and valued than communication using new technologies. We socially determine and construct this subordination in language and construct realities through it.

In particular, identities of difference (adult/child, developed/ developing, white/black, straight/gay, masculine/feminine, etc.) are constructed through differences that produce 'othering' to produce cultural standards of normality and superiority. As Campbell explained:

> Identity and difference are inextricably entwined. You cannot have one without the other (. . .) Interrogating identity is to highlight how 'otherness' is constructed.
>
> (Campbell, 1992, p. 8)

Practices of inclusion and exclusion rely on these binaries, the cultural standards they produce and the identity differences between people that they establish. For instance, in Western Minority World liberal democracies, binary oppositions (e.g. Australian/non-Australian, us/them, citizen/non-citizen, responsible/irresponsible, civilised/uncivilised, legitimate/illegitimate) are used politically to exclude or 'other' particular groups of people. Otherness is used to create and then legitimate practices of exclusion and inclusion (Bailey and Gayle, 2003).

Similarly, in early childhood classrooms, binary oppositions between 'managed' and 'controlled' expressions of emotion (refer above) are used to plan behaviour modification programmes for young children and to decide who needs to be included or excluded from these. They are also used to decide which parents should be advised or not on the importance of predictable environments for young children.

Derrida's work has powerfully critiqued how writing produces 'otherness'. He linked writing to the hierarchisation of meanings that produce the possibility of otherness:

> It has long been known that the power of writing in the hands of a small number, caste, or class, is always contemporaneous with hierarchization, let us say with political différance; it is at the same time distinction into groups, classes, and levels of economico-politico-technical power, and delegation of authority, power deferred and abandoned to an organ of capitalization.
>
> (Derrida, 1976, p. 130)

Derrida argued that the 'other' is not only socially constructed but it is often repressed and/or silenced. Deconstruction tackles its repression/silencing by showing how pairs gain their meanings from each other, how one word (meaning) has more advantage and status than the other. It forefronts this advantaging as socially decided rather than inevitable. Deconstructing (taking apart) binary oppositions by showing that each side depends on the other ('other') for its meaning aims to point to the relations of power between the binary oppositions and to show '. . . that the privileged term derives its position from a suppression or curtailment of its opposite or other' (Grosz, 1990, p. 95).

Peters (1999) explained the politics of 'othering' and the role of deconstruction in challenging 'othering' as follows:

> Western countries grant rights to citizens – rights are dependent upon citizenship – and regard non-citizens, that is, immigrants, those seeking asylum, and refugees, as 'aliens'. Some strands of poststructuralist thought are interested in examining how these boundaries are socially constructed, and how they are maintained and policed. In particular, the deconstruction of political hierarchies of value comprising

binary oppositions and philosophies of difference, are seen as highly significant for currents debates on multiculturalism and feminism. . . .

(Peters, 1999)

For instance, feminist poststructuralists (e.g. Davies, 1989; Davies, 1993; Alloway, 1995) have extended debates on ways to approach gender equity in early childhood by showing how the binaries – boy/girl and masculine/feminine – are constructed, maintained and policed in classrooms and that children work to position themselves as one or the other. In this positioning girls 'other' boys and vice versa. However, Davies (1989) argued that the 'power resides in the male' (p. 138) in the male/female binary. Further, it is the male/female binary that holds gender inequity in place by insisting on differences within it. Davies (1989) argued for finding ways beyond this binary (dualism) in gender work with children:

> If the dualism were rejected and people were free to position themselves as a person in terms of their interests and abilities quite independently of the set of genitals they happen to have, and were free to dress and move through the world without being obliged to mark themselves as male or female, then there would still be many people who would recognizably be what we now think of as female or male, and there would be many who were not.
>
> (Davies, 1989, p. 135)

Children should not be limited by having to choose to be 'masculine' and, therefore, 'not feminine' and vice versa. Davies called for pedagogical work to make the terms 'archaic' (1989, p. 141) and to celebrate diverse ways of being that are neither masculine nor feminine. If educators can learn how gender binaries are 'maintained and policed' (Peters, 1999) in classroom life they have an entry point to disrupting the maintenance of the binary thus freeing children to 'be', rather than to 'be gendered'.

Revealing the 'other' and 'hingeing it' to remake its politics

Derrida believed that revealing the 'other' involves taking a particular word or concept and using reversal and/or displacement to create a new term which Derrida calls a 'hinge word' (Grosz, 1990). Thus, reversing the binary opposition between, for instance, gay and straight involves giving gay the privileged position; and displacing existing meanings by creating a new term involves hingeing them to show their links rather than their opposition. The hinge word becomes gay–straight. A new or altered word, for instance, a hinge word, makes new meanings possible. Derrida was interested in attempting to erase the boundaries between binary oppositions, and thus show that the implied values and hierarchy within them can shift.

Language and our efforts to fix meaning: the role of logic and logocentrism

The politics of language is not only fixed by binaries. Enlightenment understandings of language and meaning fix meaning though making a logical connection between a sign (such as 'child') and what we choose it to signify/represent (a younger person). Language in this sense represents rather than reflects reality. Derrida (1976) refers to the views that the word (or sign), especially the written word, carries real meaning as opposed to conventional views, as logocentrism (Grenz, 1996).

Poststructuralists, following Derrida, upset this logic and logocentrism by arguing that there is no necessary and logical link between the two. We have constructed the link so it is possible that the sign 'child', as a text it represents through metaphor, could as readily mean learner or cute. Meaning is not fixed in specific words and images; it is generated in how we historically and thus politically link signs and their meanings.

Meanings are networked (linked to each other) rather than inherent in a fixed sign (Grenz, 1996). For instance, the meaning we give to the sign 'child' is networked with the meanings we give to 'young', 'person' and 'adult'. It is through these meanings we can assign meaning to 'child'. For this reason, as we perform language we 'perform' with reality or construct reality rather than represent it (Royle, 2002) through creating social conventions about what meanings *should* link with a specific sign. To learn a language is to learn these social conventions and with them to learn the politics of meaning (the norms and standards) embedded in them. It is, for example, to learn whether or not it is normal for a child to be dependent on an adult.

More specifically, poststructuralists argue that meanings of a particular sign are textually/culturally derived, rather than inherent in it because:

• Meanings are like links in a chain. The meaning for one word (one link in the chain) derives from the other words (links) that surround it in a text (written or oral), or chain. Words have to defer to other words in the text for their meanings. They have no inherent meanings. The link means nothing without the chain. It cannot be a link unless it is in a chain. Hence, we cannot know what 'child' means until we know what 'young' means, etc. Structuralists would say that what a child means is inherent in the sign, rather than linked to meanings beyond it.

• Texts (words and images) are redolent with meaning traces from other texts in which their words and images have been used. These traces are cultural traces – evidence the word has been used before (Spivak, 2002). Meanings are networked in the present and to the past in that they 'recede' or link back from one text into a previous text. For instance, 'dog' has specific meanings in one text (e.g. as a pet to be loved or an animal to be feared) because of how we have met it before. If we have seen or read *101 Dalmatians* the traces of this will be found in how we next read a text with 'Dalmatians' in it. If we have read or seen a text in which a 'Dalmatian dog' has devoured a child or fiercely attacked a stranger then traces of this will arrive in our next reading of 'Dalmatian dog'. Hence, meanings can shift depending on where the traces lead us and what uses the word has had before. The same is so for 'child'. Child has a specific meaning in one text as 'a developing person', as 'sexually desirable' or as 'a learner' because of where we have met it before.

• As these cultural traces (networks) of meanings shape how we understand a text in the present, we do not 'make' meaning; meaning is made external to us through how texts are constructed by their cultural histories. How these traces are networked in a particular text can be unpredictable because we each have a different history of meeting specific texts and therefore a different history of meaning traces that arrive in a reading of a text. For instance, a person who has seen Disney's *101 Dalmatians* and a veterinary surgeon who has studied veterinary texts about dogs will each arrive at the sign 'dog' with a different set of cultural traces through which to give meaning to the sign 'dog'. However, if they are each Anglo-Australian they will also share cultural history that will give them some shared understandings about what 'dog' means. Similarly, a person who has read a Piagetian developmental text on children's cognitive abilities will arrive at the sign 'child' differently to a person who has read a Vygotskian developmental text. But, they will share an understanding that the child has 'cognition'.

• Different past meanings and the unpredictable networking of a word produces contradictions in what a word can mean. For instance, a 'dog' can mean 'pet', 'feared animal', 'cute cartoon character', 'Disney toy', 'food' and 'marketable product'. A child can mean 'learner', 'sexual object', 'cognitive being', 'cute', 'dependent' and so on.

There is no objective, true meaning for a sign or specific text, only meanings that are linked, cultural, historical, contradictory and shifting. Which meanings you bring to the sign will be linked to your own cultural history. They will be linked to the texts you have accessed in your own culture and how these link over time, how they contradict each other over time and how they have shifted over time. A child has variously been understood as 'cute', 'a young worker', 'a person with rights', 'a chattel' and 'a learner'. Therefore, a child can still be understood in these ways but not always.

Derrida characterised this 'flexibility' of meaning through the term 'différance' (a pun in French), that means to *differ* and to *defer* to. Meanings in a sign differ and they have to defer to traces of meaning in other texts. A sign (e.g. 'dog' or 'child') in and of itself can never convey a single 'true' meaning. Even if we reach to the dictionary to fix a meaning for 'dog' we would find a definition such as 'any four-legged flesh-eating animal of the genus *Canis*, of many breeds domesticated and wild, kept as pets or for work or sport' (Fowler and Fowler, 1990, p. 345) that requires us to know what signs such as 'sport', 'domesticated' and 'wild' mean. To fix these meanings we turn to the dictionary again and we find ourselves constantly deferring the meaning of dog to the next definition in the dictionary and so on. In this process of deferral we can define 'wild' through its opposite 'tame' or 'domesticated' but each of these defers to yet another set of signs and so on. 'Child' offers the same challenges. If we take just one of the definitions – 'a young human being below the age of puberty' (Fowler and Fowler, 1990, p. 195) we need to define 'puberty', which requires us to define 'sexual maturity' and so on. Each sign defers to another.

Curriculum is a sign that is redolent with 'différance' that matters to the everyday world of early childhood studies. Consider Angela's opening comments. It is defined in different texts in different ways and it relies on different cultural traces and histories to give it meaning in a specific text. How we define curriculum matters to how we 'practise' it with children and/or how others expect us to 'do' curriculum. If we take Derrida's point that there is no objective, true meaning for it then there is no objective, 'true' way to 'do' curriculum in early childhood.

The tactics of deconstruction: the politics and ethics of affirming and attending to the 'other'

Deconstruction . . . 'reveal[s] the necessity with which what a text says is bound up with what it cannot say' (Grosz, 1990, p. 97) because of the assumptions about language and meaning discussed above. For instance, it reveals how a text in which the sign 'dog' appears or 'early childhood curriculum' is bound up with what it doesn't say because the cultural traces and histories that enable us to 'read' the text and give the sign 'dog' meaning are not able to be said in the text. Deconstruction involves 'deforming, an accredited, authorized relationship between a word and a concept' (Derrida, 1983, pp. 40–41). It means showing the impossibility of saying with any authority that this word (dog or child) means this because of what cannot be said in the text.

Identifying what is not said and 'deforming' the link between link and concept involves looking at what knowledge is privileged within the text/discourse using the two Derridian concepts: 'différance' and 'otherness'. Through this process we can create new meanings to challenge the current relations of power in our ways of understanding the world and in the texts we use in it.

In what follows I present some basic tactics for deconstruction: binary analysis, erasure, metaphor making and mapping meanings.

These can be applied to any classroom texts, e.g. classroom fashions, books, symbols, talk, routines and rituals. Again they are not certain guides but possibilities to explore and to expand in their use.

Binary analysis: some basics for attending to the 'other'

> I talk often to parents about school readiness. I had never wondered about what the opposite of readiness meant – reluctance. School reluctance – what can that mean? I never talk to parents about a child's reluctance to do something as part of thinking about when they are ready for school. Now I am thinking, how much readiness is linked to the idea that children need to be willing to do what I think is necessary for school. Could it be that a child doesn't do what I think makes them ready for school because they are just reluctant to? What might make them reluctant? Which children are reluctant? What would need to change to make them keen (ready) for school? Would I be keen on school if my language wasn't spoken? What would make me reluctant to go to school? It is unsettling and I find I am thinking about how many ideas I use are full of politics like this.
>
> (Janine, early childhood educator, research
> interview, Trembarth Project)

There are many tactics for deconstructing meanings using 'différance' and 'otherness' that begin with engaging binary analysis and – in Derrida's terms – ethically attend to and affirm the other:

> [D]econstruction is – if it is – an ethics. [I]f you call this an ethics of affirmation, it implies you are attentive to otherness, to the alterity of the other, to something new and other.
>
> (Derrida, 2002, p. 180)

Deconstruction using binary analysis inverts and subverts binary meanings and it ruptures logic to create alternative meanings (Coole, 2002). It uses this rupture to attend to the 'other' in texts so as to affirm and celebrate diversity. This can productively point to new possibilities for living within diversity using the texts of classroom life. In daily classroom life, attending to the other is an ethical stance consistent with challenging discrimination and marginalisation. Discrimination relies on 'othering'. Learning to attend to what is being 'othered' in daily classroom texts forefronts the dynamics of discrimination and the points at which it can be challenged. If we reflect on the following texts of conversations with young children we can see how 'othering' links to simple acts of discrimination between children:

Sally and the sandpit

Teacher: Why can't Sally (four years of age and female) play in the sandpit? She is very upset she can't play with you.

Charles (four years of age and male): She can't play with me because I need boys to dig.

Girls are 'othered' in this moment as 'people who cannot dig big holes', boys are privileged and Charles discriminates against girls playing within him in the sandpit.

Yuk, can't eat with me

Teacher: Jana (four years of age, female and Nigerian) needs somewhere to sit for milk and fruit today. I'd like her to sit on this chair next to you please.

Bella (four years of age, female Anglo-Australian): Dirty, dirty yuk. She can't eat with me till she washes clean (and she points to her own face).

Bella 'others' being 'dark' skinned in this moment by privileging her own face as 'clean'. She uses this to discriminate against who she will eat with at milk and fruit time.

To deconstruct a concept, idea or word, first identify the binary oppositions it brings into play (dirty/black skin – clean/white skin). Then identify the politics of the opposition – which term is 'othered' and which term is privileged. Next, attempt to show how each term in the binary opposition is not in opposition but necessary to the other. We cannot talk of 'white' skin as clean without the binary for 'white' – i.e. 'black' skin that is dirty. The intent is to 'disintegrate' the hierarchical meanings attached to the concept and become ethically attentive to the 'other' by asking who and what is privileged by the maintenance of the binary. For instance, which skin colour does Bella privilege in this moment? What is she 'othering'?

It is also to show the contradictory and shifting ways in which the concept, idea or word can be understood by playfully showing how what is privileged as normal or desirable in a particular text (e.g. classroom conversation) is exceptional and problematic. For instance, digging big holes may not be the only skill required in the sandpit, and/or maybe Sally will be able to dig a very big hole because she is very persistent and determined, and/or not all boys can dig big holes. Playfully showing children the contradictory and shifting ways in which you can see 'digging holes' and 'girls' and 'boys' can point to their views as exceptional or problematic.

In overview, a text or sign can be deconstructed using the following basic steps:

• Identify the binary oppositions that it brings into play by asking, 'What binaries does this text rely on for meaning? What are the silenced others in this text?'.
• Identify the politics of the opposition by asking, 'How does this specific text create assumptions about what is normal or desirable?'.
• Identify the necessity of each term to the other by asking, 'How does each term in the binary depend on the other for its definition?'.
• Ethically attend to the 'other' by exploring who and what is privileged by maintaining the binary by asking, 'Who benefits in this text from how the word or idea is used and its binaries constructed?'.
• Disrupt the meaning hierarchy by showing how the normal is what is exceptional and asking, 'How is the norm exceptional?'.

Take, for example, the following statement made in an article about how to teach children collage using children's art books and fine art illustrations. It contains many binary oppositions that it relies on for meaning, including 'authentic'/'fake', 'fine art'/'gross art', 'truly'/'falsely' and so on:

> As children create collages with cut and torn papers, photographs, fabrics, natural objects and other materials, they are practicing an art technique used by many fine artists. Introduce children to artists such as Pablo Picasso, Henri Matisse, Romare Bearden, and Charlene Marine, as well as illustrators Steven Jenkins, Bryan Collier, and Jeannie Baker.

By linking fine art and picture book illustrations with children's art lessons, the activities become more authentic and
truly art focused.

(Prudhoe, 2003, p. 10)

If we attend to the 'other' in this excerpt of text we can disrupt
its assumed standards of what is normal and desirable art:

*   The silenced others include 'fake', 'bad art' and 'false(ly) art'.
*   The text creates assumptions that there are 'objective' stand-
    ards for judging art and its value and that all readers can share
    these assumptions. The norms for judging art refer to (or in
    Derrida's terms, defer to) European 'master' artists such as
    Picasso and Matisse and published children's illustrators from
    the US.
*   'Fine' art depends on the idea of 'gross' art for us to define
    it, In doing so, it fixes the assumption that values and judge-
    ments about art are accepted universally.
*   The definition of 'fine' art through deferral to, for instance,
    European 'masters' links art standards to European art tradi-
    tions. Where are the judgements of Majority World artists?
    How might indigenous artists be judged? Is their art 'gross'
    art and if the children's teacher draws on these artists will the
    lesson be 'fake' and 'false'? Can we have unbiased judgements
    of 'fine' art? Whose cultural traces and histories are present
    in the definition of 'fine' art and whose cultural histories and
    traces of what art is and what it means are silenced or margin-
    alised in how the text uses 'signs' with each other to fix
    meanings (norms) about art and art lessons? The question of
    what is 'art' and who decides? What is silenced in the sign
    'art'? What does it defer to for its meaning?

Attending to the 'other' within Prudhoe's text we arrive at questions about how 'art' norms and standards are established within
early childhood classrooms. To what extent are ideas about what
art is, how to judge it, how to use it and how to teach it built
through deferral to European art traditions and within which art
traditions? What assumptions does it make about the resources
that should be available to children? What does it assume about
art as teachable and by whom? Consider the following statement
in which 'needs' and 'shoulds' again establish standards and make

assumptions about what art looks like and what place it should
play in a child's life:

> The art center provides materials for creative expression as
> well as art appreciation. It needs easels with space for two or
> more children, primary colors along with tan, brown and black
> paint, and a water supply. Crayons and marker pens in skin
> tones and other colors should be available. . . . Low tables and
> chairs for collage, clay, and other activities should be provided.
> Art work representing various cultures should be displayed at
> a child's eye level.
>
> (Read, Gardner and Mahler, 1993, pp. 55–56)

What does it mean to display art 'representing' various cultures?
What is being 'othered' in this and what is being silenced? Where
are the cultural traces that take us to understandings about
what art represents in the different cultures and therefore what
art should or should not be displayed for all to see? For instance,
for indigenous peoples in Australia art carries their 'dreamings' –
deeply spiritual stories and histories, some of which are 'secret'
business. What does it mean to 'display' this at a child's eye
level? What might happen if we traced the cultural histories and
links between different early childhood texts on art in early childhood? Where would we learn about the spiritual and ritual place
of art for some groups of people? What traces would lead us
to the meanings of colour, form and shape for particular groups
of people? What texts do we need to take us to these cultural
meanings?

Deconstructing professional texts, such as those written by
Prudoe and Read, enables educators committed to equity and
social justice to sharpen their comprehension of how their classrooms' understandings and practices produce cultural standards
of normality. For instance, they can examine what is 'othered'
in how they 'do' art, science, literacy, music, numeracy, social
and environmental studies, etc. They can learn to 'read' the physical environment of their classrooms for how it 'others'.

Engaging in binary analysis can help those of us working in
early childhood studies to analyse the specific politics that we bring
into being through the texts used to make sense of classroom
life. We can analyse every text we use for how the binaries within
it produce norms and standards of practice and expectation.

It is a practical way to reflect on the effects of cultural traces and histories in our work with children and a jumping-off point for realigning the even power effects we find. We can 'do' art differently if we can think about art differently.

Erasure: some basics for 'wondering' other meanings

> I'd always used the word program, and when I stopped and thought about it, what does this mean, I started to think about 'to program, 'to program a child', 'to program a machine' – I'd never thought of it, I'd just always used the term and never stopped to think what it actually means or could mean. I'll put that under erasure now.
>
> (Jina, early childhood teacher, research
> interview, Critical Teaching Project)

Another way to disrupt truths at the local level is to engage the tactics of erasure to show that a meaning of a specific word/idea/concept is provisional, rather than fixed. In doing so, you disrupt the idea that it has a single meaning that is fixed for all time and that its meaning is 'real', rather than culturally 'based/biased'. Erasure can also help us to 'wonder other forms of knowledge' (Hyun, 2001, p. 24). For instance, Jina has begun to see the word programme as problematic when describing how she frames/plans/enacts her work with young children. It is associated with issues of control and input of data that feel out of step with how she thinks of her work with young children. To represent this to others and to remind herself of it, she can put the word under erasure. Derrida drew on Heidegger's concept *sous rature* meaning to put something 'under erasure', to attack specific concepts that are necessary to us because we have no alternative at present but they are inadequate for what we wish to say (Wong, 2002). Davies (2001) talks of erasure as casting a shadow over a specific word, concept or idea. Orton talks of it as creating a 'strategic indecidability' (Orton, 1989, pp. 38–39).

When a term is put under erasure it can be physically 'scored' through to show its inadequacy at present. For instance, Jina decided to put the word programme under erasure. She would do so by scoring through the word thus – ~~programme~~. In doing so, Jina shows that she is 'wondering' other meanings for what she does that she has until now described as 'programming'. Given the discussion above about 'art' in early childhood classrooms we could put art under erasure to indicate that we recognise its problematic cultural traces in most contemporary early childhood texts. We could wonder other meanings for art and highlight our 'strategic indecidability' (Orton, 1989, pp. 38–39) about how it should be understood and practised in early childhood classrooms. It highlights our efforts to attend to the 'other' and to wonder 'other' meanings. It shows that we mistrust a word and its meanings.

Race is a term that has been put under erasure in contemporary times because its meanings are mistrusted because race does not exist, except as a social and political construct. It is a term that has been developed to classify people into distinct groups based on physical and genetic differences (e.g skin colour). It has been used to create hierarchies between groups of people and to establish one group as superior to another. Generally this has placed white Europeans at the top of the hierarchy and black African people at the bottom (Ashcroft, Griffiths and Tiffin, 1998). But the distinctions used to group people racially are regularly undermined through relationships between different groups of people that blur genetic traits and through contemporary research that suggests that there are more shared physical and genetic characteristics between 'racial' groups than there are differences. Despite this, the distinctions are still invoked to justify discrimination and oppression and so while they are mythical differences that the term race defines, it has very real material effects. To talk of those effects, for instance as racism, we still need the term race despite its problematics. To indicate these problematics some people put the word in quote marks, like so: 'race'.

Metaphor: tactics for deforming and contradicting meanings

> There is nothing that does not happen with metaphor and by metaphor. Any statement concerning anything that happens, metaphor included, will be produced not without metaphor. There will not have been a meta-metaphorics consistent enough to dominate all its statements. And what gets along without metaphor? Nothing.
>
> (Derrida, 1978, p. 103)

When we encounter something new we explain it by comparing it with something we have already experienced. Through metaphors

we move meaning from one context into the unknown in order
to explain the unknown (O'Sullivan *et al.*, 1983: Chandler 2002).
You could use the metaphor, 'the meeting *sparkled* with ideas
for rethinking planning', to explain what happened at a staff meeting to someone who wasn't present. It assumes that that person
knows what 'sparkle' means in other contexts (e.g. the effervescence
in champagne, the flash of sequins or lurex) and it applies this
meaning to describe a meeting in which there was an energetic
emergence of new ideas.

Metaphor can also be used to shift our understandings about
something that we know by reframing how we see it. Derman-
Sparks and the Anti-Bias Task Force (1989) used the metaphor
of a 'tourist curriculum' to shift the meanings associated with
tourism (e.g. visiting a place briefly, seeing the sights, learning often
trivial facts about the culture and then returning home) to
tokenistic approaches to diverse cultures in early childhood curriculum. This metaphor reframed how multicultural curriculum
can be evaluated in early childhood by pointing to the ways in
which children 'visiting' a culture for a day or a week in the classroom and then 'returning home' shows the dominant cultures
as 'home' and other cultures as 'exotic', 'foreign' and 'strange'. In
Derrida's terms, it 'others' them.

Davies (1989) drew on metaphor to shift understandings of
gender as a simple binary between male and female in children's
lives and to call attention to the different ways in which young
children can 'do' being male or being female. Her metaphors
included:

• the rough, tough princess who took up ways of being female
  associated with 'wealth and privilege' (p. 118);
• the sirens who took up ways of being female that were 'alluring
  and seductive' (pp. 118–119);
• the 'home corner' girls who took up ways of being female that
  emphasised 'the position of the domestic nurturer' (p. 121);
• the superhero boys who 'were often aggressive towards girls
  and younger boys' (p. 122);
• the articulate intellectual boys who were 'sensitive and articulate' (pp. 124–125).

For Derrida, metaphor is an important tactic of deconstruction.
In metaphor is the evidence that our meanings are not fixed but

rely on each other. For instance, to understand girls as 'sirens' we have to rely on knowing that sirens are 'alluring and seductive' and in doing so 'sexualise' young girls. In metaphor is the logic of meaning and language. We know what a word means because of the others we use to picture it, or what a concept means because of the narrative we use to describe it. It highlights that meanings are nested in other meanings. Metaphor allows us to enter nested meanings. Consider how we might come to understand who we are in a child's life through the following metaphors. Each present the child as a passive receiver of cultural information:

- A child is a blank slate waiting for the world to write its stories on it.
- A child is a sponge who learns about gender roles and differences through osmosis.

In contrast, other metaphors represent the child as an active constructor of meaning. For instance:

- A child is pre-programmed like a computer to process information in and through its own stories.
- A child directs a play, actively using the props of the world about them and the scripts in it to create their own gender play.

Metaphors bring us the possibility for rereading/reseeing the world. But they can be contradictory. For instance, how can a child be both a blank slate *and* pre-programmed, or a sponge *and* a director?

As we call on metaphor we call on cultural knowledge and its biases. In producing metaphors we can disrupt the local politics of truth and attend to other possible ways of knowing. Early childhood educators can deploy metaphor to explore and unsettle the local politics of truth expressed in specific words/ideas/concepts/texts. Theilheimer and Cahill (2001, p. 103) introduce the metaphor of a 'messy' closet to unsettle the idea that early childhood classrooms are free from sexual 'messiness' and to emphasise exploration of the politics of sexuality in early childhood classrooms:

Classrooms for young children are supposed to have well-organized closets. Yet, we are finding a messy virtual or metaphorical closet in the field of early childhood. In it is a jumble of myths, beliefs, norms, and representations of sexuality and child that spill out into the room, affecting how teachers and children see themselves and others. In an effort to open the door and clean the closet, this chapter investigates ignorances, assumptions, and silences about sexuality, using stories from our own experiences.

(Theilheimer and Cahill, 2001, p. 103)

This metaphor highlights the possibility that the daily practices and understandings that fill early childhood classrooms attempt to lock out the effects of sexuality. It places sexuality in the classroom.

Matoba Adler draws on the metaphor of racial and ethnic mirrors to re-see how culture and identity form in early childhood classrooms. She applies it to her own experiences of visiting a Hawaiian immersion school in Honolulu of which she wrote:

As we observed through our own cultural lenses, I couldn't help hiding my elation, knowing that those Hawai'ian parents, teachers, and children were defining themselves in mirrors, rather than appropriating identities assigned to them by others.

(Adler, 2001, p. 157)

This metaphor places the cultural identities of educator firmly in the spotlight pointing to how the educator 'others' through the reflection (or lack of it) of a child's culture in the culture of the educator.

We can generate metaphors that unsettle dominant truths in all aspects of early childhood studies. Producing metaphors that highlight what is silenced locally becomes a strategic political act. Sheralyn Campbell's metaphors of snakes and puddles (refer to Chapter 2) help her to:

negotiate the risky business of doing equity work with children, staff and families in our community. I think of puddles as a sign that we have had some rain. While they are familiar they are also uncertain terrain. They sit on the surface of the ground and can be deceptive – shallow or deep. They reappear unexpectedly. I think of snakes that lie quietly – openly sunning themselves or hiding in the long grass that surrounds us. They are dangerous and can be aggressive when threatened, or timid and slither away.

(Sheralyn Campbell, 2005, pp. 8–9)

She finds herself negotiating equity work in uncertain and shifting terrain in which issues appear and reappear in different forms and with different effects. Racism can 'openly sun itself' or 'hide in the long grass'. It can be 'aggressive when threatened, or timid and slither away'. This metaphor presents racism as complex and shifting, needing reflexive and specific responses. It can be used to help others think about how racism 'suns itself' or 'hides away' in their own work. It disrupts the idea that racism does not exist (it could be hiding away), that there is a single and universally applicable response to racism or that there is a guaranteed effect from challenging it. Racism 'slithers away' in response to challenges but it may also 'fight back aggressively'. The metaphor prepares us for these possibilities.

Mapping meanings – practising the tactics of deconstruction

Well why would you want to look at the word curriculum? A curriculum is a curriculum why pull it apart? Just leave it alone and go with the flow. . . . but I reflected on the word curriculum and I was thinking well who it is that we do the curriculum for and how do we do them, and what do we want as the end result and it got all the way up to the Department and government policies and reflecting on what type of children and adults they wanted to produce. At the end I thought wow that's scary because that's a really big picture, rather than focusing on one little centre and one little curriculum.

(Angela, early childhood educator, research interview, Trembarth Project)

Drawing on the work of Derrida and Foucault, I have been playing with ways to trace key ideas back to their origins and to 'read intentionally for trouble' using what I call a 'Meaning Map'. The 'Meaning Map' (Mac Naughton, 2001e) is my attempt to produce a practical tactic for educators intrigued by possibilities of 'deconstruction' (Derrida, 1976; Derrida, 1978) for the 'deliberate practice of liberty' (Keohane, 2002). The Meaning Map can be used to invert and subvert meanings, rupture logic and produce new meanings that highlight our responsibilities in a local politics of truth. More specifically, the 'Meaning Map' and its associated processes aim to help users become sceptical about their everyday texts, especially the understandings and practices that they have taken for granted and to examine and take them apart in order to reveal how power operates.

The Meaning Map builds from the ideas in Chapter 1 and Chapter 2 on the dynamics of power and knowledge and their implications for equity and social justice. It suggests a stepped process that can be used locally in early childhood studies:

1   Seek multiple meanings by asking, 'How many meanings can you find for this word?'.
2   Seek meaning traces by asking, 'How are the meanings we give linked to other words?', 'To where can we trace the origins of these meanings?'.
3   Seek the limits to meaning by asking, 'What are the assertions, assumptions, contradictions and irrationalities within your understandings and practices?' and, 'How do meanings limit what you consider possible for yourself and others?'.
4   Seek the power effects of meaning by asking, 'Who benefits from the meanings?' and, 'What meanings/voices are silenced, suppressed or marginalised?'.

For instance, we could begin to map the meanings of 'curriculum' as follows:

1   *Seek multiple meanings* by asking, 'How many meanings can you find for this word?' For instance, curriculum is:

• a set of courses, programme, syllabus (Fowler and Fowler, 1990);
• everything that happens in an educational setting (Reid and Johnson, 1999);
• a carnival (Coyne, 1996);
• National (Parker, 1997);
• a gift (NSW Early Childhood Curriculum Framework – check for specific reference);
• anti-biased (Derman-Sparks and the Anti-Bias Task Force, 1989);

- 'an historical accident' (Longstreet and Shane, 1993, p. 19);
- a phantom, tacit, hidden (Longstreet and Shane, 1993);
- 'formal aspects of teaching and learning' (Lovat and Smith, 1995, Introduction).

2 *Seek meaning traces* by asking, 'How are the meanings we give linked to other words?', 'To where can we trace the origins of these meanings?'. For instance: we can trace curriculum to a Greek meaning for 'race course' (Fowler and Fowler, 1990) or a fixed course of study. So, curriculum can read as a fixed place for running with a fixed course of study. This meaning trace can be used to raise the questions: What is that course of study in early childhood? Is it or should it be the same for all children? Do all children have an equal start in the race? Do all children run the course in the same way? Who decides what is fixed and where the course is run?

On the other hand, Coyne's (1996) characterisation of curriculum as 'carnival' enables curriculum to be traced to meanings of 'intense colors, music, religion; all expressions of the joy and warmth' (Coyne, 1996) and of merrymaking and revelry (Fowler and Fowler, 1990). Can curriculum be seen as merrymaking and revelry full of intense colours, music, religion and all expressions of joy and warmth? What might this mean for what a classroom might look like? What is the course of study that would enable all expressions of joy and warmth to be? How might a teacher's role be transformed through seeing curriculum as a festival? And, so on. Thus, why call it a curriculum, not a carnival?

3 *Seek the limits to meaning* by asking, 'What are the assertions, assumptions, contradictions and irrationalities within your understandings and/or practices?' and 'How do meanings limit what you consider possible for yourself and others?'. What are the limits in seeing curriculum as a 'racecourse' or as a 'carnival'? How do your ways of seeing curriculum limit the colour, music and emotional expressions redolent in seeing curriculum as a carnival? What are the contradictions between the different ways of seeing curriculum and who do these effect? Can a curriculum be everything that happens in an early childhood centre and a carnival? Who would win the curriculum 'race' in your centre? Who does the merrymaking and revelry in your centre? When and why do children 'make merry' and 'revel' in the course of study that is your curriculum? And so on.

4 *Seeking the power effects of meaning* by asking, 'Who benefits from the meanings?' and 'What meanings/voices are silenced, suppressed or marginalised?'. Who benefits when we think of curriculum as a race course? Is it only the children who 'win' in everything that happens in an early childhood centre? Do all children win in the moments in which they 'make merry' in your classroom? Whose colours, music and emotional expressions race for the advantage and the position of privilege in your early childhood centre? Where is the place for sadness and anger in a carnival? Who might need to express anger when the merrymaking begins? Is sexism reinforced by the competitions (races) in your classroom? Where is anger against racism possible in festivals of joy and warmth? And so on.

Playing with meanings and beginning to map their possibilities in how we work and how we think about work in early childhood studies is a tactic for re-wondering the possibilities of how we 'do' early childhood studies. It is playful and it is serious. When we act from one set of meanings it silences others and it silences possibilities. This is serious. To know this is to be provoked to a choice. It is to be provoked to be playful for new possibilities.

Tactics of deconstruction to engage ethical and political responsibility

Education is about choices – for example, choices to 'do' curriculum in particular ways, choices to prioritise one set of goals over another and choices to address an issue or not. Each of these choices is linked to a set of meanings about who a child is, what education is for and who should take decisions about what the child needs. Deconstruction can help us to confront those choices in the daily ideas, words and concepts we choose to use in early childhood studies. As Parker puts it:

> What the postmodern teacher recognizes is that we have a choice in education: that every decision to teach this way, or assemble that collection of subjects on a curriculum, or organize one's classroom according to this set of principles or anec- dotes, is ungrounded in reality, has no ultimate, compelling justification. Every decision involves potentially endless levels of choice which we can contrive to forget or conceal but which deconstruction is always ready to uncloak. We are responsible

for those decisions in a most extreme way. We have a responsibility for our decisions that the world cannot excuse since the
world is, itself, an outcome of our deciding so to take it.

(1997, pp. 143–144)

Parker sees that educators have an 'extreme' responsibility for their
decision-making because they cannot escape the choices it brings.
Deconstruction brings us choices about how we make our local
meanings and how we remake them. It opens up possibilities for
ethically attending to the 'other' in the meanings we make and
acting in and through this attention. These choices and their possibilities bring us what has been termed an aporia. Aporia is a Greek
term meaning puzzle, but in Derrida's work it means an impasse
or paradox in how we give meaning to an idea/word/concept
(Derrida, 1993).

Making this practical in daily lives with children is not easy.
Yet, it is in our daily texts (words and images) that the possibilities of 'othering' exist. In these moments attending to the 'other'
is challenging. It is especially challenging as 'others' engage with
us. In the following vignette Karina Davis (researcher, lecturer,
early childhood educator and mother) shares her efforts to 'attend
to the other' in her everyday conversations with her children. The
'other' has been powerfully brought to her through postcolonial
theorists who have focused on deconstructing relations between
colonisers and colonised. Karina's research has focused on
rethinking the place of indigenous perspectives in the early childhood curriculum, and postcolonial theory pushed her to attend to
the othering of indigenous perspectives and the privileging of
whiteness in contemporary Australia. She writes of this in Chapter
5 (see p. 179). However, in the conversation that follows she draws
on her understandings of 'othering' to disrupt the othering of
homosexuality in a simple but deeply gendered conversation with
her daughter Kiana.

KARINA DAVIES
Princesses are beautiful Mummy

I am aware of how straightforward applying theory and recommen-
dations for changing practice can seem to someone immersed in
academia – someone who is not practising with children, parents and
colleagues in a day-to-day situation. I am constantly drawn back to

conversations with my own children and my stumbling, clumsy and constant attempts to question and challenge their developing ideas on gender, race/culture, abilities, sexuality, class, inclusion and exclusion. The conversations that follow bring forth the powerful ways in which heterosexuality and gender are becoming in the lives of my daughter (Kiana) and my efforts to disrupt this. This is one such conversation in which Kiana asserts and reasserts heterosexuality and heterosexual marriages as the norm:

Kiana: Princesses are beautiful Mummy.
Karina: Are they?
Kiana: Yes.
Karina: What makes them beautiful?
Kiana: They just are.
Karina: Is there anything about them that is just so beautiful?
Kiana: Yes. They wear beautiful yellow dresses.
Kiana: I'm going to get married one day.
Karina: What does it mean – to get married?
Kiana: You wear a white dress and get married.
Karina: Who do you marry?
Kiana: Someone.
Karina: Do you always have to wear a white dress?
Kiana: Yes.
Karina: I know someone who got married and wore a black dress and someone else wore a red dress.
Kiana: Oh.
Karina: And do you know what else?
Kiana: No. What else?
Karina: Some people we know aren't married at all. Not everyone gets married.
Kiana: Who isn't married?
Karina: Matty and Sam aren't married and Jane and Janine aren't either.
Kiana: What are they then?
Karina: They love each other and that's pretty special. And some people just love themselves you know.
Kiana: Who loves just themselves?
Karina: Matt does and Stu does.
Kiana: I'm going to get married though.
Karina: OK.
Kiana: To Matty and Sam.

In these excerpts, my experiences as 'parent' and as 'teacher' merge for me as I realise that the questioning is similar. I now question how I approach/ed the topics, what I say/said and how I phrase/d things.

Postcolonial and whiteness theory now has me questioning not only how I say things about 'race' but also about gender, sexuality and class. It also has me questioning what I choose to say (or not) in response. While this questioning could be unnerving and destabilising and possibly has been in the past, I am glad of it. It keeps me focused, it helps me see issues and find entry points into conversations more clearly. It has the effect of not being able to dismiss 'innocent' comments. I am sometimes seen as aggressive and emotional and I feel like I can never relax because I am surrounded by colonialism and whiteness. I see its structures and influence more clearly now all around me. These influences and structures are reflected in my life, in my children's lives, in the courses at university, in the research that I work in and/or help structure, and in all of our understandings and actions.

Deconstructing for possibilities

Deconstruction becomes tied to a politics of possibilities as it offers us ways to imagine new ways to 'continuously wonder other forms of knowledge' (Huyn, 2001, p. 24). If we attend to the 'other', create metaphors, and place terms under erasure we are imagining that there is another way to see a text – another way of knowing it. We are drawn to 'wonder' what other ways might be. For instance, when we place art, under erasure (art) we are drawn to wondering what other ways of knowing art there might be.

Deconstruction cannot remove inequities and injustices but it can be a tactic to help us to remain ethically attentive to them. As Attridge (1995b) argued, it makes the ethical and the political unavoidable:

> We now know – or have no excuse for not knowing – that deconstruction is not a technique or a method, and hence that there is no question of 'applying' it. We know that it is not a moment of carnival or liberation, but a moment of the deepest concern with limits. We know that it is not a hymn to indeterminacy, or a life-imprisonment within language, or a denial of history: reference, mimesis, context, historicity, are among the most repeatedly emphasized and carefully

scrutinized topics in Derrida's writing. And we know – though this myth perhaps dies hardest of all – that the ethical and the political are not avoided by deconstruction, but are implicated at every step.

(pp. 109–110)

Beyond the basics: taking deconstructive turns in the everyday

There is not just one set of deconstructive tactics to uncover the politics of language and meaning that lie at the heart of the possibilities of truth and regimes of truth. Miriam Giugni uses the tactics of metaphor to 'strip back the coats of wonder' of the meanings she gives to working with your children. She adopts the metaphor of 'the epistemological shudder' to enter the politics of meaning she gives to gender and sexuality in her interactions with children. Put simply, epistemology is the study of meanings and, as Miriam explains in detail below, the metaphor of the 'epistemological shudder' is used by Losinsky and Collinson (1999) tocapture what happens (emotionally and cognitively) when people encounter the 'marvellous' that incites unexpected meanings or ways of knowing.

Miriam also uses inversion – inverting her understandings of wonder and marvel of the child – and producing multiple readings to attend to and to affirm the other. In what follows she takes a deconstructive turn to her work with young children, using these tactics to produce other ways of knowing the child and her relations to the child to those offered through the lens of developmental psychology. Her metaphor, inversion and multiple readings of a moment of conversation with young children offers her new insights on the politics and practices of sexuality in young children's lives and her relations to that as an educator.

MIRIAM GIUGNI
Practising for liberty, taking a deconstructive turn: the epistemological shudder

This case study is drawn from a research study that constituted my honours thesis that I undertook at the University of Western Sydney. The project was designed to investigate the processes by which children constitute their 'identity work' in the context of popular culture. I deployed a poststructural framework to design, implement and analyse the study. More recently, in search for a new tool to strip back the layers of my thought of how to 'read' children's play I happened across a 'marvellous' interrogative contraption named by Losinsky and Collinson (1999) as the 'epistemological shudder' (p. 3). The 'epistemological shudder' makes conceptual space for a range of theoretical positions to be used as ways of 'knowing'. These theories are often contradictory, but can be *deliberately* used to create points of resistance in order to theorise everyday practice.

The 'epistemological shudder'

The 'epistemological shudder' (Losinsky and Collinson 1999, p. 3) can best be described as an affective response to an encounter with things marvellous. The term 'marvellous' here refers to a concept of 'difference', 'out of the ordinary', 'unexpected' rather than the often dichotomised meaning of such adjectives in the 'good/bad' binary. This affective response entails the 'cracking apart' or 'fragmentation of contextual understanding'. Losinsky and Collinson (1999) argue that '[a]n epistemological shudder occurs when a person's preferred representations of their known world prove incapable of immediately making sense of the marvellous' (pp. 3–4). In other words, when a person encounters the marvellous, astonishing or different, the response entails a splintering of the prototypical representation, the known, and perhaps the 'truth'. Losinsky and Collinson (1999) argue that this response creates a process of two parts. First, a phenomenological experience of the unexpected and chaotic; and second, the cognitive process of 'placing' the new knowledge within the displaced and fractured contextual understanding.

I argue that there is a third part of the epistemological shudder which embodies the physical, that is: the effect of the shudder inscribes the body and produces body knowledges, such as facial expressions, which are manifest through embodiment and disposition. This experience is not simple or straightforward, rather it is constituted by a series of unordered actions dependent on the specificity of the context. Losinsky and Collinson (1999) argue that the effects of the epistemological shudder result in an aporia (puzzles and paradoxes) in understanding. An aporia cannot last because 'a representation can always and must always be found to assuage the shudder' (p. 4). Here, the epistemological shudder offers an understanding of how we deliberately come to experience uncertainty.

The epistemological shudder in action – painting a new pedagogy

In the following pages I demonstrate one example of the workings of the epistemological shudder. First, I use a table to present a detailed discourse analysis read through the epistemological shudder, followed by my interpretation of the analysis. Second, I show the effects of the shudder I experience while analysing the data. Finally, I explore the usefulness of the epistemological shudder as an everyday pedagogical and reflective tool.

This vignette illustrates the conversation of four four-year-old boys huddled together discussing some serious secret boys' business. By secret boys' business I refer to the ways in which the children engage in dialogue that is 'secret' in two ways. First, because it is not really the usual genre of conversation these boys would have with an adult and second, the children's talk is explicit, sexist and sexualised. In this way their conversation embodies a kind of secret and covert way of being a boy, discussing dangerous issues while a female adult educator listened in. The conversation was audio taped by the children as they sat, tightly tucked underneath a trestle and jumping board in the middle of an outdoor area in Long Day Care Centre in Sydney, Australia. I was sitting on top of the jumping board, 'eaves dropping', as they spoke. Their voices were gruff, their bodies stiff and puffed up, shoulders hunched up and legs sprawled. I on the other hand was crunched up in a little ball holding my legs and feeling like my eyes would burst with perplexity and astonishment, feeling as if I would fall and crash into the conversation at any minute. They knew I was there, listening, above them.

This vignette shows the dynamism of the epistemological shudder as a way of viewing, interpreting and questioning a given situation, but by no means telling the 'truth'. It shows how knowledges are created through interactions and can be read through particular frameworks to expose particular features or perspectives. For example, Colm appears to have a significant role as the holder of knowledge and the provider of answers (truths?) and the keeper of fragments to fix the shuddering epistemologies of masculinity of the other boys. Specifically, this interpretation shows how dominant discourses can act to govern the epistemological shudder through renaming, reiteration and resistance. This is evident by the way Tonio, Nicolo and Mardi question Colm for important information about the required discourses of masculinity to deploy correct superheroness. Although it appears that

Vignette	Epistemological shudder
Colm: . . . and Poison Ivy's got poison on her lips they're poison and Batman wanted to kiss her. [the boys' eyes open wide in amazement]	Sharing the marvellous: the dangerous and the forbidden.
Mardi: Did he love her?	Assuaging the shudder with conceptions of the 'proper' methods of kissing and 'love'.
Colm: No. He just liked her because she is bad.	Cracking apart the 'proper' with the 'bad'.
Mardi: Did she fight?	Attempting to act logically linking representations of badness and fighting.
Colm: No. she couldn't fight that's why she has poison on her lips.	Rationalising the substitute of poison and fighting – masculinity and femininity.
Mardi: So did she want to destroy Batman?	Contributing a familiar storyline, suggesting some kind of quest for masculinity to prevail, a dominant discourse to assuage the shudder.
Colm: No, in this episode they don't get destroyed. We can make up our episode, Nicolo and we can have Power Man and Diamond Man and we can like Poison Ivy. Do you think that is excellent?	The shudder: a challenge to masculinity. Drawing on a series of cultural resources which fill the cracks with normative back up representations and dispositions. Authorship: certainty, knowledge, truth.
Tonio: What if Batman loves Barbie? (he giggles)	Deliberately deploying the epistemological shudder?: the power of disruption.
Colm: No, can't happen. Batman doesn't need girls. He doesn't have love. They only love him. It . . . It . . . It's silly, Barbie looks silly. Batman only likes Bat Girl cause she's cool and Poison Ivy cause she's bad. Barbies aren't strong because they're just girls, they're just normal toys.	Fixes contextual fractures with truth. Renders discourse's hypermasculinity by stripping this form of emphasised femininity down to the normal, weak and silly: anti-feminist. Culturally affirming femininity that represents lust, desire, power.

Vignette	Epistemological shudder
Nicolo: Does Barbie got anything?	Cracking apart of representations and embodiment of Barbie style emphasised femininity.
Tonio: Yeah . . .	
Colm: No she's got no power at all . . . she's only beautiful. She's not like Bat Girl and Poison Ivy and Robin.	Fracturing the beauty myth? Setting factions of femininity apart – through their identification with masculinities. Fracturing of beauty – all girls are the same?
Tonio: Why?	
Colm: No . . . because she just wants to get married he doesn't like her because [Barbie] doesn't have a suit. She doesn't have brains she's just beautiful. She's silly. She just wants to get married. I'm not marrying anything.	Marriage fractures the individualist and independent life of the Superhero – free from the need for femininity unless by choice. Resisting hegemonic heterosexual life path.

Tonio and Nicolo could be deliberately challenging the relationship between Batman and Barbie, their epistemological framework is built around the masculinity/femininity binary. As a result, they do not disrupt Colm's position on issues of love, marriage, desire and sexuality. Here the complexities of discursive power relations become visible. So the interrelated social categories that we name in order to specify parts of identity such as gender, language and (hetero)sexuality are viewable as dynamic and interwoven. In turn, this visibility enables a view of and specifies the various different knowledges, and ways of knowing, that these children have of gender, language and (hetero)-sexuality and the cultural institutions, such as marriage, by which they are sanctioned.

This exemplar of reading children's conversations also shows how the shudder comes in bits and pieces, and many shudders are experienced and are never ending. For example, the boys each play with multiple themes in their discourse through which power is manifest, while maintaining a collective interest in the precarious relationship between Batman and Barbie. Nonetheless, each of the boys presents his curiosity from the curiosity of their own supply of cultural resources and subjectivity. Moreover, the body positioning of these cultural actors was shaped by the ways in which words were spoken throughout this conversation. Eye contact was intense, eyebrows furrowed held fast with the concentration that shaped every crevice of the forehead as the shudders sporadically fractured the boys' epistemologies with each piece of new or naughty information, and chests grew in size, bellowing up with each hegemonically masculine (/anti feminist and oppressive) comment. So, shudders collide and overlap, influencing and interrelating, confusing and clarifying, collecting and culturalising.

To make sense of the effects of the epistemological shudder, it is useful to draw on the concept of 'fractals', a feature of chaos theory. The relationship between fractals assumes everything can be broken down into bits and pieces but still remain complex, defining and redefining into new fragments of complexity, but never fragmenting to the point of nothingness. In other words, fractals act as a '[f]ractional dimension [which] becomes a way of measuring qualities that have otherwise no clear definition: the degree of roughness or brokenness or irregularity in an object' (Gleick, 1987, p. 98). So, these fractured conceptions of childhood, or fractals, now created new complexities within the complexities – another shudder. Here we see the ways that the fractal-induced epistemological shudder operates in and through existing power hierarchies. For example, Colm fractures the relationship between Barbie-style beauty and power when he states that 'she's [Barbie] got no power at all ... she's only beautiful' which are commonly assumed to be intimately linked as an image of powerful and emphasised (hegemonic) femininity. Contradictorily, and perhaps refreshingly, there is room for the fragmentation of this hegemony, through thoughtful and critical pedagogies of questioning and deconstruction. These practices might include revisiting the conversation with children and offering deliberately opposing views. Notwithstanding, children easily and skilfully also execute pedagogies concerned with maintenance of the status quo to create points of resistance as safety from a dangerously fragmentary epistemological shudder. Colm demonstrates this resistance by beginning each response by stating 'No' and inverting each of the other boys' questions and statements with his form of evidence – 'truth'. Colm skilfully resists any threat to his conception of 'truth' about women; subsequently, he maintains his discourse of hegemonic masculinity and control of this friendship group.

So, Colm demonstrates how these pedagogies are deployed. His representation of gender acts as a will to 'truth' in the Foucauldian sense (1977d). So to protect his truth, from the aporia left by the shudder of amazement, Colm uses a will to truth manifest through knowledge spoken expressively and body positioning, which demonstrates the physical, embodied component of discourse, to maintain his use of the known and familiar 'fractal' to detail and fix the fracture. Thus, he uses his evident knowledge of an 'M' rated film, a valuable cultural currency, nicely facilitated by the undivided quizzical curiosity of his peers, which allows the fragmented space to become a space for reiteration and reassurance for Colm to reproduce 'knowings' of gender through popular cultural products, within this friendship group. Additionally, through the logical fixing and filing of the boys' curiosity, Colm contributes to and maintains the hegemonic gendered hierarchy of men and women. As a result, Colm reiterates his representations of gendered identities, gendered hierarchies and sexuality. He permits this kind of desire and discussion of women as part of the 'business of friendship', that is, a particular type of hegemonic masculinity (Hughes and Mac Naughton, 2000; Giugni, 2003). Therefore, dominant and hyper discourses of gender and gender order remain intact.

Because representations of three- and four-year-old children can appear to be convincingly static, the epistemological shudder is not foolproof. Rather, it requires deep understanding and a long-term commitment, specifically when battling some of the mortar that renders the value of interest-based learning pedagogies that are produced, gloriously, without critique. The exemplar presented above is one attempt to highlight the rapid fashion by which the maintenance of sedentary 'knowings' act to fix, fill and file the fragments of truth. And so, conversations are easily shut down to avoid the shattering affects of uncertainty. In addition, conversations are not pursued owing to fear of uncertainty, 'innocent' images of the child and pedagogies that allow normative knowledges to form the content of the daily curriculum.

Shudder upon shudder

These effects on my 'knowings' of children, childhood and identity, using the epistemological shudder as a critical and reflective tool, have stripped back ten years of 'knowing' and created an aporia, remembering 'that a representation can always and must always be found to assuage the shudder' (Losinsky and Collinson, 1999, p. 4).

So, new conceptions of the child, their epistemologies and an awareness of the unexpected ameliorate the shudder, along with the
required risk-taking to make use of this thought-provoking tool! But
beware – the shudder is not always an easily explainable process, it
is complex and dangerous.

As a witness to this conversation, I experienced a fragmentation of
contextual understanding. I shuddered at the way the boys delighted
in being in the company of one another relishing this conversation
and producing unequivocal statements and understandings about
love, marriage, sexuality, gender, exclusion and hierarchy – the unknow-
ing child fragmented. I struggled to digest the language these children
used to describe each of the characters they discussed so intimately
– the innocent and influential child fragmented. And I was astonished
by the way that detail of the boys' conversation inscribed their bodies
– the innocent physically underdeveloped sexual body fragmented. Furthermore, I cringed at the thought of discussing such a conversation with
their families and I felt fear about documenting such an interaction.
I shuddered at the smooth exchanges of cultural currency inciting the
marginalisation of women and femininity – the sexist child visible and
tangible. I shuddered at my own response to the children's conversation – defining my own sexism(s) and ageism – the essential child
fragmented – the knowing adult fragmented.

I remember feeling confronted by Colm's comment, perhaps the
familiar experience of shattering and shuddering, unable to make a
decision about what to do with this aporia, this moment of uncertainty. I was paralysed by silence. I revisit it because I realise that
this was just one conversation. How many of these conversations
occur in a day? How many children are continually shattering and
shuddering only to grasp onto dominant images and representations
to alleviate the 'cracking up'? What does this mean for educators
who are committed to equity and social justice?

How does the epistemological shudder fit into current early childhood curriculum? Are we bound by the practice of the learning of
knowledge uncritically? Do we feel we have permission to question
'the way we have always done things' or what we choose to engage
children in as 'quality learning'? Do regulating bodies support our
growth as early childhood educators who work for social justice and
equity? What are the ramifications for early childhood educators who
see themselves as intellectuals and retheorise their work? What are
the ramifications for early childhood educators if they do not?

Recall, rethink and retheorise

The epistemological shudder dances through our conversations, our actions, our being: the observer, the listener. But here, it has become a useful tool for *me* researching, analysing and revisiting everyday interactions and exploring equity and social justice issues. Because I now have this new tool for the development of transformative pedagogies I am compelled to use it, to construct myself as a 'transformative intellectual' (Aronowitz and Giroux, 1985, p. 36) and intervene, subvert the business of maintaining truth. Moreover, I am inspired to reject notions of the 'innocent', 'romanticised' and 'extraordinary' child and thus I strive to capitalise on the 'epistemological shudder'. If an aporia is created then we as early childhood educators and researchers have the opportunity to dive in and offer other, new, alternative and diverse ways of 'knowing' before the familiar representations mitigate the shuddering space into normativity (producing norms). We have the opportunity to deliberately create points of resistance and to create a culture of strategic questioning. Such a process is necessary in order to delve into any kind of understanding of the culture of the 'other'. This process can be likened to deconstructive practices, rewording binaries, exploring power relations and other fun activities. So get fragmented and shudder with this last thought: question everything.

Becoming critical meaning makers: expanding strategies and tactics

It is possible to strategically understand and begin to disrupt the regimes of truth that govern the field of early childhood by coming to know your will to truth and by learning to read for equity. This work can be deepened and localised by using the tactics of deconstruction to trouble the politics of knowledge of specific signs and texts (written, spoken and visual) embedded within a regime of truth thus coming to know them afresh. Miriam brings the metaphor of the epistemological shudder to this task. In particular, she uses it to deliberately produce puzzles and paradoxes in how she 'reads' her interactions with children. In refusing to maintain a 'truth' about these interactions she acts deconstructively in the epistemological shudder to defer 'truth'.

Tactics of deconstruction can be used to build a more complex and dynamic understanding of how specific truths within a regime of truth touch daily pedagogical practices. Knowing the specific effects of specific truths in specific early childhood institutions, such as 'innocent' or 'extraordinary' child, is necessary if new possibilities are to emerge in specific local sites. Deconstruction allows for that possibility and thus for ways in which local early childhood educators can 'do' the work of practising for liberty in their daily work with children. It also allows for that possibility for researchers and policy makers in the field as they come to know how their texts do and don't attend to the 'other'.

The next chapter layers into these possibilities by using the tactics of rhizoanalysis to produce 'other' possibilities for giving meaning to work in early childhood studies.

For reflection

- How does binary thinking enter your everyday discussions in early childhood studies?
- What is silenced or othered through the hierarchical thinking in these binaries?
- What everyday words could you put under erasure to help you wonder new meanings and actions for social justice in your classroom?
- What metaphors could you generate to help you attend to the 'other' in your daily work with parents?
- How does metaphor help Miriam attend to the 'other'?
- Where are your epistemological shudders?

Chapter 4

Deliberately practising for freedom

Tactics of rhizoanalysis

I came to explore rhizoanalysis as I searched for a tool with which to understand how the child, the parent and the early childhood professional learn, develop, relearn and change their complex, multiple, contradictory, contingent and shifting understandings of themselves, of others and of the world.

(Kylie Smith, early childhood educator
and researcher, Victoria)

The rhizome operates by variation, expansion, conquest, capture, offshoots . . .

(Deleuze and Guattari, 1987, p. 21)

Rhizoanalysis

Deliberately practising for liberty creates new and multiple meanings in early childhood communities. This chapter explores how to use rhizoanalysis to understand the child in early childhood studies. More specifically, it shows how to weave alternative 'readings' into the everyday work of observing, documenting and analysing children, their learning and their relationships. To do this it:

• provides an overview of rhizomatic logic as a tactic for meaning making;
• demonstrates how this logic can be used to reframe the meaning given to children's play;
• outlines simple moves you can make towards rhizomatic logic by interrogating your texts of the child, being nomadic in how you frame them and seeking surprises in how you read them;

- shares a vignette of how one early childhood educator has created new co-ordinates for observation as a political practice for social justice.

Rhizoanalysis is a way to explore the politics of a text in order to create new texts. For instance, we can use rhizoanalysis to explore how an observation of a child from within a developmental perspective links to the politics of gender, 'race', class, ability and sexuality in early childhood studies. Rhizoanalysis both deconstructs and reconstructs a text. It deconstructs a text (e.g. a research moment or a child observation) by exploring how it means; how it connects with things 'outside' of it, such as its author, its reader and its literary and non-literary contexts (Grosz, 1994, p. 199); and by exploring how it organises meanings and power through offshoots, overlaps, conquests and expansions (Deleuze and Guattari, 1987, p. 21).

Rhizoanalysis reconstructs a text by creating new and different understandings of it; and it does so by linking it with texts other than those we would normally use. For example, we can use rhizoanalysis to replot the links between an observation of a child, and a child development text, a feminist text and a popular culture text. Later in this chapter, Kylie Smith does just that – she 'reads' an observation of a child by linking it with popular culture texts (including *Buffy the Vampire Slayer* and *Harry Potter*) to reconstruct her understanding of gender, 'race' and class in that observation. As she constructs a rhizome of gender meanings in the observation, she rethinks what it means to 'do' gender at four years of age and how she might see and work with children's gendering in early childhood services.

Rhizoanalysis builds from the philosophical and cultural theories of Gilles Deleuze and Feliz Guattari (1987). They used the contrast between rhizome (e.g. ginger, iris, agapanthus) and tree as a metaphor of the contrast between two forms of logic. The tree's linear structure – from roots through the trunk to the branches – is a metaphor of the fixed, determining and linear logic that explains things in terms of cause-and-effect relationships. The rhizome's contrasting 'lateral' structure – a collection of mutually dependent 'roots' and 'shoots' – is a metaphor of a dynamic, flexible and 'lateral' logic that encompasses change, complexity and heterogeneity.

For example, consider this description of gender development:

> How do children learn about gender? How do they learn
> gender stereotypes? . . . Parents teach with rewards and disci-
> pline. They might praise girls and punish or discourage boys
> for the same thing. That is one way to create gender stereo-
> types. For example: Mom might praise her daughter when she
> picks flowers for her, but she might be upset with her son for
> doing the same thing.
>
> (Putnam, Myers-Walls and Love, 2003–2004)

That explanation relies on linear logic with fixed and final results: parental rewards and discipline cause gender stereotypes. In contrast, the rhizome – a metaphor of 'lateral' logic – implies a world that is dynamic, ever-changing and always 'becoming' in a never-ending process. A rhizome is never finished, it is always 'becoming' through crossovers between offshoots, through expansions of one form of growth into another and through the death and decomposition of outdated elements. Thus, rhizoanalysis explains things in terms of a dynamic, ever-changing 'becoming', rather than a fixed and finished 'being'; and a particular rhizoanalysis – e.g. of gender – is never fixed and final, but is always becoming. One meaning expands into another, some meanings become outdated and new meanings shoot forth. 'Rhizomatic' logic is associated with poststructuralist ideas because Deleuze and Guattari sought to move beyond a (linear, universal) logic that produces stable and universal truths of the world, towards a (lateral, local) logic that produces shifting and multiple truths.

From a 'rhizomatic' perspective, we can never 'be' gendered in a fixed and final way; instead, we are always 'becoming gendered' as fashions, expectations, experiences, values, beliefs, opportunities and desires associated with genders change over time and between cultures and geographies. From a 'rhizomatic' perspective, the development of gender stereotypes in young children requires more complex explanations than the cause-and-effect relationships between, for example, parents' expectations and children's behaviour posed by Putnam, Myers-Walls and Love (2003–2004). The 'lateral' logic of rhizoanalysis challenges the idea that one act causes another and that one idea or meaning inevitably leads to another. It highlights instead how relationships and meanings link in complex and shifting ways in our 'becoming'.

For example, a rhizoanalysis of the growth of gender stereotypes in young children would show how those stereotypes overlap with cognition that, in turn, overlaps with cultural experiences that, in turn, overlap with parents' expectations, that, in turn, overlaps with their age that, in turn, overlap with their experiences of early childhood settings that, in turn, overlap with geographical location that, in turn, overlaps with national identities that, in turn, overlap with history that, in turn, shifts over time. And so on and so on. If gender stereotypes grow rhizomatically, this implies our ways of seeing and planning for gender stereotypes need also to be rhizomatic – overlapping, multi-focal and shifting with time.

Rhizoanalysis challenges the idea that one moment in a child's life (caught through observation) is caused by, say, her stage of child development or by her gender or by what another child did or said. Instead, it highlights the complex and shifting links between gender, cognition, class, 'race', etc. and how these links shoot in unpredictable ways into a particular moment in a child's life. It highlights how those links overlap with, for example, the understanding/s of gender held by adults who work with the child; peers' gender practices; and the presence and absence of gender in the 'text' (the stories, songs, teacher talk, child talk, rituals, routines, etc.) that is the early childhood setting.

Similarly, we can also explain family relationships using rhizomatic logic. Family relationships are traditionally pictured as linear – descending through a paternal family tree. However, family relationships could be pictured as rhizomatic, as Mansfield explained:

> Patterns of intermarriage and birth infinitely expand from any one point. Your birth connects you to two families via your parents: through them to four families via their parents and so on. The complexity of the picture is intensified by lines of flight cojoining you to your siblings, cousins, their children, their partners, their partners' families, and so on to infinity.
>
> (Mansfield, 2002, p. 146)

Families' rhizomatic relationships overlap, turn back on themselves, disperse, compose and decompose in a complex pattern that can't be captured in the traditional family 'tree'. Mansfield argued this was 'no accident' because the single line of 'paternal inheritance connects with traditional masculine authority' (ibid.). From a 'rhizomatic perspective', power is never fixed and finished in our lives. Instead, it is always 'becoming' through dispersed and shifting relationships and through new connections and inter-connections between our becoming and that of others. Power that is dispersed and shifting in this way, continually composing and decomposing, requires radically different strategies for change to those required by power that is fixed and finished.

A rhizoanalysis of children's play

Using rhizomatic logic, we can look within and beyond a text for unlikely connections between diverse data fragments (Alvermann, 2001). Diverse data fragments are observations or sections of an observation that differ in terms of who was observed, when, where, how, why and by whom. If we apply this idea to observing and analysing documentation in early childhood studies, we can generate some questions about the data fragments that will help us to link and map data in unlikely ways. For example:

- What are some of the diverse fragments of this data on an observed child? (E.g. who is present and absent, how, when and why are they present or absent?)
- How do these data fragments connect to each other? (E.g. how do they overlap, cojoin, disperse, shift, etc.?)
- How do these data fragments link with other data fragments from texts outside of it? (E.g. What are the overlaps and shifting links between them?)
- How do these data fragments connect with me? (Alvermann, 2001)
- What do these data fragments connect with each other? (E.g. What discourses do they bring to life and what are the impli-cations (Davies, 2001)?)

I will illustrate this by drawing on some outcomes of a research project known as the Preschool Equity and Social Diversity project (PESD) that is summarised in the Appendix. In the PESD project, I videotaped children during their 'free' play with four anti-bias persona dolls (Willie – Vietnamese-Australian doll, Tom – Anglo-Australian doll, Shiree – dark-skinned Indigenous Australian doll, and Olivia – Anglo-Australian doll) then used rhizomatic logic to develop new ways to interrogate and understand my 'data'. (See Mac Naughton, 2003 for an earlier iteration of this work.)

VIGNETTE 1
Diverse fragments from 40 minutes of 'free' play

Fragment 1: Four anti-bias persona dolls had been carefully placed in a play area defined by large outdoor wooden blocks under the verandah near the door that led from the inside play area of the centre to the outside play area. The play area also contained several large pieces of cloth, some cooking utensils and a stove.

Fragment 2: A video camera on a tripod was pointed at the area. The children could clearly see that as they entered the area they would be videotaped.

Fragment 3: A researcher sat nearby, noting who entered the play area, when and for how long.

Fragment 4: Two Anglo-Australian girls were the first children to enter the area. They began to play with the dolls by moving the two Anglo-Australian dolls, Olivia and Tom, to an area on the edge of the play area. This began a lengthy (nearly 35 minutes) of elaborate dramatic play in which the girls fed and talked to the dolls and put them to bed. During this play, the girls rearranged the blocks with great care; and at several points they used adjuncts such as pieces of cloth and eating utensils.

Fragment 5: The girls' dramatic play was punctuated on five occasions by the entry of individual boys, and on one occasion by the entry of a group of three boys. The boys hovered at the edge of the play area for minutes at a time before making forays into the girls' play. The boys jumped on the blocks, moved the pieces of cloth, handled Shiree roughly, moved Willie aside, stood menacingly in front of the girls, and shouted in several bursts of a minute or two.

Fragment 6: The girls used several tactics to ignore the boys, such as turning their backs and getting on with their play and successfully suggesting that the boys leave them alone.

Fragment 7: Throughout the play, Mai – a Vietnamese-Australian girl – sat to one side watching silently.

Fragment 8: As the girls and the boys left the play area, Mai entered it and picked up Willie. She sat him gently on a block and began talking to him.

How do these data fragments connect to each other?

Questions that invite the rhizome to map how power is organised in these fragments include: What does Fragment 8 'do' to the other data fragments? How does it overlap, cojoin or rupture what has come before? What new lines of understanding can it offer of all that has come before? Was Mai on the edge of the play watching because of what was in Fragment 4 (two Anglo girls entered the play area and chose Tom and Olivia) and in Fragment 5 (the boys moved Willie aside)? Did Mai stay at the edge of the play area because she understood that the 'racial' politics within it excluded her? How can we link Mai, Tom and Olivia with racism in this vignette? How does this vignette link with the wider issues of 'race' in Australia?

How do these data fragments link with other data fragments from texts outside of it?

To address this question using rhizomatic logic, I will use fragments from five texts beyond the research vignette to attend to the data inside it and to generate questions about what are appropriate ways to attend to children's voices in research:

- an article in an early childhood journal that explores the construction of identities (O'Loughlin, 2001).
- an article in an educational journal that explores the effects of the presence of ethnic minority teachers in education (Quiocho and Rios, 2000).
- an article in a childhood education research journal that explores solitary–active behaviour in preschools (Coplan, Wichmann and Lagacé-Séguin, 2001).

- a second PESD research vignette.
- a book on researching young children.

Identificatory positions as consequential to children: how does it connect?

What happens in young children's lives influences how they 'become'. This seems so obvious as to be not worth saying. However, many poststructuralists (e.g. Butler, 1997; Davies, 2001) argue that 'becoming' is full of tensions as children negotiate different possibilities for themselves as gendered, 'racialised' and classed beings and attempt to clarify which forms of 'becoming' are risky, possible and/or desirable. In and through their 'becoming', children learn to identify with specific ways of thinking and being, and to resist, reject or 'disidentify' (O'Loughlin, 2001) with others. O'Loughlin suggests that the development of a 'racial' identity depends on the 'Other':

> While it would seem, intuitively, that identification with one's own racial or ethnic group is essential to identify formation, some writers suggest that, at least for Caucasians, the development of a white racial identity may depend as much on defining an Other that they are not, as on defining some essential characteristics of whiteness with which to identify.
>
> (O'Loughlin, 2001, p. 50)

In Vignette 1, what were the possible ways of 'becoming'? How did the research influence the children's 'performance' of the discourses associated with them 'becoming' 'racial' beings? What was Mai becoming? Was Vignette 1 a significant discursive moment for all the children or just for Mai? O'Loughlin invites us to consider the former:

> The one thing we do not want to do, I think, is assume that subject formation is inconsequential, or that we need to do nothing because the inherent innocence of children will protect them from performing hateful acts.
>
> (O'Loughlin, 2001, p. 63)

Connecting Vignette 1 with O'Loughlin's text prompts me to ask several reflective questions. Would this moment have existed if the research didn't exist? Can we assume that research moments in which children are active participants are inconsequential and innocent moments and merely observe who and how they are 'becoming'? Can research ever be innocent? As we 'merely' observe children, are we colluding with their particular 'becoming'? With what in children's 'becoming' do I want to collude? O'Loughlin's text is outside of research, but shooting it into the middle of my research text raises new questions about the role of researchers in children's 'becoming' because of how power and race are in the middle of his text.

The power of presence of the 'Other': how does it connect?

Quiocho and Rios (2000) summarised the results of research between 1989 and 1998 about the experiences of minority group teachers during their preservice training and their entry to the education profession:

> One theme that has emerged is the perception of the 'margin-alized' teacher. In Feurverger's (1997) study of immigrant teachers in Canada, the teachers' personal narratives were used to talk about the complexities of being marginalized. . . . In spite of the training they received, these teachers were treated as second-class citizens and began to see themselves as such. They found themselves catapulted into a culture that refused to recognize either their strengths or the strengths of their students.
>
> (Quiocho and Rios, 2000, p. 509)

Quiocho and Rios were not writing about early childhood education or young children's dramatic play. However, overlapping it with my research prompts new questions of how power works in young children's lives. When does marginalisation of minority groups grow in education? Did Mai experience such marginalisation and what are the implications for early childhood education? Do young children from minority groups in a particular early childhood programme or a particular moment from a research project 'become' and see themselves as second-class citizens? What did Mai learn through her involvement in my research project? How did her experience in those 40 minutes of the research project link with and overlap her experiences beyond it? The moment when Mai sat on the edge of the play with the persona dolls, watching silently, has become, in my view, the central and most consequential fragment in the research text. Would that moment have happened if the research project didn't exist and (how) does it shoot into other moments in Mai's life?

Solitary play as dysfunctional: how does it connect?

Giving children a 'best' or a 'head' start through early education is so great a concern that children's positive adaptation to early childhood programmes is a source of interest and concern to researchers. Coplan, Wichmann and Lagacé-Séguin (2001) studied the dysfunctional effects of solitary play behaviour (non-social play, reticent behaviour and solitary–passive behaviour in preschools). They defined reticent behaviour thus:

> *reticent* behavior involves such activities as sitting/standing unoccupied, and observing others without subsequently attempting to join the interaction. . . . The display of reticent behavior in the preschool seems to be reflective of social anxiety and wariness. In this regard, reticent behavior in the preschool has been associated with maternal ratings of child shyness and negative emotionality, as well as teachers' ratings of children's internalizing problems . . .
>
> (Coplan, Wichmann and Lagacé-Séguin, 2001, p. 165)

They suggest that non-social play, including reticent behaviour, is connected to 'different forms of social and emotional maladjustment in this milieu' (ibid., p. 164). What happens if we use rhizomatic logic to place this argument in the middle of Fragment 7 in Vignette 1? Mai's reticence to join in could be explained as shyness and as evidence that she has internalised emotional problems. It could signal her social and emotional maladjustment to preschool. How does this logic connect to the texts of marginalisation (Quiocho and Rios, 2000; O'Loughlin, 2001) and how young children perform and experience 'race'? Is it Mai who has internalised emotional problems, or is it the children who never notice her and never invite her or Willie into their play? What is the consequence? How is racialised power 'becoming' in this research moment? How is working of power silenced by Coplan, Wichmann and Lagacé-Séguin (2001)?

VIGNETTE 2
'But she might like it' and what happens if I connect it?

Ten children (five boys and five girls) sit listening to a story about Olivia, the Anglo-Australian persona doll. Olivia is from a rich family, who have just moved to a new house and Olivia is choosing new curtains for her new bedroom. Her choices are fabric with pink hearts, or with pink and blue cats and dogs, or with fire engines or with bulldozers. The children are asked which fabric that they think that Olivia will choose. A majority say that she will choose the fabric with pink hearts, but one child dissents. A girl (Sandy) says uncertainly, 'I think she might like the fire engines'. The other children laugh at her suggestion and restate their choice loudly. Nevertheless, Sandy says again and with a little more determination, 'I think she might like the fire engines'. She repeats her view four times before finally hanging her head quietly and staying silent for the remainder of the discussion.

What do these two vignettes 'do' to each other? Mai and Sandy are two different girls in different places and parts and times of the research project. Do they overlap through texts about marginalisation, reticence, resistance and how being non-social might be produced in preschools? Did my research project – designed to explore and respect children's views – create their silences? How was power organised through observing children at play with physically diverse dolls and talking with children in groups about gendered choices?

How do these fragments connect to me?

To discover children's knowledge of 'race', class and gender, researchers in the PESD project used well-known and respected methods – we watched children and talked with them. The use of such naturalistic observation methods has a long history and continues to influence observational practices in early childhood studies. An equally acceptable way to bring children's voices into research is through interviews with individuals and groups (Dockrell, Lewis and Lindsay, 2000). My concern here is not so much with the techniques themselves, but with how I 'explain' what happened as I employed them.

Dockrell, Lewis and Lindsay (2000) remind researchers to be objective and to deploy clear strategies to find 'true' indicators of what children think and know. They warn researchers against devaluing their data through two types of error:

> Errors that occur because we underestimate a child's competence (commonly called a type 1 error) and errors that occur because we overestimate a child's competence (commonly called a type 2 error).
>
> (Dockrell, Lewis and Lindsay, 2000, p. 53)

My research in early childhood studies and, in particular, my use of rhizomatic logic to re-see what is 'becoming' gendered and 'racialised' in children's play could lead me to commit each type of error. I may have underestimated what children can and do know about gender, 'race' and class and I may have been drawn potentially to overestimate 'race' as a factor. For example, I may have colluded in Mai's marginalisation by not intervening as the other children marginalised Willie and Shiree and left Mai on the 'sidelines' of the play. However, using rhizomatic logic, of placing texts that map power and 'race' in the middle of my research, I can recast type 1 errors as underestimations of how the research organised power and its effects. Similarly, I can recast type 2 errors as overestimations of my capacity to do objective research that reaches a single, fixed and final truth, i.e. research that generates answers, not questions.

Towards rhizomatic logic: what do these fragments 'do' to each other?

I have just counterposed disparate fragments of text about research, voice, children, equity and social diversity, and explored ways to connect them that map 'race', gender and power. Doing so led me to new insights on power in the PESD, because the fragments I wove together highlighted the dangers in giving voice to young children in research without first asking:

• Which children's voices will come forth?
• What will the consequence be for each child who participates?
• How might one child's voice silence that of another?
• What can and should I do when the voices are racist or sexist?

- How might intervening as one child voices their knowledge enable another child to speak?
- How will I honour those children who struggle to make their voices heard?

These questions come to me not as the final stage of analysis but as a prompt to re-meet my 'becoming' as a researcher so that I do more than give voice to children. My use of rhizomatic logic in research analysis has led me to ask whether and how we can find ways to transform childhood research by becoming politically engaged researchers who transform children's (and adults') discourse and its effects on our 'becoming' rather than merely reporting how it works. To engage with the politics of our reporting the child is to go beyond merely reporting. To do so requires some simple moves towards rhizomatic logic:

- generate your texts of the child;
- interrogate your texts;
- 'be nomadic' and find texts beyond your own;
- place these other texts in the middle of your own text and see what they 'do' to each other that surprises you;
- use your surprises as points from which to practise afresh for liberty.

Generate your texts of the child

Rhizomatic logic can start anywhere with any text. But, it starts with generating and/or locating texts. In early childhood studies, it can start with generating and/or locating texts of the child. A child observation can be a good point to start.

Interrogate your texts

Ask of your text questions that push issues of equity to the fore and locate your own understandings of the text at present. Reworking the questions above, early childhood educators can ask of their child observations:

- What is happening in this observation?
- What are the texts I would normally refer (defer) to in a search for an answer?

- Which children's voices are present in my observations?
- What are the consequences for a child being present in my observations?
- How might my observations privilege one child's voice and silence that of another?
- What can and should I do when the observations I produce are racist or sexist?
- How might I use my observations to intervene in one child's voicing of their knowledge to enable another child to speak?
- How will I use my observations to honour those children whose voices struggle to be heard?

Rhizoanalysis isn't an alternative logic with which to analyse texts, so much as an invitation and permission to challenge traditional/ dominant ways to do so.

'Be nomadic' and find texts beyond your own

To explore these questions, rhizomatic logic suggests the need to seek texts beyond those that are normally used to create meanings about child observations. You need to break and cross the borders that say 'this is an early childhood text' and 'this is not'. Challenge the hierarchy that says an early childhood text will be better than other texts to 'read' the child. To explore what you can and should do when the observations are racist or sexist locate texts from early childhood educators but also cross the borders into texts from activists and scholars who have experienced racism or sexism and place them in the middle of your own. For instance, black feminist scholars placed in the middle of your analysis may deviate from what you had thought or known and enable you to trace new ideas through it. Treat the search for texts a little like being a nomad (Deleuze and Guattari, 1987). Search around and move from one to the other as you find the need to multiply your understandings.

As Best and Kellner explained:

> Rhizomatics is a form of 'nomadic thought' opposed to the 'State thought' that tries to discipline rhizomatic movement both in theory (e.g. totalizing forms of philosophy) and practice (e.g. police and bureaucratic organizations). Universalist state thought is exercised through 'state machines' and nomadic

thought combats them through its own 'war machines' such as rhizomatics.

(Best and Kellner, 1991, p. 102)

The choices you make about what texts to layer into the meanings of your observations will link to the rhizome you aim to build – to your political intent. The aim in rhizomatic logic is to link meanings (semiotic chains), such as gender meanings, with how power is organised and efforts to struggle for equity and justice:

A rhizome ceaselessly establishes connections between semiotic chains, organizations of power, and circumstances relative to the arts, sciences, and social struggles.'

(Deleuze and Guattari, 1987, p. 7)

If you wish to build a rhizome that challenges racism, then texts in which this challenge is present will produce lines of entry to it. If you wish to build a rhizome that challenges sexism, then texts that talk to this challenge, that are themselves in the middle of it, will link your observation with this work. Feminists – activists, scholars, policy makers, writers, film makers – are in the middle of this work.

To find the texts that provide new entry points to ways of making sense of child observations disrupts what was and links to what might be – it links it to becoming differently in how to make meaning in work with children. It links to struggles for social justice and to questions of how power moves through our meaning making in early childhood studies.

Place these other texts in the middle of your own text and see what they 'do' to each other that surprises you

Ask what is in the middle of your text (e.g. child observation) by placing other texts in the middle of it. What do the texts do to each other? Do they reinforce each other? Do they rupture each other? Do they connect with each other? Do they overlap? Do they point to the same direction? Do they call on the same discourses? Seek surprises in this work so that you can disrupt the familiar and the obvious in what you know about how power organises. Building new logic about what is happening in your text is about building new understandings of its relationships to other texts.

Use your surprises as points from which to practise afresh for liberty

In searching for tactics to practise for liberty, rhizomatic logic can orient you towards new lines for action, new ways to understand the child and the ways in which dominant discourses of gender, 'race', class, geography, age, sexuality and ability twist in on each other in the daily lives of early childhood. It is to search for what is now redundant in these discourses, what is resurfacing and remaking itself and what lines of attack against prejudice and bias are shooting now. As Deleuze and Guattari warn us, discourses do not disappear:

> A rhizome may be broken, shattered at a given spot, but it will start up again on one of its old lines, or on new lines.
> (Deleuze and Guattari, 1987, p. 9)

Kylie Smith used rhizomatic logic to create new ways to 'become' an observer of children. In the text that follows she shows how this has helped her to ask new questions about how to make sense of children's lives in and through observation – particularly a child called Isabel. She built her rhizome with the political intent to 'practise for liberty' and her choice of texts reflects this. She deliberately chose texts that question dominant discourses of the child, of gender, of 'race' and of class. Her efforts to link what is in the middle of them with what is in the middle of her observation mark a search for complex, shifting, social–political understandings of the child to guide her work as an early childhood educator and researcher. Kylie argues that 'There is a political framework embedded in rhizoanalysis'. She works to see what her texts 'do' to each other and to see how she can come to know who to 'be' in Isabel's 'becoming'.

KYLIE SMITH
Rhizoanalysis: a tactic for creating new co-ordinates for observation as a political practice for social justice

Rhizomes are about mapping new or unknown lines and entry points, not tracing which records old lines or patterns (Alvermann, 2000; Deleuze and Guattari, 1987). Deleuze and Guattari (1987) further argue that when mapping there is no starting point or ending; rather, they discuss middles.

To begin to examine this mapping and the complexity, a tracing is placed over the top so that deviations, breaks or ruptures can be identified, and the effects of these can be examined within the text (Alvermann, 2000; Deleuze and Guattari, 1987). By layering or juxtaposing text that is not necessarily related to early childhood, questions can be raised about dominant discourses within society and what that might tell us about the speech we take up (Alvermann, 2000).

I came to exploring the place of rhizomatic patterns in my understandings of the child, parent and early childhood professional in a search for a tool that supported the exploration of the child within a gaze that recognised the complexity, multiplicity, contradictory, contingent and shifting ways that the child, the parent and the early childhood professional learn, develop, relearn and change how they understand themselves, the world and others. Further, I wanted to recognise that identities are socially, historically and politically constructed. Gilles Deleuze and Felix Guattari's (1987) idea of rhizomatic structures provided an entry point to do this.

In what follows I use rhizoanalysis to:

- disrupt discourses that provide a gaze that sees and assesses the child, the parent and the early childhood professional as developing and learning through a linear progression by raising questions about the principles of rhizomatics;
- map the multiplicity of the child, parent and early childhood professional and their understandings of the world;
- use different texts to make visible points of rupture or inequity within the data and examine how they might do it differently.

To illustrate rhizoanalysis and its possibilities for our work with children I draw on three popular culture texts: *The Paper Bag Princess, Harry Potter* and *Buffy the Vampire Slayer*. I believe these books can illuminate some of the complexities and multiplicities about the child that traditional (modernist) discourses cannot.

Why choose The Paper Bag Princess, Harry Potter and Buffy the Vampire Slayer?

It was with political intent that I chose the books: *The Paper Bag Princess* (Munsch, 1980) *Harry Potter and the Philosopher's Stone*

(Rowling, 2001), *Harry Potter and the Chamber of Secrets* (Rowling, 1998) and *Buffy the Vampire Slayer, Power Of Persuasion* (Massie, 1999), and specific texts from those books to illuminate the complexity of culture, class, 'race', gender and sexuality. I did this to create dissensus for social justice in 'Spider room'. I chose *The Paper Bag Princess* (Munsch, 1980) and *Buffy the Vampire Slayer, Power Of Persuasion* (Massie, 1999) because they provided feminist perspective to female characters. *Harry Potter and the Philosopher's Stone* (Rowling, 2001) and *Harry Potter and the Chamber of Secrets* (Rowling, 1998) were chosen because the text illustrated the presence of class, gender, culture and 'race' in circulation. I was also political in my intent when I chose theorists such as Judith Butler (1997, 1990), Bronwyn Davies (2000, 1994, 1993, 1989), bell hooks (2000, 1990), Glenda Mac Naughton (2003) and Valerie Walkerdine (1990). I purposefully chose these theorists because they engage with and challenge how class, gender, culture, sexuality and 'race' intersect and circulate within and through discourses and the effects for social justice. Randomly choosing text, discourse and theorists would not have produced the same effects for social justice. The intent of a rhizoanalysis is to use text, discourses and theory to 'cast a shadow' over mapped text to create tracings that disrupt and challenge what has been mapped.

Randomly chosen text, discourses and theorists would merely re-map the epistemology of the child. Mapping documents constitutes and re-constitutes the 'truth' about the child and her world. Mapping does not question, challenge or trace to 'cast a shadow' over the patriarchal, white, middle-class discourses circulating within and through early childhood education to place social justice to the fore-ground of pedagogy.

To illustrate rhizoanalysis I'll start with a piece I call 'Do I need a thousand million pieces of paper?'

Rhizoanalysis of 'Do I need fifty thousand million paper?'

This episode began when Isabel, Malcolm, Nell and Zane were working at the drawing table and Isabel asked the other children if one of them would like to bring the A3 colouring book to her. Before beginning the analysis I will introduce Malcolm, Nell, Zane, and Isabel.

Malcolm was three years and eight months of age. He was the only child of professional middle-class white Australian parents. He had been at the service from the age of three months.

Nell was four years and six months of age. She was the only child
of Chinese parents who came to Australia from Hong Kong to study.
Cantonese was the family's first language. Nell had been at the service
for 18 months.

Zane was four years and seven months of age. He was the only
child of Chinese parents who immigrated to Australia from China.
His father was working while his mother, who was a doctor in China,
was studying so that her medical qualifications would be recognised
in Australia.

Isabel was four years and seven months of age. She was the only
child of professional middle-class white Australian and New Zealand
parents. She had been at the service from the age of six months.

*Being a girl in Spider room: the text of the observation
and locating popular culture texts*

At the time I was videotaping children's play and writing in my field
notebook while Gemma and Onya (the teacher–researchers in Spider
room) were working with the children in Spider room. Through my
observations of Isabel's social and language skills I had understood
her as a dynamic female who could cross over gender boundaries
and challenge patriarchal expectations of what it was to be a girl in
Spider room. However, in revisiting the data and considering other
texts, questions begin to emerge for me about the political effects
of being a girl and being knowable in Spider room. The rhizome of
this I have built begins with placing the language used by Isabel
in Spider room with the language used in *The Paper Bag Princess, Harry
Potter* and *Buffy the Vampire Slayer* beside each other. I will then look
at what they 'do' to each other.

THE CHILD OBSERVATION TEXT

VT7 22.9.99   10.08am   Isabel from Spider room

41 *Isabel*: Who's going to get me a sheet of paper so I can draw
       a picture?
    [Nell raises her hand.]
42 *Nell*: I want a present. I want a flower.
    [Malcolm, Nell and Zane all say 'me' at the same time and race
    to get a piece of paper for Isabel from the shelf right next to
    Isabel. They then hand Isabel a several pieces of paper each.]

43 *Isabel*: How much paper do I need? Do I need fifty thousand
   million paper?
44 *Malcolm*: And another one.
45 *Isabel*: Oh you know ... no Zane.
46 *Malcolm*: Another one to draw a flower.
47 *Isabel*: No.
48 *Isabel*: Oh no I can't draw on here. Ok. Who's going to put that
   on the ground and I'll come over here.
49 *Nell*: Me!
50 *Malcolm*: I will.
51 *Nell*: No I said ...
52 *Malcolm*: Nell!
53 *Isabel*: Nell, Malcolm said first so Malcolm you get it.

THE PAPER BAG PRINCESS

Elizabeth decided to chase the dragon and get Ronald back.
She looked everywhere for something to wear but the only
thing she could find that was not burnt was a paper bag. So
she put on the paper bag and followed the dragon. He was easy
to follow because he left a trail of burnt forests and horses'
bones ...

HERMIONE FROM *HARRY POTTER AND THE PHILOSOPHER'S STONE*

The toadless boy was back, but this time he had a girl with him.
She was already wearing her new Hogwarts robes. 'Has anyone
seen a toad? Neville's lost one' she said. She had a bossy sort of
voice, lots of bushy brown hair and rather large front teeth.
'We've already told him we haven't seen it,' said Ron, but the girl
wasn't listening, she was looking at the wand in his hand. 'Oh, are
you doing magic? Let's see it then.' She sat down. Ron looked
taken aback. 'Er – all right.' He cleared his throat. 'Sunshine,
daisies, butter mellow, turn this stupid, fat rat yellow.' He waved
his wand, but nothing happened. Scabbers stayed grey and fast
asleep. 'Are you sure that's a real spell?' said the girl. 'Well it's
not very good, is it? ... I'm Hermione Granger, by the way, who
are you?' She said all this very fast. Harry looked at Ron and was
relieved to see by his stunned face that he hadn't learnt all the set
books off by heart either. 'I'm Ron Weasley,' Ron muttered.

'Harry Potter,' said Harry. 'Are you really?' said Hermione. 'I know all about you, of course . . . Anyway, we'd better go and look for Neville's toad. You two had better change, you know, I expect we'll be there soon.'

And she left, taking the toadless boy with her. 'Whatever house I'm in, I hope she's not in it,' said Ron.

(Rowling, 1998, pp. 79–80)

BUFFY FROM *BUFFY THE VAMPIRE SLAYER*

Buffy sighed. 'The Moon sisters preach that to be female means to be all things, smart, musical, determined, and in control. I hardly know what it means to be Buffy Summers most of the time, much less the bearer of the title "feminine." Yeah, I still have stuffed animals in my bedroom, but I have a couple old Hot Wheels, too. I may freight-train my way through a batch of vampires like nobody else can, but I also like to cry at sad movies. Are there rules for being feminine and masculine? And if so, who made them up? Okay, the Moons are insane maniacal demonesses of destruction whose goal is total female rule in the high school and likely the whole town of Sunnydale and maybe even the world, but it's made me wonder about nature. How are things supposed to be? What is normal?'

ISABEL – FEMINIST OR MAN-AFFIRMED WOMAN?

ISABEL

41   *Isabel*: Who's going to get me a sheet of paper so I can draw a picture?

48   *Isabel*: Oh no I can't draw on here. Ok. Who's going to put that on the ground and I'll come over here.

THE PAPER BAG PRINCESS

'Elizabeth decided to chase the dragon and get Ronald back.'

HERMIONE

She had a bossy sort of voice, lots of bushy brown hair and rather large front teeth.

'Whatever house I'm in, I hope she's not in it,' said Ron.

BUFFY THE VAMPIRE SLAYER

> I hardly know what it means to be Buffy Summers most of the time, much less the bearer of the title 'feminine.' Yeah, I still have stuffed animals in my bedroom, but I have a couple old Hot Wheels, too. I may freight-train my way through a batch of vampires like nobody else can, but I also like to cry at sad movies. Are there rules for being feminine and masculine? And if so, who made them up?

I have drawn text from the four pieces of data to begin to bring into focus some of the ways it means to be a girl for Isabel in Spider room. Initially in September 1999 when this episode was recorded I saw Isabel's statements as displaying a strong female identity within Spider room. I saw Isabel as a feminist who directed the boys in play and was able to cross gender boundaries through language rather than taking the role of the helpless female in need of rescue (Butler, 1990; Walkerdine, 1990). However, in revisiting the text using rhizomatic logic and through reading work by feminist writers such as Judith Butler (1997, 1990), Bronwyn Davies (2000, 1994, 1993, 1989), bell hooks (2000, 1990), and Valerie Walkerdine (1990), I have begun to trouble my initial gaze of Isabel's text. Further still by tracing text from *The Paper Bag Princess*, *Harry Potter* and *Buffy the Vampire Slayer* over this map I am able to see points of rupture in my initial reading and cast a 'shadow' (Davies, 2000; Mac Naughton, 2002) over the co-ordinates of observation.

What might The Paper Bag Princess *tell us?*

Does Isabel get to be what I saw as a powerful female only through the approval of the males in Spider room, in this case Malcolm and Zane? hooks (2000) discusses the concept of women needing the approval of males in fulfilling and affirming their lived experiences as 'man-identified woman' (p. 95). This places the boys in the culturally dominant position as superior. Does Isabel collude with the boys to maintain the male/female dualism (Davies, 1994)? Was Isabel in fact performing in the role of helpless female by asking the other children to get paper and move books for her? In *The Paper Bag Princess*, Elizabeth the princess does not ask or wait for assistance when the dragon steals her prince away. Instead, she gets up and goes after the dragon and prince, battles the dragon and then rescues the prince. Why did Isabel not get up and get her own paper or move the book?

What might happen if she did? Can I ever know Isabel? Do I have a right to know her? By attempting to know Isabel through my gaze I need to be vigilant that I am not just reflecting the images of the co-ordinates of observation that are about who I am and the discourses that are circulating in and through my identity. hooks (1990) cautions that when trying to subvert discourses and revision co-ordinates, old narratives should not become a re-vision of imperialist masculine white culture in a different image. For example, I could have intervened and told Isabel to get her own paper to subvert my understandings of Isabel's reliance on the boys. This could encourage Isabel to be a strong self-reliant female. Or it could re-vision Isabel as a female who should not make demands of the males in the room and mark her needs as unimportant, positioning her in a role that serves the males' needs, not her own.

How might Harry Potter *cast a shadow over the knowable child?*

When text from *Harry Potter* is traced over Isabel's text, further questions trouble the singular gaze of the knowable child and glimpses of the rugged terrain of the unknowable child begin to immerge. Isabel is a white, blonde haired, blue-eyed female. Hermione in *Harry Potter* studies extremely hard to be a knowledgeable witch and frequently shares her opinions on how Harry and Ron should conduct themselves. On the surface Isabel and Hermione appear to be similar in sharing their opinions and directing others. However, while Malcolm, Zane and Nell seem to do Isabel's bidding, Hermione is assessed as 'bossy' and someone that Ron would not want to be stuck in the same house with. This site of rupture raises the question: does Isabel appear to have power within Spider room in this episode because she has a strong feminist identity or because she is the desirable image of the beautiful white imperialist female? Hermione has 'bushy brown hair and rather large front teeth'. Does her body image and the way she looks position her as undesirable to the boys? To shift power relations with the boys what does she have to give up to be desirable?

Did Isabel become the docile body, where she performs the political action of being the object of Malcolm and Zane's desire to shift power? Or within this patriarchal discourse does Isabel have the agency to do this, or do Zane and Malcolm place her in that position? bell hooks (2000) said that feminism is for everyone, but what are the political effects of being a feminist? For Hermione she is labelled as 'bossy' and ostracised by Ron. By asking Isabel to be a feminist within Spider room and challenge the image of desirable female due to her sexuality, would it place her in the margins and exclude her from other children or activities? For me this is confronting because I am asking children to be part of political discourses that I struggle with myself. My identity is complex and shifting depending on the situation I am in. I practise my gender and sexuality in multiple ways depending on the social context that I am in. At times I give up who I am as a feminist so that I fit within a discourse and am accepted within the rules and beliefs of that social group because it is desirable for me to be part of the group and not excluded. I don't want to sit in a corner by myself at a party. I want to be part of the group. What would it be like for Isabel to have to play in isolation in Spider room?

Intersections of Isabel and Buffy the Vampire Slayer

The character of Buffy Summers from the *Buffy the Vampire Slayer* has been acclaimed by some as portraying a powerful feminist role in popular culture on television and through fictional novels (Helford, 2002). When Isabel's text and text from *Buffy the Vampire Slayer* are juxtaposed it begins to illuminate the complexity of gender identity and the struggles to understand one's self let alone be assessed by another. Can a girl or woman always be observed as a strong independent female whose actions and questions challenge the dominant patriarchal discourses? How might co-ordinates of observation that make visible the confusion of gender identity support the observer and the observed to be seen in multiple, shifting and contradictory ways? How might these co-ordinates make visible the desires and the sacrifices of being a feminist or a subservient object? How might Isabel describe her images of what is to be a girl in Spider room? How might that description be different for Isabel in a different social context? Examples of what this might look like could include:

- Isabel as a female in the nurturing mother role volunteering and helping the early childhood professional to set up lunch.
- Isabel as a liberal feminist who demands a space and equal rights to the monkey bars alongside the boys so that she can swing upside down.
- Isabel as a feminist who attempts to discard or deconstruct male/female dualism through negotiating storylines in play to identify that females don't exist because of the category of male

(Davies, 1989). She may attempt to reverse these categories to female/male. This may be what she is doing when she says, 'Who's going to get me a sheet of paper so I can draw a picture?', reversing categories so that she is in the dominant position of female in the dualism.

By recognising Isabel's multiple and shifting femininities it is possible to explore the political and strategic choices a child chooses to speak and act.

My certainty about understanding and knowing Isabel and her identities has been shattered by tracing text from *The Paper Bag Princess*, *Harry Potter* and *Buffy the Vampire Slayer*. These texts have enabled a rhizomatic structure that raises questions and challenges current co-ordinates of observation that provided a gaze that draw me to an understanding of Isabel as knowable. The rhizome I have attempted to create has enabled me to make visible different co-ordinates to observe and assess Isabel that draw me to the conclusion that I will never know Isabel as she is shifting, contingent, multiple and contradictory within a political, historical and social context. What I can do is use every changing co-ordinate of observation to add to the complexity of Isabel's rhizome. What guides my choices will be based on social justice. My subjectivity of what constitutes social justice is blurred with my white, working-class, and heterosexual, catholic gaze. Hence, I need to enter into dialogue and consider texts that open up multiple choices about speaking and acting gender, culture, 'race', class and sexuality.

Final reflections

Rhizoanalysis is not only about mapping and re-mapping multiple views of the child through the use of text. There is a political framework embedded in rhizoanalysis. Rhizome co-ordinates of observation bring into focus and cast shadows over 'utterances' that provide a gaze about the multiplicity of who a child might be and how she might understand her world. It is with political intent that I used popular culture text to illuminate some of the precarious struggles for children around issues of gender, sexuality, culture, 'race' and class. My political intent is guided by the need to demand respect and support for all people to have safe spaces to explore, challenge, change, re-imagine and perform their identities and to have these identities acknowledged as valid and important. Choosing just any text would not produce the same points of rupture for social justice. The possibilities of continuing to develop more complex rhizome co-ordinates of observation are endless. How might my gaze shift and change in how I see and assess the child and myself when I trace other texts such as an autobiography by Nelson Mandela or text from Hansard (the minutes from the sittings from the Australian Commonwealth Parliament) or the narratives from indigenous women? My gaze would shift to recognise the child, the parent and myself as unknowable and multiple, and at the points of rupture in text, these sites would create space for descensus for me about my understandings of truth, power and knowledge in that moment. Rhizoanalysis creates a space for freedom and social justice for me as it allows me as the observer to examine, question, debate and pose other possibilities about the political, historical and social construction of gender, sexuality, 'race', culture and class for me and for the observed.

Constructing and reconstructing rhizomes for re-becoming

The link between political intent and rhizomatic logic was a powerful element of Kylie's work with young children. It highlights the connections between gender 'out there' and 'in here', i.e. between the world at large and the world of early childhood. It maps power and puts gender in the middle of each and blurs a certain reading of Isabel's 'becoming'. This logic ruptures the idea that Isabel is knowable through observation; what is knowable, however, is the politics and partiality of not only the observer's gaze but also the texts that we use to 'read' the child in early childhood studies. This rupture is not a void but a space for new lines of inquiry, for other ways to know Isabel and to know the place of gender in young children's lives.

Orienting rhizomatic logic to our 'readings' of children and classroom and research texts in early childhood studies is a practical way to 'build' complex and diverse pictures of 'the child', of 'observation' and of 'research'. It is also a practical way to expand the range of discourses through which meaning is generated in early childhood studies. Using rhizomatic logic, we can deconstruct and reconstruct meanings and, in doing so, challenge our 'will to truth' and find strategies to 'become' differently. We can map other possibilities and other ways of knowing, while remaining open to rewriting them:

The map is open and connectable in all of its dimensions; it is detachable, reversible, susceptible to constant modification. It can be torn, reversed, adapted, to any kind of mounting, reworked by an individual, group, or social formation.

(Deleuze and Guattari, 1987, p. 12)

Rhizoanalysis offers a tool for critically reflecting on how meaning is produced through the choices we make about what we use to map them. Patrick Hughes, a colleague, recently described it this way in commenting on this chapter:

Rhizoanalysis is a form of critical reflection, but on the 'reader' (researcher), rather than on the text. It illuminates the process of meaning-production, rather than illuminating the meaning/s in/of a text. It highlights the 'framing' that is at the heart of meaning-production by applying 'frames' that are 'other' to the traditional/dominant frames. This 'othering' could be carried to the point where the choice of 'other' frames is random. However, choosing frames with political intent displaces the nihilism and anarchy of randomness with action for (e.g.) social justice. Thus, Foucault's 'deliberate practice for liberty' comes to include the always-becoming knowledge (not truth) of how we do and could 'frame' events and the consequences of our choice.

(Patrick Hughes, e-mail communication, 2 April 2004)

For reflection

- What are the texts you would normally refer (defer) to in order to make sense of child observations?
- What lines of inquiry could you follow to expand the texts you use to make sense of child observations?
- How might you draw on rhizomatic logic to map power in your work in early childhood studies?

Chapter 5

Seeking the 'Otherwise'

Re-meeting relations of 'race' in early childhood classroom histories

> Knowledge of Whiteness and postcolonial theories has enabled
> me to critique my practice in new and exciting, if somewhat
> painful, ways . . . – it provides me with a structure to question
> monocultural assumptions about teaching and learning,
> contributes to my knowledge of the strategies used by 'Whites'
> to disengage and disassociate with issues of 'race' and racism
> and with new ways 'in' to question resistance.
>
> (Karina Davies, early childhood educator
> and researcher, Victoria, Australia)

> The multicultural national will, like all national will, tolerates
> national otherness, but only in so far as this national otherness is
> in no danger of constituting a counter-will.
>
> (Hage, 1998, p. 12)

Re-meeting history

This chapter presents ways for activist early childhood educators to use histories of the present and seeking the 'Otherwise' to
tactically challenge relations of race in early childhood research
and classrooms. It weaves together Foucault's ideas of writing
histories of the present and postcolonial theorists' tactics of 'seeking
the Otherwise' to extend the tactics and targets of anti-bias/
anti-discriminatory education in early childhood classrooms.

It aims to undermine the possibilities of racism in early childhood studies in the present. Specifically it:

• suggests how the tactics of postcolonial theorists can be used
  to 're-meet' histories and learn to 're-act' against racism;

- outlines the place of relations of 'race' in early childhood class-room histories;
- explores how this links with contemporary 'race' politics in Australia;
- draws on conversations with young children to point to how in their lives 'race'-colour matters, 'whiteness' is desirable, 'Otherness' is marginal and exotic and the dark 'Other' is to be feared;
- shares vignettes from an early childhood researcher and an educator who have attempted to 're-meet' their histories of 'whiteness' to re-meet their relations to 'race'.

The chapter begins with Foucault's argument that our future overlaps and is inextricably linked with our past and that history is a struggle of forces.

Foucault on history

> I am fascinated by history and the relationship between personal experience and those events of which we are a part. I think that is the nucleus of my theoretical desires.
>
> (Foucault, 1998, p. 124)

Foucault believed that the past and the present are intimately and politically connected; and that these connections produce contested and overlapping ways of thinking and being in our world. For Foucault, we should not ignore the past if we wish to understand the present. The past has effects and so to re-meet our history is to have effects and power in the present. Re-meeting history is to look again at what has been and to see it in new ways that provoke us to act and to see differently in the present.

Foucault argued that effects of the past and its power in the present are often silenced in traditional historical accounts which present history as a set of undisputed chronological facts or events caused by 'great men' who make discoveries, pass laws, govern countries and explore continents (e.g. Foucault, 1998). For instance, traditional accounts of events, such as the 'discovery' of Australia by white Europeans in the 1700s, produce a chronological set of undisputed events and facts in which 'great men' make history (discovering 'new worlds') by travelling the globe in ships and discovering new lands. As I learnt the history of Australia in the 1950s in my primary years I learnt the dates that specific European explorers sighted and landed on Australia. I was taught the history of Australia through the dates of key events and people that were deemed to have 'made' contemporary Australia. In this history, 'firsts' were important, starting with the arrival of the first fleet in 1788. We learnt when the first convicts arrived from Britain, the first free settlers, the first cattle and sheep, and the date that gold was first discovered. To learn the history of Australia was to learn the dates of events and the names of those involved in those events and to know the correct chronological order in which they happened from 1788 through to the 1950s. In contrast, Foucault's historical accounts (e.g Foucault, 1985) pointed to connections between non-chronological events, highlighted disputed facts, presented multiple perspectives on events and their effects and pointed to discursive struggles that shaped the pasts and the present.

History is 'made' through discourses

Foucault showed that 'great men' are shaped by their times and the dominant discourses of their time and that they act to reproduce those discourses. In other words, history doesn't just happen because 'great men' do something. It is made because particular ways of thinking about what should be done and how it should be done dominate specific epochs. History for Foucault was 'an ongoing chaotic struggle between different forces, and according to different levels – or patterns – of time' (Danaher, Schirato and Webb, 2000, p. 101). To understand history was to understand the discursive struggles, the different forces, the gaps and the contradictions that produced our pasts and that overlap with our present. Therefore, history could never be a simple chronology where one event logically led to another. Events may have no effect on the future and an event in one century may mark time before its effects are seen in another time and place, but events may be linked through discourse, i.e. shared ways of making sense of the world. For instance, the history of Australia is linked through colonial discourses of 'race' that emerged in the 1700s to justify its colonisation that have ever-present effects in contemporary relations between Indigenous and non-Indigenous Australians.

History is histories with losses and gaps

For Foucault, there wasn't just one history of a time, i.e. one set of facts and events that capture what happened in our past. Instead, there are many histories. For instance, the histories of women, of people with disabilities and of indigenous people are often buried in traditional accounts of the past that don't seek out and share their lives (McNay, 1995). To seek these histories is to find new insights into their lives and our contemporary institutions. For instance, to find new insights into 'race' in early childhood classrooms we must seek the histories of 'race' that have been buried over time, such as indigenous histories of 'race', but niggle at our present.

To find the untold histories is not simple. Documents that illuminate histories can be lost, oral histories and stories disappear as languages disappear and some people never meet historians or leave material that enable their stories to be told. Danaher, Schirato and Webb (2000) argued that these losses 'continue to "haunt" this (historical) record through their silences, opening up gaps within the historiographic enterprise' (p. 101) and they cite examples of the stories of European peasants and of indigenous people. These losses, gaps and silences in what we know from our past demonstrate that our history is not whole. It is partial, it can be understood differently by different people and it is, therefore, contradictory. History *is* these partialities, contradictions, gaps and silences. Consider the following statement from one of my primary school texts in which a 'white' Australian tells of what 'white' invasion of indigenous lands meant for Indigenous Australians:

> Captain James Cook saw other natives on the east coast in 1770, but he, like Dampier, was only passing by and did not get to know them well.
>
> It was different in 1788, when the first shipment of white men came to Australia to settle. From then on life began to change for the Stone Age people who had been the only inhabitants of the country for so long. . . . In some places the aborigines put up a fight against the white man, speared his sheep and cattle, and sometimes his family and servants. Then white men raided the native camps and killed members of the tribe. Some aborigines learnt to work for white people.
>
> (Pownell, 1960, p. 35)

From a Foucauldian perspective, history is always associated with a politics of truth. To 'tell' history always and inevitably involves struggles over meanings that are discontinuous and partial and that overlap with the present. Therefore, someone with a Foucauldian perspective on history would ask questions about that account such as: Where in that account do Indigenous Australians say what it meant to have their land stolen from them, what they lost in learning to work for 'white' people and why they chose to do this? What has been silenced in and by this account of Indigenous Australians' encounter with 'white' Australians? For example, where is any intimation of the widespread deaths that accompanied white 'settlement'? Rowley (1986) tells of 'piles of (Aboriginal) human bones in the bush' (p. 5) being commonplace as Aboriginals struggled against their land being stolen and as cattle denuded the land that had fed them. Where is any discussion of whether you can 'settle' land that is not yours in the first place? In searching for answers to such questions we re-meet history and, as we do so, we can see the 'racialised' present afresh – and act differently in it.

History is comprehensible through genealogy

Foucault used what he called a genealogical method to explore the traces and absences of the past in our present. He traced the power/knowledge practices of specific institutions (e.g. schools, prisons, police organisations, asylums, factories, barracks and hospitals) to show how their particular ways of organising people and ideas came to be. His genealogical works that explored these institutions included:

• *Discipline and Punish* (1977 trans.)
• *The History of Sexuality* (1978 trans.)
• *Madness and Civilisation* (1965 trans.)
• *Mental Illness and Psychology* (1976 trans.).

In his genealogical work, Foucault sought to know the present differently by 'analysing and uncovering the historical relationship between truth, knowledge and power' (Danaher, Schirato and Webb, 2000: p. ix), a task that he saw as central to his ongoing intellectual project:

There are times in life when the question of knowing if one can think differently than one thinks and perceive differently than one sees is absolutely necessary if one is to go on looking and reflecting at all.

(Foucault, 1985, pp. 8–9)

Engaging genealogically with our pasts and their traces in our presents can offer powerful insights into how we organise institutions and relationships in them (e.g. early childhood institutions). However, Foucault's genealogies can also help us to think differently about those institutions and relationships in the present, so Danaher, Schirato and Webb (2000, p. 97) characterised them as 'histories of the present'. For instance, a genealogy of early childhood institutions in general, or of specific early childhood classrooms, would trace their struggles over truth and knowledge, highlighting losses, gaps and silences to encourage us to think differently about them through a 'history of the present'. A Foucauldian genealogy of 'race' in early childhood would be a critique of early childhood norms about how to be and how to act in an early childhood classroom. It would ask questions such as:

- Whose understandings of 'race' in this classroom have I silenced?
- Whose experiences of 'race' are not recorded? Whose perspective is missing?
- Whose documents have produced the current norms? Whose documents are absent?
- What have I not seen or understood about 'race' relationships in this classroom?
- What have been the struggles between different ideas, practices and relationships of 'race' over time, for instance, in how we organise the classroom or how we plan for learning?
- What forces have produced those struggles?
- What forces have produced the gaps in my knowledge of this classroom?
- What are the effects of these historical issues on what we can know now and on current 'racialised' power/knowledge relations?
- How does the 'racial' past appear in what we do now and how do its absences affect my understandings and actions?

Such questions can help us to think differently and critically about the present and they offer a critical basis from which to re-imagine and reinvent current inequitable or unjust institutional practices and relationships (e.g. relations of 'race' in early childhood classrooms). As McLaren (2002) argued, Foucault's analysis of social institutions and practices is a critique of sociological and philosophical norms that reduce our possibilities for freedom and justice because it shows these norms to be partial and biased. For instance, Western Minority World child development norms are based upon Western Minority World expectations of children and ways of studying them. Hence, they are not universally applicable but culturally limited (biased and partial) in their application. Understanding this enables us to rethink how we might be different, and we might seek greater freedom and justice for all. If we know what has been lost from history, we can change how we see and understand our relationships with each other now. We can seek to produce new histories in an effort to produce new presents and in doing so to practise for liberty in them. The point of history for Foucault was not to understand the past but to understand the present in order to find new possibilities in it (Alvesson, 2002).

Re-meeting 'race' histories

Histories explore shifts and struggles in relationships between people's experiences and the events of which they are a part (Foucault, 1998). Histories also explore relationships between groups of people and the power/knowledge politics of the institutions that structure these relationships. In 'race' histories, the relationships between people in different parts of the world (e.g. Europe, Africa and Australia) come to the fore. Colonisation of one part of the world by another has been the colonisation of one group of people by another. Colonisation is the history of exploitation of people and their physical (e.g. mineral and natural) resources by 'invaders'. Geopolitics is the study of these histories and relationships.

Geopolitics and postcolonialism

Geopolitics explores the politics of relationships between people in different parts of the world and the effects of geography on their power/knowledge relationships. For instance, it is about the politics of colonisation and how they are linked to a country's geography – its natural resources, its climate and its landscape. When the British colonised Australia in the 1700s, the combination of the natural landscapes and climates of Australia, together with the ways in which the British stole land from Aboriginal people, and how they used it, significantly threatened Aboriginal survival. In the dryer areas of Australia, the British grazed cattle on Aboriginal lands and their cattle – inevitably – competed for scarce water with Aborigines and with the indigenous animals that had been Aborigines' traditional food sources. The results included the 'piles of bones in the bush' that Rowley (1986, p. 5) referred to.

When we apply Foucault's genealogical studies to geopolitical histories, such as relationships between groups of people living in Europe and Australia, we emphasise how discourse operates as a colonising force, connecting people living in different times and producing overlapping and contested ways of understanding and practising relationships between them (Danaher, Schirato and Webb, 2000). For instance, we can consider how 'racialised' discourses of 'whiteness' that produce it as preferable to 'blackness' allowed Britain to invade Australia and take land from indigenous peoples in the 1700s connected to the institution of a 'white' Australia immigration policy in the 1900s. The challenge by indigenous peoples in the 1700s to a 'white' invasion and the challenge by groups of Australians to the 'white' Australia policy in the 1900s show oppositional and overlapping 'race' discourses at play across different times.

So, while the 1700s and 'bones in the bush' might seem far removed from the pedagogies and possibilities we construct for each other now in Australian early childhood classrooms, in what follows I point to possible ways to re-meet relations of 'race' in contemporary Australian early childhood classrooms by linking them with the geopolitics of the 1700s and beyond. The conceptual tactics used to do this, borrowed from Foucault and from postcolonial theorists, allow us to trace the power/knowledge relations that produced pasts and the overlaps with presents. While these tactics are applied to the geopolitics between Australia and Britain, they can be used also to produce additional critical geopolitical histories that allow people living elsewhere to think differently about pedagogies and relations of 'race' in early childhood classrooms in the present. They do this by raising questions about how 'race' discourses that act as 'snakes' (borrowing from Sheralyn's metaphor in Chapter 2) in Australia now might slither across into other times and places.

Foucault and postcolonialism: a note

While Foucault is rarely referred to as a postcolonial scholar, he has been widely used by key postcolonial theorists, such as Edward Said (see *Orientalism*, 1978), to trace the construction and operation of racist orientalist discourses. In this groundbreaking work on the effects of racial imagery and politics of the 'oriental', Said established that Western knowledge of the 'East' and the 'Orient' was fundamentally biased and embedded in relations of power between the 'West' and the 'East'.

Postcolonial scholars have shown how to deconstruct and reconstruct 'racialised' geopolitical histories of the present (Said, 1978; Nandy, 1983; Spivak, 1985, 1990). Postcolonial theorists like Said draw on several of Foucault's ideas in their efforts to explore specific instances of knowledge/power relations and geopolitics. These ideas include but are not limited to the following:

- The colonial is a discourse in which power and knowledge are cojoined (Ashcroft, Griffiths and Tiffin, 1998).
- Discourse is a relation of power that is open to resistance, for instance by the colonised and dispossessed (Loomba, 1998).
- Knowledge (e.g. of 'race') is discursive and thus intimately connected with the operation of power between different groups.

(Said drew heavily on these ideas in *Orientalism* (Loomba, 1998).)

Postcolonialists' tactics: tracing 'race' histories, tracing 'whiteness'

The postcolonial is a time (after colonisation has ended), but it is also a way of thinking that seeks to investigate colonialism's effects in the present. Ghandi (1998) defined colonialism succinctly and powerfully as the 'historical process whereby the 'West' attempts systematically to cancel or negate the cultural difference and value of the 'non-West' (p. 16). Postcolonial scholars study the knowledge/power geopolitics produced by encounters between 'West' and the 'non-West'; for instance, the creation in the 'West' of distinctions between the 'civilised' and the 'non-civilised 'and its application in the colonisation of the 'new world' which included Australia. The original habitants of colonies such as Australia were seen as non-civilised and 'genetically pre-determined to inferiority' (Ashcroft, Griffiths and Tiffin, 1998, p. 47). The British invented the term 'aborigine' in the mid-1660s to distinguish indigenous inhabitants of its colonies from its 'settlers'. But also embedded into its meaning were the derogatory links with the primitive and the savage. This idea of the 'savage and primitive' Australian Aboriginals persisted through time.

Some 200 years later, my 1960s primary school text – *The World We Share* – maintained those distinctions. Its 'Section B – Primitive Man in Modern Times' introduced us to 'the Negritos of Malaya', 'the Aboriginal People of Australia' and 'the Eskimos' (Pownall, 1960, pp. 29–41). It told us that the 'Aborigines' 'lived very much like the Stone Age people of other lands' and that 'when white people first saw the aborigines they thought them savages who lived more like animals than humans' (Pownall, 1960, p. 31).

Colonialism was linked intimately with cultural and economic exploitation and oppression in colonies populated by indigenous peoples, such as Australia. These possibilities were intimately linked to an ideology of 'race' that ensured that the colonising 'races' saw themselves as superior to those that they colonised (Ashcroft, Griffiths and Tiffin, 1998). As Mac Naughton and Davis (2001) explain:

> This ideology of race was strongly rooted in Social Darwinism and its core elements (which continue to construct an ideology of race today) were, firstly, that it is possible (and desirable) to classify people into distinct groups by noting their biological, genetic and physical characteristics. Secondly, people's behaviour is related to those biological, genetic and physical differences. Thirdly, the simplest way to distinguish between groups of people is on the basis of their physical characteristics, especially colour. Finally, some groups of people (races) are more competent and advanced than are others with the most advanced groups of people (races) being the Europeans and Aryans. The construction of this ideology of race provided a

justification for the behaviours of European colonizers towards indigenous peoples.

(p. 86)

Postcolonial scholars revisit, remember and interrogate our colonial past (Ghandi, 1998) to show its effects on our present 'racial' politics and imagery and to highlight its omissions. Their work challenges what Crowley called 'the mystifying amnesia of the colonial aftermath' that produced 'the extraordinary ordinariness of "whiteness"' (Crowley, 1999, p. 106) in countries such as Australia. Their work also links to Foucault's concern with 'histories of the present' (Danaher, Schirato and Webb, 2000), encouraging us to engage with our past and its silences by 'reading for Otherwise' (Chow, 1993). Reading for Otherwise involves imagining how people 'Other' to the culturally and 'racially' elite and privileged (for instance, white Australia) might understand something. It implies and requires access to an 'Other' wisdom – the wisdom of the dispossessed, oppressed, marginalised and silenced (Loomba, 1998). For example, reading for Otherwise requires me – a white Anglo-Australian – to seek wisdom beyond that given to me by my white privilege to understand gender, 'race' and class in children's lives. How might I understand gender, 'race' and class if I was not a 'white' Australian? How have discourses of whiteness shaped 'histories of the present' (Danaher, Schirato and Webb, 2000) in Australian classrooms and how do they continue to do so? To answer these questions I turn to the histories of the present from the Preschool Equity and Social Diversity (PESD) project (refer to the Appendix, pp. 216–217) and a re-meeting with my 'whiteness'.

Re-meeting 'whiteness': histories of the present in a research project

As I engaged with the young children in the PESD, I saw themes recurring in how they constructed their knowledge, desires, experiences and ideologies of 'race'. In particular, I was confronted by the 'extraordinary ordinariness of whiteness' (Crowley, 1999, p. 106) in their early lives. This was apparent at a time (the late 1990s) of persistent struggles in public discourse about who had the right to be considered a 'real' Australian. I was haunted by the paradox that in Australia, whiteness is both extraordinary and ordinary and this paradox challenged me to think about the place of 'whiteness' in my own life as a 'white' Australian. It pushed me to respond to Foucault's challenge to produce a history of the present that could help me to re-meet 'whiteness'; and to respond to the challenges of postcolonial theorists to read for the 'Otherwise'. Starting with what had been ordinary in my own life about 'whiteness', I sought gaps, overlaps and silences in my early years and in the PESD.

Seeking gaps, overlaps and silences: my early years and the PESD

Many things helped to produce the ordinariness of 'whiteness' in the early years of my life. I grew up in 1950s and 1960s Australia. Like me, my family, my neighbours, my teachers, my local shop-keepers and my friends were all white, Anglo-Australians. This was not an accident but an effect of British colonists being white and of British laws being enacted in its colonies that inserted white British values and institutions into all aspects of Australian life. Schooling was no exception.

My primary school texts were implicated in my view of whiteness as ordinary and their images and ideas connected me with colonial views of Indigenous Australians as the 'primitive aborigine' (Pownall, 1960, p. 31). My storybooks accomplished the ordinariness of 'whiteness' as much through how they portrayed the 'other' to whiteness – non-whiteness – as through how 'whiteness' was lived by those within them. The 'non-whites' were the exotic and strange 'red Indians' and the silly and scary 'black' golliwogs. All that was magical and good in those early years – Santa, God, the tooth fairy, the Easter Rabbit and my storybook princesses – were white. I knew without knowing that being 'white' was good, desirable and normal.

My early knowledge of 'whiteness' was shaped and reshaped by the social and cultural landscape of a 'white' Australian in which 'whiteness' was what I knew, desired, experienced, practised, believed in and was. My schooling did little to challenge the ordinariness of 'whiteness' in my early life – indeed, it did much to reinforce it. British textbooks, British history, British folk dancing and British poetry were only a few of the very British and, within this, very 'white' and 'Anglo' ways of thinking, knowing and being that were part of my daily life at school. What does all that matter now? I was young and I was innocent of Australia's racist past and present. I was innocent of 'white' Australia's history of genocide against its indigenous peoples and its constant pursuit and enactment of a 'white Australia' immigration policy. I did not know about the history of colonisation that had led to the fact of 'whiteness' and it ordinariness in my life.

However, even the knowledge of the young is not accidental, it is touched inevitably by the knowledge of others and by the geo-politics and the power/knowledge relationships of a particular time and place. Australia still operated a 'white Australia' immi-gration policy and so post-war immigration had little impact on Australia's cultural and social landscape. Australian immigra-tion patterns and policies and relationships between Britain and Australia touched my early life even if I was not aware of it. If we take a Foucauldian position on this knowledge, Australia's educational and social institutions were not innocent in their artic-ulation and production of my knowledge about whiteness. They were profoundly connected with the operation of 'white' power within an Australian society that presupposed 'blackness' as prim-itive and savage. Loomba drew on Foucault to remind us that, 'knowledge is not innocent but profoundly connected with the operations of power' (Loomba, 1998, p. 43).

Since that time, much has changed. Australia is now one of the most racially and culturally diverse countries in world with immi-grants from over 150 countries (Australian Government, 2004) arriving in the late 1990s. Nonetheless, what children in PESD knew and said about 'race' showed traces of the then-in-the-now. The histories of whiteness were present in the identities of young Australian children in the present and have produced four discur-sive traces of colonialism and of the 1950s in the present:

- race-colour matters;
- 'whiteness' is desirable;
- 'Otherness' is marginal and exotic;
- 'the dark Other' is to be feared.

Race-colour matters: discursive traces of colonial histories in the present

Skin colour mattered to most of the Anglo-Australian children we interviewed in the PESD project. For instance, approximately two-thirds of the Anglo-Australian children sorted the four persona dolls by skin colour and other physical attributes including hair colour, eye colour and clothing rather than by equally obvious differences produced by gender or clothing. Spivak (1990, p. 62) calls this process of basing decisions on skin colour 'chromatism'. The children introduced and used the terms 'black', 'brown' and 'white', not the researchers. For instance:

Researcher: At your house. Oh I see. All right so, which doll here looks, do you think, looks the most like you? The most like you, Sally.
Child: This one.
Researcher: This one. You chose Olivia.
Child: Cause this one's got brown skin.
Researcher: Oh. And what colour is your skin?
Child: White.
Researcher: If you have a look at your skin, which doll has skin like yours?
Child: I have white skin, it's that one (pointing to Olivia).

Some children struggled to find the words to accurately describe the colour of the persona dolls, but many were clear that they themselves were 'white'. They used this term to identify themselves in relation to the dolls and in particular to describe how they were different from Willy (the Vietnamese-Australian doll) and from Shiree (the Indigenous Australian doll). Nearly half of the of the Anglo-Australian cohort of children introduced and used the term 'white' to describe themselves and others.

A small group of children saw 'white' and 'Australian' as insep-arable. James exemplified most powerfully these children's clear view that 'whiteness' constituted 'Australian':

James

Researcher: These dolls all live in Australia. I was wondering . . . do you live in Australia?
James: I was born in Australia.
Researcher: Do you think all of these dolls were born in Australia?
James: No.
Researcher: Can you tell me?
James: [interrupts and points to Shiree] That's Aboriginal isn't she?

Researcher: Yes that's right. So, was she born in Australia?
James: [Shakes his head.]
Researcher: No? Where do you think she was born?
James: In Aboriginal. (Did he say 'Aboriginal land'?).
Researcher: In Aboriginal land. And can you tell me about Australia? What it means to live in Australia?
James: That you all have white skin.
Researcher: So what about Willy? Do you think Willy was born in Australia?
James: [Says nothing.]

Additionally, these children said that:

• Willy couldn't be Australian because he was born in Australia, but he is still Vietnamese.
• Willy and Shiree are not Australian because 'they've got different faces'.
• Willy and Shiree must ask God if they want to be Australian. God might allow Shiree to be Australian but not Willy.

Anglo-Australian children also used 'whiteness' as a category when deciding which doll looked most like them and when discussing Shiree. One child's *only comment* during her interview was in response to the question, 'Which doll looks most like you?'. Pointing to Olivia (the Anglo-Australian doll) she said, 'I'm white'. She was an Anglo-Australian child.

Why did skin colour matter to these young children living in multicultural Australia now? Why did some young children prioritise this in their efforts to describe themselves in relation to our dolls? What difference had the past 200 years made in how those of us in 'white' Australia had come to see and know ourselves? Did the fact that these children knew that their skin colour was 'white' express the racial power/knowledge relationships of their time? Or were they innocent or ignorant of such colonial power/ knowledge relations? Postcolonial theorists would argue that they weren't and can't be. The creation of the 'racialised' 'other' is at the heart of the possibility of racism (Hall, 1996). To racialise the 'other' one must racialise the 'self'. One must know how one differs from the 'other'. For white Australia, skin colour is how one knows oneself. The learning of this begins early. But for racism to flourish it is the desire for 'whiteness' and the fear and marginalisation of the 'other' – the 'non-white' – that makes skin colour matter. Constructing 'whiteness' matters when desires are constructed in and through it. This takes me to the second trace of the then-in-the-now.

'Whiteness' is desirable: discursive traces of colonial histories in the present

You may recall that in my early years, all things good and lovely were 'white'. I knew I was 'white' and all around me told me that 'white' was good. To know whiteness, as many children in the PESD did, is one thing. To find goodness and beauty in that 'whiteness' is another. My next conversation I call 'Lovely is lighter' and it is taken from my first interview with John, a four-year-old Anglo-Australian child. In this conversation, the link with knowing your 'race-colour' and the desires within this knowledge is undeniable.

Lovely is lighter

Researcher: Well this is Olivia and this is the last of the dolls you will meet today. Is there anything you can tell me about Olivia?
John: She is very pretty.
Researcher: What makes her pretty?
Researcher: What's that you are pointing at, her dress. Is there anything else that makes her pretty?
John: This does.
Researcher: What's that, can you use your words to tell me?
John: Legs, these are knees.

[John then looks at Olivia's face very closely for several seconds. The researcher picks up on this cue and asks a question.]

Researcher: What about her face, is there anything about her face you can tell me?
John: Her face is lovely like mine because it's lighter. It's like Tom's.

John was not the only child to find 'white' desirable and good. Most (70 per cent) of the Vietnamese-Australian girls in the study identified themselves consistently with the white-skinned and fair-haired doll. Kim was one such girl. Kim was a four-year-old Vietnamese-Australian girl who attended an early childhood centre that was strongly committed to including multicultural perspectives in its programme. (Kim's teacher believed that Kim spoke sufficient English to participate in the project, but when Heather, my co-interviewer, interviewed Kim, a Vietnamese-Australian bilingual worker at Kim's centre was also present.) Kim entered the room where she was to meet the persona dolls for the first time. I sat ready to take notes of the interview. Kim was holding Heather's hand tightly. Her attention quickly fixed on the dolls. I-was not sure which of the dolls held her attention so tightly but I could see her staring at them. Kim sat down and listened closely as Heather introduced the dolls to her. She looked closely at each doll as Heather told her about it. Heather then said to Kim that we'd like to ask her some questions.

Kim's blushes

Researcher: Do you understand, Kim?
Kim: [Nods.]
Researcher: When you look at the dolls, can you tell me which doll you think looks most like you?
Kim: [Silence. She looks at Heather then casts her eyes down and points at Olivia. As she does so, she blushes very strongly.]
Researcher: I see. Can you take a good look for me and be sure?
Kim: [Nods and then points again at Olivia, this time holding the researcher's gaze. She blushes again.]

Kim was silent but responded clearly and unambiguously to our questions. She told us that she looked like Olivia, not like Willy, Tom or Shiree. This was especially noteworthy as later in the interview she identified facial and skin tones as the main differences she saw between the dolls.

Kai was a Thai-Australian girl who also seemed fascinated and enamoured with Olivia to the exclusion of each of the other dolls. When asked why she had chosen Olivia as her favourite doll, she said, 'Olivia is good' and said that she didn't want to talk about Shiree or Willy. How has this come to be for John, James and for Kai? Why did Kim choose so determinedly to self-identify with Olivia? What is it about the knowledge/power relations of those children's time and place that produces these possibilities? How have children come to know this? How have they come to express a position that sits so comfortably with Principles Seven and Ten of Pauline's Hanson's One Nation Policy Document on Immigration, Population and Social Cohesion? Hanson was a controversial Australian politician who formed the One Nation Party in the late 1990s. The policy document stated:

> Principle Seven: Our migrant intake will be non-discriminatory on condition that the numbers do not significantly alter the ethnic and cultural make up of the country.
>
> Principle Ten: The Government institutionalised, publicly funded policy of Multiculturalism is not in the best interests of migrants, nor of Australia, and will be abolished.
>
> (Pauline Hanson's One Nation Policy Document:
> Immigration, Population and Social Cohesion
> www.gwb.com.au/onenation/policy/immig.html,
> downloaded 21 November 2002)

I am certain that neither James, Kim nor Kai had read this document. So what knowledge/power conditions produced it and produced Anglo- and Asian-Australian children's sense of the desirability of 'whiteness'? Are they linked? Borrowing from Gilroy (1996, p. 22), can we find 'cues and clues' in these three children's words to explain how desires about 'race' and 'whiteness' merge then and now, in children and in adults? Gilroy argued that:

> Both colonisers and colonised are linked through their histories, histories which are forgotten in the desire to throw off the embarrassing reminders of empire.

How do the 'embarrassing reminders of empire' in Hanson's policy documents link to James and Kai? How is that history precipitating a desire for whiteness now? I thought that I knew the answer. Fifty years of research on children and 'race' says:

- Black children consistently choose white dolls as those that they'd like to play with and as the ones that look pretty (Gopaul-McNicol, 1995).
- Black children showed a bias towards lighter skins (Averhart and Bigler, 1997).

- Black children showed racial preference to whites (Kelly and Duckitt, 1995; Johnson, 1995).

On the other hand, maybe I was just making too much out of a small moment in Kim's life and her response had nothing whatever to do with racial identification and the desire for 'whiteness'. Maybe Kim's choice would have been different if we had included a female Vietnamese-Australian doll? Indeed, many have commented to me that it would have been. I have now told the story of 'Kim's Blushes' to diverse audiences in the US, UK, Singapore and elsewhere in Australia. Not surprisingly, responses to my questions about 'Kim's Blushes' have been varied. I have been asked:

- Have I considered that it's impossible to answer the questions without more information about Kim, her background, her language skills, etc.?
- Could I have framed the research questions in ways that confused or were misleading?
- Did Kim not understand what we were asking?
- Did Kim think that is how she looked because she doesn't see skin colour as an issue? Is it possible we are the ones making it an issue?
- Maybe Kim just wanted to go to the toilet or go out and play.
- Did Kim choose Olivia because she thought that would please us as Anglo-Australians?
- Aren't you making a lot out of something that wasn't really that important?
- Did Kim chose Olivia because she was a girl and we didn't have a Vietnamese-Australian doll who was female?

Each of these comments came from early childhood professionals who are 'white' Australians, as I am, or are 'white' North Americans or 'white' New Zealanders.

As I reflected on these possible answers to 'Kim's Blushes', Spivak's (1990, p. 21) caution to be ever vigilant in these postcolonial times and to reflect on what is 'edited out' of our accounts of 'race' jangled in my mind. I began to reflect on what was omitted through my explanations of 'Kim's Blushes' and became drawn to the tactics used by 'postcolonial' scholars to redress the silences in contemporary accounts of 'racial' politics and 'racial' imagery. 'Whiteness' has been and is part of the 'racial' imagery and politics that continue to touch the lives of all Australians.

To understand how 'whiteness' touches our lives and the lives of the children we work with, such as Kim, postcolonial theorists challenge us to engage with our past and its silences in the present by 'reading for Otherwise' (Chow, 1993). As highlighted earlier in this chapter, reading for Otherwise involves imagining how people 'Other' to the culturally and 'racially' elite and privileged in white Australia might understand something. It requires access to an 'Other' wisdom – the wisdom of the dispossessed, oppressed, marginalised and silenced (Loomba, 1998). For example, to read for Otherwise, I as a white Anglo-Australian must seek wisdom beyond that given to me by my white privilege to give meaning to 'Kim's Blushes'. How might I understand Kim if I was not a 'white' Australian?

Seeking the Otherwise: some beginnings

To try to understand 'Kim's Blushes' outside of my own experience of 'whiteness', I sought the views and interpretations of those that have been where I cannot go because of who I am and what my life has been as a privileged 'white' Australian. There is a rich and powerful literature that shares with us migrant experiences of the ordinariness of 'whiteness'. For example, Gunew's writings on the Australian 'migrant' experience, born of her own experience of immigration, challenge us to think about the violence associated with the need to speak English in Australia. She asks:

> If you are constructed in one particular kind of language, what kinds of violence does it do to your subjectivity if one then has to move into another language, and suppress whatever selves or subjectivities were constructed by the first?
>
> (Gunew, 1990, p. 66)

I had not thought that our research project could be a 'violence' towards Kim and that her choices about which doll she identified with might be tied to our demands that she rebuild her ways of thinking and being in English as she talked with us. To what extent was our use of English forcing her to suppress her Vietnamese self? How might this have affected what she chose to do and feel? These questions have stayed with me as I search beyond what I first knew. They were certainly edited out of the possibilities I saw when I turned to the research on 'race' and children literature (see Mac Naughton, 2001a, b, c and d)

Hage (1998) offered another powerful and yet difficult insight into why Kim might resist identifying with Willy – the doll that later in the interview she told us had skin like other people in her family. He wrote that:

> The multicultural national will, like all national will, tolerates national otherness, but only in so far as this national other-ness is in no danger of constituting a counter-will.
>
> (p. 112)

Commenting to me on this statement, a colleague from the US wrote:

> So very true. Don't I know it. Intuitively, I have always acted keeping this in mind. I know when to be silent and when to voice my opinion.

Did Kim know that being 'Other' than 'white' was dangerous and only tolerated if it does not produce a 'counter-will'? Did Kim know that refusing our question was safer than answering it? Had Kim already learnt intuitively to know her place as a 'non-white' Australian? These uncomfortable questions took me beyond what I knew, and forced me to think 'Otherwise'.

Finding the Otherwise: sharing stories with diverse audiences

My forays into the writings of migrant Australia continue but I also found a second way to go beyond what I had known and to begin practising for liberty. My ways of reading 'Kim's Blushes' have been especially challenged through sharing her story in diverse fora from small professional development sessions, lectures in undergraduate teaching through to large early childhood confer-ences where I have been privileged to listen to the responses of people who are not white. (Some of these people would label them-selves people of colour, some would label themselves 'black', some would prefer 'ethnic minority', some Aboriginal, some Indigenous and some I did not ask, which means that a collective term is problematic. My apologies to these people for my awkward efforts to 'collectify' them in what follows.)

Not one woman or man who is 'not white' who has spoken with me has doubted that 'Kim's Blushes' and her choices were linked to issues of skin colour. Why, then, did so many Anglo women – including myself – doubt it? The responses to 'Kim's Blushes' from people of colour have always been brimming with emotion ranging from sadness through to desire, gratitude and recognition and often accompanied by tears. How can 'white' women remain rational and objective as they share their explanations? Each person 'of colour' who has spoken with me has drawn directly from their personal experience as a way to make sense of 'Kim's Blushes'. Not one of the Anglos did or could. I certainly cannot. Some of the comments I have noted include the following:

- 'I could feel my skin creep as you told Kim's story – I just knew what she felt.' (Indigenous Hawaiian female.)
- 'I felt I wanted to cry because I knew those blushes well.' (Japanese-American female.)
- 'Very powerful. I am truly emotionally feeling a bit teary eyed and choked up when I read this.' (Indian-American female.)
- 'I know how Kim felt. When I was four years old I asked my mother to wash my skin so that the colour would come off. I was the only dark skinned child in my kindergarten. I want to thank you for telling Kim's story. It is important that people know how it feels.' (Indian-Australian female.)
- 'You know that story has meaning for me. My niece she is now six years old. When she was four years old she came home from kindergarten and at bath time and she asked her mother to wash her skin so that it would be lighter.' (Singaporean-Indian female.)
- 'Kim's story is very true for me. I always wanted white skin.' (Malaysian-Australian female.)
- 'I want to thank you for that. You have just told the story of my sisters. My wife and I have been close to tears as you talked but you have said what needed to be said.' (Indigenous Australian man.) (A long discussion followed about how his sisters' lives had been spent trying to pass as white and the tragic implications of their sense of not being able to 'pass' which had included drug abuse and suicide.)
- 'It hits you where you live. I felt very tearful when I read it.' (A Female Indigenous Australian early childhood consultant.)

Some responses have been non-verbal. I once shared Kim's story during a conference dinner, where participants were served by a variety of catering staff. I was told afterwards that in the midst of the story, one of the staff – a Vietnamese-Australian woman – stopped serving dinner, leant against a support post and listened. As she listened, she began to nod. Apparently several of the catering staff began talking about the story in the kitchen afterwards. The next day, as the catering staff who had heard me tell Kim's story prepared morning tea for the conference, they asked the organisers to thank me for the story as it was so true of their own school experiences.

The intimate connections between skin colour, experience, desire and emotion link people of colour across national borders in their responses to 'Kim's Blushes'. Explanations other than skin colour link white Anglo people across national borders. Would I have ever doubted whether 'Kim's Blushes' were linked to skin colour, experience, desire and emotion if I had been a woman of colour? Despite my search for the Otherwise to explain 'Kim's Blushes', I will never finally know why she did what she did and why she blushed. I have come to see that what is important is how I seek to understand 'Kim's Blushes' and whose knowledge I privilege in doing so, rather than finding the answer. bell hooks (1987), an African-American feminist writer, reminds me that my 'whiteness' does not necessarily prevent me from seeing 'Otherwise', but it can get in the way of me wanting to.

I am now listening hard for the 'Otherwise' that might help me to understand how Australia's 'white' past touches Kim's present and my sense of it. Racial amnesia and the ordinariness of 'whiteness' in this country are deeply linked with what I can know. Racial amnesia is a choice for me. I can choose not to see 'race' as a factor in Kim's story as many others have who have heard the story. But for people of colour who have shared their responses to Kim's story with me, racial memory is ever present. As a 'white' Australian, I have to remember not to forget that 'racial' politics and 'racial' imagery are ever present in our actions and choices. How could I forget it as an Indigenous Australian? How would I forget it as a non-Anglo immigrant to Australia? Will Kim ever be able to forget it?

How do the stories of Kim, Kai and James link with the positioning of the 'other' – the 'non-white' – in contemporary Australia?

For many children we spoke with in PESD, the 'other' was regularly positioned as exotic and marginalised. This is the third trace of the 'then-in-the-now' of 'race' that I will now turn to, drawing from the words of children's conversations from the PESD.

'Otherness' is marginal and exotic: discursive traces of colonial histories in the present

My first remembered encounter with Indigenous Australians was on a holiday to Gippsland, a country area in south-eastern Victoria. We visited an Aboriginal reserve to see the 'blackfellas'. I remember the occasion as extremely disturbing. I wasn't sure why we were there, but I remember feeling the strangeness of their difference to me and I remember my father's fascination with their odd and exotic cultural artifacts. In these feelings, I was joined with 'white' Australia as I learnt about myself, and about the 'other'. I learnt that 'they' were different from me and that 'they' were 'strange' in their difference.

The representation of indigenous cultures as exotic and/or primitive and the colonisers' cultures and worldview as normal and natural was and is central to the creation and maintenance of an ideology of race. Most Anglo-Australian children in the here and now who we interviewed in PESD expressed traces of these colonial ideas. For instance, they saw Aboriginal people through 'their' difference from 'us', and these differences were seen as primitive and/or exotic. For many of these children, Indigenous Australians were still the strange 'other'. The following extracts show how these understandings were clearly based on inaccurate information.

Culture as primitive

Researcher: And what sort of things do you know about Aboriginal people?

Child: Well, do you know that they can make their own fire, by rubbing two sticks together. Without matches.

Researcher: Alright, anything else about Aboriginal people?

Child: Yes. When they get hurt they put a leaf like a Band-Aid or oil. And did you know there were no shops?

Researcher: Where were there no shops?

Child: In Aboriginal land, Aboriginals made spears and boomer-
angs. There were no shops or houses. They had to make little
huts.

Culture as exotic and/or strange

Researcher: What can you tell me about Aboriginal people?
Child 1: Um . . . They don't, they only drink water and they don't
drink other things that we drink.
Researcher: They only drink water, you think. They don't drink
things that we drink.
Child 1: We drink water, but we drink other things as well.
Researcher: Is there anything else you know about Aboriginal
people?
Child 2: Um . . . They don't eat other food that we eat.
Researcher: What can you tell me about Aboriginal people?
Child 3: They are bad, they will come and kill you in the night
with their knives. They will kill you dead.

No child in the PESD shared any information that suggested that
Aboriginal-Australians and Anglo-Australians have anything in
common or that there are differences in how Aboriginal-Australians
lived their lives. Instead, they had learnt that Aboriginal people
were odd and different, and at times, bad. Some children had also
learnt that they were to be feared.

'Otherness' is frightening: discursive traces of colonial histories in the present

The fear of the dark 'Other' is central to colonial racism but it
wasn't until my teenage years that I remember knowing how
fearful the 'dark' other could be. I had just seen *Guess Who's Coming
to Dinner?*, the Hollywood film starring Sydney Poitier. At the
Sunday lunch table, which in our house was always a place of
great chatter and debate across three generations, I declared in
protest at something my grandmother said that I would marry an
Aboriginal person if I wanted to. If I loved him, and of course, I
would, Gran would just have to get used to it. Of course, in my
mind, he would look like Sydney Poitier and I would bring him
to Sunday lunch. I immediately learnt about the power of my
declaration to horrify and shock and to give me some power over

the adults in my family. During my teenage years my grandfather saw 'reds under the bed' and I was regularly warned against them and the 'hordes of yellow peril' that would invade Australia in their millions overnight unless we and Arthur Calwell kept a close watch. Calwell was Australia's first Minister for Immigration in the post-war period and became infamous for his racist retorts such as 'two Wongs don't make a White'!

In the PESD project, I found much of the discomfort and fear of the 'dark' other that I knew in my family. A small number of Anglo-Australian children (6–14 per cent) reacted to Shiree's dark skin colour with uncertainty, discomfort and, at times, actively rejected her. Most often, this discomfort and rejection was felt through powerful silences. The only silences in Jamie's interview followed questions about Shiree. They were full of discomfort. While Jamie never said 'lighter is lovelier' there is a clear message in her reactions to Shiree.

Put it back

Researcher: Shall we choose another one? Which one would you like to choose next?
Jamie: [Silence, then points at Shiree.]
Researcher: That one. Would you like to pick her up?
Jamie: [Silence, then shakes her head, shifting nervously.]
Researcher: What do you notice about this one?
Jamie: [Silence. Averts her eyes. Then . . .] I don't know.
Researcher: I shall tell you that her name is Shiree, and Shiree is an Aboriginal doll. Do you know any Aboriginal people?
Jamie: [Silence. Shakes head.]
Researcher: No. Have you heard about Aboriginal people?
Jamie: [Silence.]
Researcher: What do you know about Aboriginal people?
Jamie: [Silence. Then . . .] No. Put it back.

The other five children's responses to questions about Shiree were accompanied by a strong verbal or physical refusal to touch or hold Shiree and one refused to stay in the room if Shiree did. For example, Sally had wanted to hold each of the other dolls, but when the researcher asked her if she would like to hold Shiree, Sally responded, 'No, Yuk'. Further, Jamie asked the researcher to put Shiree ('it') back with a powerful expression of disapproval.

The other children's refusal to touch, talk about or look at Shiree was consistent with research in the US (see Aboud and Doyle, 1995) and in Australia (Black-Gutman and Hickson, 1996) showing that white children are often negatively biased against black children.

I am sure that these young children have not read what Pauline Hanson wrote in her newsletter (*The Truth*) about multiculturalism.

> Abolishing the policy of multiculturalism will save billions of dollars and allow those from ethnic backgrounds to join mainstream Australia.
>
> (Pauline Hanson, *The Truth*, p. 9)

I am as sure that they have not read what Ron Casey (a prominent public figure in Australia) said in 1998:

> The conspiracy exists among prominent politicians to stifle any debate on the immigration issue, and among ethnic leaders in the community to defuse any opposition to unlimited Asian immigration. The facts are plain to see. The majority of Australians are against it, but nothing is done to ensure that their wishes are fulfilled.
>
> (Ron Casey, cited in Hage, 1998, p. 212)

Nonetheless, it is clear that the terrain of Australian 'racial' politics that touches the lives of adults and children then and the now is disturbingly similar. What does this mean for early childhood education policy, training, research and practice?

Re-meeting 'whiteness': histories of the present and the equity terrain

What children in PESD knew and said about 'race' showed clear traces of the then-in-the-now. The events and consequences of 11 September, including Australia's harsher treatment of asylum seekers, and the emergence of 'Islamophobia' (EYTARN, 2001, p. 1), are likely to do little to challenge this knowledge. They may in fact cement it. Much in this possibility should concern those of us committed to building democratic communities that assure human rights for all. Much in this possibility should trouble those

of us committed to building democratic early childhood communities that enrich children's rights. As we connect with children we
must act now to cement a different future by rebuilding the equity
terrain of young children's lives. If we seek the geopolitics of our
time and understand how the racist knowledge/power politics of
the past construct our current discourses then we have the possibility of reconstructing them in ways that undermine racism and
its possibilities in the equity terrain of our times and places.

As Foucault reminds us, power is everywhere because its effects
are through all of us. It is networked and systematised in discourse
and our institutions. For instance, 'white' Australia's exercise of
the power of 'whiteness' operates like a weather system shaping
and reshaping 'racial' knowledge, desire, experience, practice in
our specific equity terrain. For Australian children 'whiteness' and
the accomplishment of its 'extraordinary, ordinariness' rumbles
dangerously and continuously in the foundations of our equity
terrain as we live and practise the power of 'whiteness' in our early
childhood research, policies, training and practices.

I use the equity terrain as a metaphor to capture how ideas and
practices about equity and social diversity come together at a
specific point in time to produce how we understand, practise and
shape relationships with each other. The equity terrain is built by
how the past inures itself into the present. It does this through a
complex meeting of our histories, knowledges, desires, experiences,
practices, and positions.

Nowhere has this power been more saddening than in the
conversations I have had with young Anglo-Australian children in
the PESD about who they think they look like, what they think
Aboriginal means and about what they know about being Australian. I have been haunted in these conversations by the racist
foundations of the equity terrain of my youth built of the geopolitics of a Western, 'white' colonisation of Australia. I have seen
the traces of my equity terrain overlap in the foundations of theirs
and re-met my own 'whiteness' through it. Currently,

• some Anglo-Australian children's first and only meeting with
  Indigenous Australians is when they go holiday and build a
  picture of them that is about superficial and specific to their
  tourist experiences;
• some Anglo-Australian children's images of being black and
  desirable still arise in the popular culture that comes to us from

the US – Michael Jordan or Oprah Winfrey rather than (say)
Cathy Freeman, an Olympic-winning Indigenous Australian
runner or Patrick Dodgson, a leading Indigenous Australian political figure;

•   colour and relationships between black and white are rarely
    spoken of and to see a lot of black people around you in a
    kindergarten is still odd if you live in predominantly Anglo-
    Australian suburbs or regional towns;

•   some Anglo-Australian children know that skin colour links
    Australia and Britain, that 'real' Australians are white and that
    Asians are yellow.

How can this be? All Anglo-Australian children in early childhood programmes could and should know the obvious facts and
histories of our life now, i.e. that:

•   Australia no longer has a 'white Australia' policy;
•   Australia is a multicultural country;
•   black people live in Australia;
•   Indigenous Australians are their neighbours.

What is it in our equity terrain that has created so little change?
Has early childhood research, training, policy and practice been
implicated in creating an equity terrain that makes it possible to
continually return to the past as we build our future?
    As I search for answers to these questions, I find myself asking:

•   Is it because much of what we have known about race and
    young children for the past 50 years has been understood via
    primarily Piagetian inspired theories that see categorisation
    and chromatism as normal developmental phenomena rather
    than as politically learnt ones?

•   Is it because our desires as policy makers, trainers, researchers
    and practitioners for constructing a racially just Australia have
    not been strong enough?

•   Is it because our own equity positions in Australian early child-
    hood policy, research, practice and training have been pri-
    marily those of the female, white middle-class Anglo-Australian
    – how might it have been different, how might it be different
    if our profession was dominated by indigenous women and
    immigrant women of colour and if their stories shaped our
    knowledge of young children?

I am glimpsing the answers to these questions as I listen to the PESD children and search for racially just ways to answer them. I have also found more questions that challenge me to take a fresh position on how 'racial' justice can and should touch my work in early childhood education.

Drawn from Foucault's histories of the present and the post-colonialists' call to read for the Otherwise I am asking to re-meet my histories of 'race' in my equity terrain questions such as:

- What power relations have already been accomplished and thus have shaped my equity terrain in the early childhood academy?
- How do these power relations touch children and their under-standings about themselves and others, and how I am impli-cated in these?
- What history, knowledge, desires, experiences, practices, ideol-ogies and equity positions have gathered in my local terrain in the early childhood academy to work for and against equitable relationships in our early childhood communities?
- Where are the dangers and possibilities for equitable relation-ships and understandings with children in my equity terrain as an early childhood academic?
- How does power circulate through my academic practices and desires and what effects is it having on the possibility for social justice in the early childhood community?
- How can I exercise power as an academic to create a sustain-able micro-climate of change for greater equity and racial justice in and through early childhood education.'

I cannot claim to have found answers to these questions. However, through these questions, I have gained a determination to resist my past in how I construct my future work as an early childhood researcher and trainer, and I have confronted the 'racial' choices I make in my work as an early childhood academic, and the need to reposition myself within the equity terrain is clear.

Taking a position in the equity terrain

As a 'white' researcher, I can position myself in Australia's racial equity terrain and the knowledge/power regimes produced within it in different ways. I can do research that aims to defend and to document what has been formed in early childhood education through our policies, training and practices. Or, I can choose to explore what has been silenced or hidden and in doing this become an inventor of what might become and what could be different. In your own work as policy makers, researchers, trainers and practitioners, you have similar choices. You can defend and document what is, or explore what you have silenced and marginalised in order to invent a different future by knowing differently now. The choices are mine and they are yours.

As we live with the after-effects of colonisation and of 11 September, I believe that it is critical to building democratic communities with young children that we revisit our choices. Foucault's urge to politicise our histories to revisit the present, and the post-colonialists' tactics for revisiting 'race' offer strategies and tactics to help us re-face our choices. They haunt me to ask of what I hear from children:

*   What power relations have already been accomplished and how do these touch children and their understandings about themselves and others?
*   What history, knowledge, desires, experiences, practices, ideologies and equity positions have gathered in children's local terrain to work for and against equitable relationships in our early childhood communities?
*   Where are the dangers and possibilities for racially just and equitable relationships and understandings with children?
*   How is racialised power circulating through us and our practices and desires and what effects is it having on the possibility for social justice in our early childhood communities?
*   How can we as early childhood professionals exercise power to create a sustainable micro-climate of change for greater equity?

Learning to remember histories, learning to act for change

To strive for justice and against racism in contemporary early childhood classrooms, those of us in 'white' Australia must fight against 'white' Australia's ability to forget. We must learn to know the histories of 'whiteness' and understand the geopolitics of colonisation in order to be haunted by the silences, losses and oppressions that link 'whiteness' now with 'whiteness' then. Our capacity to struggle against 'racism' and for more just possibilities for all children in our early childhood classrooms rests on our capacity to use our remembering to act for change on two fronts.

We must challenge the privilege to define meaning and experience that comes from 'whiteness' and we must challenge the re-emergence of white supremacist discourses. Each is an increasingly urgent task. As Hage reminds us:

> No matter how much it is maintained that multiculturalism reflects the 'reality' of Australia, the visible and public side of power remains essentially Anglo-White: politicians are mainly Anglo-White, customs officers, diplomats, police officers and judges are largely Anglo-White. At the same time, Australian myth-makes and icons, old and new are largely Anglo-White, from shearers and surfers to television and radio 'personalities', to movie actors and rock stars. . . . Anglo-ness remains the most valued of all cultural capitals in the field of Whiteness.
> (Hage, 1998, pp. 190–191)

If anyone doubted this in 1998 when Hage wrote the book *White Nation* from which this quote is taken, they surely could not doubt it now. The Tampa story, its aftermath, and all that has hardened since in Australia's acts towards asylum seekers can only reinforce the view that Anglo-ness remains the most valued of all cultural capitals in the field of whiteness. The M.V. *Tampa* was a Norwegian container ship that rescued 438 asylum seekers predominantly from Afghanistan who were stranded off the Australian coast late in August 2001 when the boat in which they were travelling to Australia sunk. The Australian government refused the asylum seekers admission to Australia. If the asylum seekers on the *Tampa* had been Scottish, Welsh or English could and would Australians have acted in this way?

No child should want to wash away their skin colour, no child should need to blush when they tell us who they are. It is our responsibility ethically, morally and professionally to ensure that they don't. To meet this responsibility we need to do three things:

* Build strong 'racial memories' that never let us forget the particular effects of 'whiteness' on each of us. 'Racial' amnesia is not an option if we want every child in Australia to feel strong and proud in who they are.

- Encourage 'white' Australia to seek the Otherwise. 'White' Australians' explanations will inevitably be limited by what has gathered in our life and inevitably limit how we connect with and understand children, colleagues and families in all their diversity.
- Act for change in the 'racial' politics and imagery of all that we do with children so that the privilege of 'whiteness' is undermined through early childhood education rather than strengthened in the living, daily experience of our communities.

Through these actions, 'white' Australia could recognise and confront discrimination, celebrate diversity, and help to build respectful and democratic early childhood communities. Barbara Creaser was the co-author of the first edition of *The Anti-Bias Approach in Early Childhood* and it was in her honour that I first told Kim's story. Barbara was certainly prepared to risk changing herself to build respectful and democratic early childhood communities:

> I discovered I was a different person from the one that I had been for so long. I found I opened up to new ideas and new people in a way that previously would not have been possible, because I would not have allowed it to happen.
>
> (Creaser, 1998, p. 210)

She wanted to:

> entice others to open to the possibilities that the anti-bias approach offers.
>
> (Creaser, 1998, p. 210)

Opening up the possibilities for reconstructing 'race' in early childhood classrooms rests on 'white' early childhood Australia learning to reknow its histories and allowing itself to open up to the possibility of the 'Otherwise' and by doing so to act as an advocate for more just ways of living. I do not and cannot know how 'white' Australians' understandings of 'whiteness' in Australia have affected other people in other places. However, I do know that 'whiteness' and its meanings have crossed national boundaries. What has it meant within your national boundaries? What does and might it mean for early childhood educators in your country?

Karina Davis, an Anglo-Australian early childhood educator, invites you to explore such questions through reading a vignette of how she has learnt to re-meet history in a search for ways to 'do' curriculum respectful of indigenous perspectives.

KARINA DAVIS
Journeys to re-meeting 'whiteness'

I will start with stories from areas of my early practice for several reasons – first, they document and highlight my understandings at the beginning of my journeying; second, they have been important in providing the base for which growths and changes in my understandings have developed and third, they provide me with sources of reflection and questionings for future action as I observe and reflect on my growth, children's growth and the possibilities available to us.

My first teaching experiences involved little knowledge of the theory that would later centre my thoughts and reflections in the way they do now. I only knew I was unhappy with the way curricula were generally constructed, thought it underestimated, silenced and left unquestioned the important and often discriminatory understandings white children were developing and realised that this left me battling with parents and colleagues about 'appropriate' curriculum content and 'acceptable' conversations early childhood practitioners were to have with children. Over the next few years, my teaching experiences were to provide me with understandings of the challenges, difficulties and rewards of working within the early childhood field that I took with me as I entered the academic world.

Here are snapshots and reflections from those years.

Reflection one

After being at this service for a number of weeks and beginning to build strong relationships with some parents in the centre, I approached the parent-run committee of management to get some funds to buy multicultural resources that were sorely lacking in the centre. I anticipated this would be a relatively straightforward request – the centre was extremely wealthy and had money for resources, the parents were well educated and had shown commitment to their children's learning and growth. I had expected that they would quite clearly see the need for building up a supply of multicultural resources and that they would see that this would only improve the centre's programmes. As such, I was completely unprepared when my request at a monthly committee meeting was dismissed on the grounds that it was unnecessary, as we didn't have any children from 'other' cultural backgrounds.

I came away from that meeting puzzled. As a naïve, new graduate I had assumed a number of things that I haven't had the luxury to assume since. I had assumed that first, the parents would believe me that these were important resources for the centre to have and buy them, after all, I was the teacher and I had decided that this was necessary! Second, I had assumed that the silence and occasional nod of agreement of parents and other staff had meant they actually agreed with my ideas on the importance of adopting a multicultural type approach with all children, regardless of the cultural makeup of the children in the centre. I went home that night complaining of ignorance and lack of social responsibility, completely thrown about working in a service that paid lip service to its philosophy of inclusion and multicultural approaches, and unsure of my next move.

Over the next few months I tried a variety of different ways to get my message heard within this early childhood community. I spoke with sympathetic parents often about the need for their children to be exposed to the broader multicultural community in which they lived, discussed the discrimination and bias faced by indigenous people, quoted from research studies that showed young Australian children growing up with incorrect and biased ideas on who our indigenous people were and towards people from other cultures in general. I spoke about people from other cultures with the children, especially indigenous people, and put transcripts of these conversations in the centre newsletters. I annoyed the committee with my persistence and had one family leave the centre because of these issues. I must admit these times were difficult, especially for a new graduate who was faced with this resistance as well as the usual issues of beginning to 'teach' and 'be in charge' for the first time. It was the continued contact with people from university who provided ideological support and the continued support from a small number of parents within the centre that ensured I didn't give up in my first intimidating battle.

Eventually, funding was supplied and I purchased a small number of jigsaws, books and posters. The catalyst for gaining access to funding had, in the end, been from a question on a government checklist designed to check the quality of the service we were offering families. Some questions asked about the presence of multicultural resources and linked this to a 'quality' programme. The funding for my resources was then provided.

Reflection two

I had just put up posters of Indigenous Australians with one brightly coloured poster having images of Indigenous Australian men in various poses and doing a variety of activities. Some were in suits and in offices, some were playing sport, others were 'painted up' and participating in a dance and there were some images of men and children playing together. A child, I will call him Mike, had been staring at this particular poster since he had arrived this particular morning and, when I had asked what he was looking at, had quickly averted his eyes and said 'nothing'. I watched Mike watch this poster for a time, even when he was participating in the day's activities, his attention was pulled back to these images.

After about an hour, I gathered a small group of children together, Mike included, and asked if any of them had noticed the posters I had put up. Some children stated they had and some children looked at them as if for the first time. At this stage, Mike didn't look at the poster at all, instead sat in the group with his head bowed as the other children asked questions about the images they could see. After a discussion on Australian indigenous people and cultures, I asked the children what they thought and had they heard words like 'indigenous', 'Aborigine' or 'Koori' before. In a rush, Mike requested, 'Karina, I don't like that one, can you take it down?' before becoming silent again. It was not common for Mike to be silent within the larger or smaller groups. He had consistently shown himself to be a headstrong, active child who was continually flanked by other boys as they moved confidently around the room engaging in play that usually involved large spaces, noise and some element of destruction.

It was apparent, after asking Mike a question about this, that he was not going to comment further on his request or the reason for his unease while we were in this group. After explaining to him that I would leave the poster up for the time being and that I would like to talk with him further about the poster, the group stopped the discussion and went back to the larger group. I worried about Mike and the reason for his discomfort with these images, I wondered if it was possible to get him to talk about his unease and I was adamant about leaving the posters where they were. At the same time I wondered about my direct approach with him, if he felt 'ambushed' now and how that would make him even more reluctant to speak further. I decided to talk to a number of children individually and to talk to him only after he had seen me talking with other children.

When the opportunity came to talk with Mike we sat together, at his request, in the block area, an area he was in often and where he felt comfortable. After asking a similar question in a number of different ways, Mike told me that he wasn't concerned about everything in the poster, just 'the man who's got paint on his face and on his body, that's scary'. Further, he told me he had seen 'that man' on television before and he was 'scary' then too and that 'those' men are frightening. And he wanted me to take the poster down.

I wondered how to set his mind at ease with this, how to provide him with opportunities to develop positive perceptions when all he had seen was positioned as negative. We discussed how there were a lot of people who painted their faces in different ways and in different colours. I promised him I would bring some more pictures in of different ways to paint faces and how people did this. I talked about how people often painted themselves and danced and that this sometimes was a way of telling stories about important things. And as I talked about all this I wondered about how much impact this was having on his developed and developing biased ideas. I thought about this responsibility I/we/white has in de/re/structuring (dismantling our beliefs and restructuring new ones) our racist systems and was suddenly overwhelmed at the enormity of this. I wondered about the focus and direction of my discussion. Had I addressed this appropriately, was it of benefit and how had I reconfirmed any racist or stereotypical idea in the direction I took? And I worried about Mike – about him feeling uncomfortable and 'scared' in a place we had worked hard to all feel safe in and accepted.

Reflection three

I had fossicked through the extensive library of this early childhood service and found only three books that focused on a culture other than white culture – three Indigenous Australian creation stories. Determined to begin exposing the children in my group to differences in cultures and beliefs as soon as possible and especially introduce them to Australian indigenous cultures, I set about reading these books to them. We had discussed the posters in the room, there was some beginning understandings that Australia consisted of more than their white families and friends, that there were 'other' people who called Australia home, even before 'we' did.

So I read the stories. Before beginning, I discussed (told) the children that everyone has different ideas on how things happened, how people and animals became the way they were and how the land was built. I discussed (told) that while we as individuals believed what we believed, it was OK that 'other' individual people believed what they believed. I highlighted this by using examples from a 'hot' topic of conversation and contention within our group at the time, that some children believed Easter bunny left eggs in the garden while others believed she left them in their bedrooms. The children, like 'good', 'well-behaved', white children, listened, nodded and agreed. And I began the story of 'How the Kangaroos got their Tails'.

This story, put simply, tells of how one Indigenous Australian group believes the kangaroos got their tails and explains that once, all kangaroos lived together all over the country. It tells of a fight that the kangaroos had and how during this fight the kangaroos threw sticks at each other that stuck in their rumps and became their tails. It then goes on to tell how the kangaroos split into two groups and one group went and lived in the hills and the other group stayed and lived on the plains – where they stay today.

After reading this story and discussing with the children how this happened, after the children's inevitable comments about fighting and stick throwing and their comments that showed, to me, their growing ideas on the acceptability of different ways of thinking, after all this and me feeling like we were 'getting somewhere', the group split up to choose play activities. As they were dispersing, Simon turned back to me and said 'You know, we all know that kangaroos tails just grew. That's how they got them Karina.' Throughout the group, there where nods and agreement as they wandered off . . .

Re-meeting my understandings with postcolonial theory

My limited understandings of postcolonial theory shaped my ideas and perceptions in those early days of teaching and academic life. While I clearly see now that I had a developing theoretical grasp of issues of othering and the influences of colonial discourse, this knowledge had not yet permeated my personal understandings in the same way. So those first initial attempts with children to explore issues and attitudes of and towards our indigenous cultures and people I now see as simplistic and problematic. At the same time, however, I am now aware that the questions and dissatisfaction with practice will always remain and this does not trouble me in the same way. I am grateful that questions remain as they urge me to tread respectfully while remaining aware of, and careful about, my position – a privileged white woman living in a colonial country who is working within the early childhood field to question how we, as white educators, are teaching our white children about cultures other than our own.

Initially postcolonial theory provided me with the concepts and theoretical basis for questioning what we do with children. I was grateful for this as before my questionings were unfocused and general – postcolonial theory provided reasons and structure for my unease. Within this theory was something I could apply – I saw how we used images and activities to 'other' indigenous people and cultures and saw within this an alternate way to practise; I became increasingly aware of how colonialism structured our social world and influenced our educational systems and sometimes was overwhelmed and sometimes was energised by the need to act. I worked on research projects that asked children about their attitudes towards difference and reflected and discussed with early childhood practitioners ways to reconceptualise our practice in the ways we present images of indigenous people and cultures. Postcolonial theory informed my understandings of these discussions and moved the conversations and ideas forward in ways that would not have been possible without it.

Postcolonial theory has allowed understandings of its concepts to seep into a small part of the early childhood field and move our practice forward – for some of us there is automatic questioning of how images of people from other cultures are presented and how they are 'positioned'; understandings that a 'colonial discourse' is in circulation, and academics and practitioners are questioning its influence within the early childhood field; the need for curriculum practices that discuss indigenous cultures as current and contemporary are voiced and heard. That these questionings and changes bring some sense of destabilisation is true, however, they also open up the possibilities for practice in new, exciting and more equitable ways.

Re-meeting 'whiteness'

My journey with postcolonial theory at this stage was focused outwards, however, and this became obvious to me only after a prolonged period away from the early childhood arena. For me, further change and depth of understandings occurred after considerable life changes and challenges were experienced. As I returned to the academic world I became restless and dissatisfied with the 'answers' postcolonial theory provided and was drawn to readings that discussed critical race theory and more specifically, whiteness. Critical race theory and whiteness encouraged me to look at my own world and culture and with this encouragement I could more clearly see how I acted and practised. As my understandings further developed I increasingly found examples and instances within my own practice and my own life where colonialism and 'whiteness' acted (and continue to act).

Looking back on the examples of my early practice, my knowledge of whiteness theory now provides me with different understandings and ways forward with the issues and conversations I had with children. I remember my conversations with Mike, question what we discussed and reflect on the major issues I overlooked and ignored in our conversations – this ignorance and avoidance of topics being due to my lack of understanding of whiteness and my connections (invisible to me at the time) to white colonialism. I didn't discuss how 'black' is represented and discussed in the media and within our white communities, didn't touch on the issues of the racialisation of aggression we see within these images, I didn't mention the disadvantage many indigenous people face in their everyday lives and how this disadvantage is linked to how indigenous peoples are portrayed, I didn't touch on issues of prejudice and discrimination.

I think back to the reading of 'How the Kangaroos got their Tails' and wonder about my motivation to read this story. Whiteness and postcolonial theory help me to question the appropriateness of 'Dreamtime' books – what benefit were they, what would the children get from this reading, how had I positioned indigenous people and culture as 'other' and had I merely widened the gap that existed for the children (and me?) between 'them' and 'us'? I think back to my teaching as a whole – I didn't attempt to contact, or invite in, the indigenous communities of the centre where I worked nor did I contact other communities that lived and worked around our centre who were not represented within it. I worked from my white, narrow and arrogant perspectives of what was needed to integrate throughout *my* curriculum with the questioning about this solely focused on the centre as my community. As the centre, and my own, backgrounds were Anglo-white this ensured I remained cocooned and safe within this white perspective even while I argued that I was attempting to work against this.

Knowledge of whiteness and postcolonial theories has enabled me to critique my practice in new and exciting, if somewhat painful, ways. Understandings of my past practice with children have new dimensions, pathways and possibilities. These are exciting and powerful tools that can provide new possibilities for challenging a dominant educational discourse which invisibilises the effects and benefits of white colonial culture while disadvantaging and oppressing 'others'.

Re-meetings for change

Australia has placed increasing responsibility on educators to work in non-discriminatory ways with children, encouraging children to accept and respect social diversity. There have been several attempts in Australia and internationally to describe how early childhood curriculum can achieve these aims. Prominent in these descriptions has been the US-derived approach known as the 'Anti-Bias Curriculum' ('ABC') (Derman-Sparks and the Anti-Bias Task Force, 1989; Dau, 2001).

James, Kim and Sally were in an Australian early childhood classroom where their teacher actively pursued an anti-bias curriculum, drawing on its goals and critically evaluating her resources and curriculum content for bias. However, for complex reasons she had not actively engaged with the politics of 'race' and how 'whiteness' and 'blackness' were generated within these politics for teachers and for children. In part, it was because politics is not normally seen to be the business of early childhood, as children are regarded as immune to their effects (Campbell, 1999, p. 2001). In part, Karina's histories and my own offer insights into why 'race' is silenced by 'white' early childhood educators.

Yet to ignore the politics of 'race' is to ignore a key discourse through which we construct our identities, become 'racialised' and thus produce racism and its effects. To ignore the effects of this discourse on young children and our relationships with them is to diminish the possibilities for 'racially' just and equitable relationships in early childhood classrooms and beyond. This is especially the case in countries such as Australia, which is tainted by a colonial past, contains social structures that continue to oppress its indigenous peoples and their cultures (O'Shane and Bickford, 1991; Partington and McCudden, 1993; Huggins and Huggins,

1994; Brennan, 1998) and in which the politics of 'Asian' immigration remains ever present. In searching for deliberate ways to practise for liberty, learning to re-meet our own racialised histories and those of the children with whom we work is an important tactic. With tactical awareness of 'race' in our lives, we cannot tactically interrupt racism.

I end this chapter by thanking Kim for where she has taken me and apologise to her for what I might not have known and seen when I met her. Through her I have learnt to re-meet my histories of 'whiteness' and I have found new ways to enter into the 'Otherwise'. But, in the struggles against the possibilities of racism in early childhood classrooms the histories of 'race' remind us to include struggles against the silences, omissions and losses that any single account brings with it.

For reflection

- What is your relation with 'whiteness'?
- What is the relation of children in your classroom with 'whiteness'?
- How do your geopolitics make your relations with 'race' in children's lives?
- How could you re-meet your own histories to expose the place of race and racism in your life and the lives of the children with whom you work?

Chapter 6

Imagining professional learning for a change

Becoming again in critically knowing communities

> Although at times we feel that we are an island of difference in a sea of conformity, we continue to share our discussions with others, to engage their interest in our debates and to incorporate their perspectives on a diverse range of challenges, since we believe that we are attempting to work, in Foucault's sense, from the 'bottom-up' to introduce change into the larger structure of power in which our work is embedded.
>
> (Dahlberg, Moss and Pence, 1999;
> quoted by Sally Barnes, early childhood educator and
> researcher, the Curriculum Club, South Australia)

> What is philosophy today – philosophical activity, I mean – if it is not the critical work that thought brings to bear on itself? In what does it consist, if not in the endeavour to know how and to what extent it might be possible to think differently, instead of legitimating what is already known?
>
> (Foucault, 1985, p. 9)

Imagining professional learning for a change

This final chapter shares a vision of how we might build the skills, passions and commitments to make a difference in young children's lives using what I have called 'Critically Knowing Early Childhood Communities' and how such communities can contribute to activist education. Specifically, it:

- explores the potential for professional learning and change among the everyday conditions of work in early childhood services;

- argues for the need to recast the content and delivery of professional learning;
- shares a vignette of how one group of early childhood educators have constructed a critically knowing community of learners;
- links the creation of Critically Knowing Early Childhood Communities to the wider vision of this book – greater equity and social justice in and through early childhood studies.

Imagine what might happen in young children's lives and their learning if every person employed to work with young children had the:

- skills to intervene in children's lives and in their learning in ways that are critically informed by the leading edge of social thinking and theory of their time. In this time that would include the social and political theories of feminists, post-structuralists, postcolonialists, critical and cultural theorists;
- passion to advocate policies based on social justice that aim to give young children respectful, equitable and joyful lives;
- commitment to act with children and the adults in their lives to create progressive social change and to extend democracy;
- commitment to embed children's rights in all that they do in the name of children.

What might we achieve with and for children if these skills, passions and commitments drove:

- government policy concerning children's services;
- funding decisions concerning children's services;
- employers' choice of early childhood educators;
- professional development for early childhood educators?

Critically Knowing Early Childhood Communities are based on the skills, passions and commitments referred to above and they seek to honour ethical engagement with children, respect diverse and multiple childhoods and embed equity in all that they do. They can be based in a locality or they can cross several localities via face-to-face networks and/or via the internet. They can embrace anyone with a responsibility for the quality of children's lives, including early childhood educators, children and their families, and researchers. They can be initiated by government or by individuals. Finally, Critically Knowing Early Childhood Communities can fuse research, policy formulation, quality improvement and professional learning into a dynamic, mutually informing process that can revolutionise how the field of early childhood thinks about and engages with policy, funding, learning and pedagogical innovation in work with young children.

However, many parts of the early childhood field are far from creating the conditions where a Critically Knowing Early Childhood Community could flourish. Instead, the everyday conditions of professional learning in much of the early childhood field starve early childhood educators of the nutrients that support them to proactively, enthusiastically and knowingly draw on leading edge theories to push the possibilities for democracy and progressive social change in their lives with young children and their families. In what follows, Australian early childhood educators paint pictures of how the structures, processes and content of their professional learning operate to starve them of the possibilities a Critically Knowing Early Childhood Community could offer them. In particular, these pictures highlight the constraints to learning and change that flow from the dominance of technocratic approaches to professional learning in the early childhood field. It begins by retuning to Cara's comments on motivation and innovation in her everyday life as an early childhood educator.

The everyday conditions of professional learning in early childhood

> Motivation is a big factor – me, I'm like a little seed in the ground, in a hole in a rut waiting to bloom. I don't want to be a wilted seed in the garden! Like a Gerbera that stands up and then goes eeeeer [she uses her hands to show how a Gerbera stands and then wilts].
>
> (Cara, early childhood educator, CRIUT, research notes)

When Cara spoke those words she worked in an Australian long day care centre with children who were between birth and three years of age. She was participating in a small action research project referred to in what follows as the Critical Reflection and Innovation Under Threes [CRIUT] project. Along with the eleven other participants she was exploring pedagogical innovation in her work with very young children.

Cara was asked in one of the CRIUT groups meetings what enabled her to be innovative in her daily work with the children. Her response grew from her previous experience of professional learning and development in one-off training days and conferences. During these days new pedagogical ideas and suggestions had poured into her 'rut' of normal practices like a heavy burst of rain forcing her to soak them up quickly. Often that soaking created in her a sudden burst of enthusiasm to put the new ideas into practice. However, equally often her enthusiasm quickly wilted as she returned to the daily conditions of working with children under three.

These daily conditions of her professional learning did little to feed and nurture her enthusiasm for a long-lived blooming of the fresh and new in her work with young children. Instead, she and other CRIUT participants were regularly starved of conditions in which critical reflection and pedagogical innovation could grow. They worked with untenable staff–child ratios (one adult to five children under two years of age) so they constantly juggled their desire to individualise their relationships with the children with the daily tasks of changing nappies, feeding children, managing staff breaks, talking with parents, responding to colleagues, briefing relieving staff and responding to children's varying needs and feelings. Brittany, a CRIUT participant who worked with babies, described her experiences at the beginning of the year as she juggled 'cuddles', feeding and crying infants:

> Cuddles – it's the start of the year and the children are infants 0–12 months. We can't do the one to one and sitting in a group its hard to do – we play and do routine things. Equity counts – its different with little babies – they all need a feed at the same time – if they don't get what they want they cry. We try to be fair and treat them the same if possible.

Being innovative in this context required more than an injection of new ideas for Cara to put into practice. An injection model of pedagogical change expresses a technocratic discourse of professional learning and change (Parker, 1997). Learning occurs through implementing 'good' practices and solving problems by applying linear causal logic to them. It relies on the reasonable teacher acting on reasonable evidence about what works as efficiently and effectively as possible. Likening one-off in-service courses for educators to 'quick fixes', Parker says:

These 'quick fixes' are premised upon the technical-rationalist
assumption that the techniques by which the problems of teaching are to be solved are universally applicable to *any* teaching
and learning context: to any child, by any teacher, in any school
whatsoever.

(Parker, 1997, p. 15)

In the CRIUT project Cara and other participants were constantly
confronted by problems in their teaching that challenged reasonable evidence about what works with any child, for any adult, in
any childcare centre whatsoever. Instead, they found ethical puzzles
and dilemmas layered through their daily lives with children and
with colleagues. Consider Daniel's puzzles and dilemmas in what
follows.

Daniel's puzzles and dilemmas centred on a child who bit other
children. Daniel, a participant in the CRIUT project, was working
with a child of 20 months who had bitten other children early in
the year. Children would 'cringe when he came near' but over
time this reaction had 'faded away' as his biting stopped. Then,
it began again. Daniel's search for the 'right technique' to stop
the biting and 'nut out' the problem became enmeshed with his
sense of the impossibility of finding:

it came crashing back today because he'd done it (biting) to
a couple of children and we came back to the situation that
we, you know they started cringing from him when he came
near them, and so I mean as I said, it's one step forward and
some back, but I'm sure if I can nut it out, or somehow persist
or, I don't know, I don't know if that's the right strategy or
put myself in his shoes, because I don't think I'll ever be able
to do that, because of his culture at home or whatever, but,
because as I've said, you know, it seemed to work that waving
and acknowledging the other child, it worked for a time, but
then whether I should have followed it up with something, it
was still new, and whether that didn't hold him enough or
it just became a pattern or something we'd say.

(Daniel, early childhood educator,
CRIUT, research interview)

Other CRIUT participants such as Viv also faced dilemmas
about how to navigate children's peer relationships:

Children push into each other – take each other or pull each other's handbags – I try to show them extra things but they keep going back to pushing.

(Viv, early childhood educator,
CRIUT, research interview)

Nath's and Pam's teaching dilemmas were embedded in their relationships as adults with children. They were struggling to decide what respectful relationships with children looked like when children rejected them as adults:

One child keeps saying go away go away. I can't actually sit with him – I want to make him stop saying go away but I also want to fit in with his little world – I want to break through so he plays with me but he usually plays by himself.

(Nath, early childhood educator,
CRIUT, research interview)

Children keep doing the opposite of what we want them to.

(Pam, early childhood educator,
CRIUT, research interview)

Relationships are notoriously difficult to control and predict. Techniques that work with one person fail with the next, irrespective of their age and their contexts. Technocratic solutions in quick fix training that flood an educator with instant solutions offer little guidance of any lasting pedagogical value in these matters. Relationships are messy, unpredictable, complex and shifting – they are rhizomatic (Deleuze and Guattari, 1987). They demand more of the educator than techniques.

The 'quick fix' technocratic models of change emphasise the place of method and technique in creating change, often ignoring the messiness, uncertainties and ethical dilemmas of relationships in teaching. In doing so, this approach to 'improving teacher quality' diminishes the very person it targets – the educator – who wilts as yet another 'simple answer' fails them. As Carla reflected:

What is more important for a child's success – the teacher or the method? There has to be a balance. How do we find the balance? Where is the middle ground? It would be nice if we could say all teachers were passionate but the reality is they're not – its got to be more. Literacy teaching is very complex. There is no simple answer but as far as the bureaucracy is concerned if teachers just were told what to do and if they would just do as they were told all would be revealed as the problem solved. But, we know it's not true.

(Carla, early childhood educator, the
Trembarth Project, research interview)

Like the bureaucracy within which Carla worked, one strand of dominant discourse within mainstream early childhood literature persistently treats the development of quality teaching and innovation in teaching as a technocratic process where method matters (e.g. Bredekamp and Copple, 1997; Honig, 1996; Mooney *et al.*, 1997; Munton and Mooney, 1999) and one-off training sessions count. In Australia, the dominant funded form of early childhood professional learning is presented in the 'Training Calendar', a document that lists the sessions to be run over a term, semester or year by 'expert trainers' to professionally 'develop' the field.

Cara's seed wilted under this technocratic 'quick fix' model of pedagogical change. Cara called for time and space so she could grow her ideas and understandings and change her practices. She wanted time and space in which critical reflection and innovation could bloom. Yet, persistently and consistently she and other educators in CRIUT were forced to survive in their daily lives with young children in conditions that stifled spaces for reflection. For many their spaces for reflection were stifled by the everyday 'housekeeping stuff' of working with young children. Lily talks of this:

Space to think about things – need systems in place and running so that not worrying about who is going to stack the dishwasher or pick up the washing. Space to think about things so that you can step back and reflect in a situation instead of worrying about the housekeeping stuff.

(Lily, early childhood educator,
CRIUT, research interview)

They were also stifled by how staff responsibilities were arranged so that the 'little things' like having time to sit with children, let alone reflect on practice, was all but impossible:

A lunch time reliever is needed not to do more routines but to give us time – they get used in the wrong way – we had three extra people – some students to do work and it was busier than ever – they needed help – an extra half hour at lunch time – not on lunch but structured to spend with the children and do little things such as today sitting with the children because there were only five in.

(Lily, early childhood educator, CRIUT, research interview)

Technocratic discourses of professional learning intersected with daily conditions of work to produce an environment in which it is hard to imagine the complex and difficult work of using much of the theory within this book to extend democracy and enact progressive social change being possible.

In the CRIUT and Trembarth Projects the educators yearned for this to be different. It mattered to them that critical engagement with their work was stifled by the everyday conditions and practices of professional learning. They longed for deeper intellectual engagement in their work. They wanted the possibility of thinking beyond the mundane to what one participant in the Trembarth Project called the 'major issues'. The major issues beyond the mundane included seeking 'social justice', 'fighting racism', talking about 'poverty', 'war', 'peace', images of the child as a learner, and as a citizen and what success means for children from diverse backgrounds.

The interviews with the teachers in the Trembarth Project were regularly punctuated by comments about their desires to bloom intellectually as teachers irrespective of the questions asked:

What is critical reflection?
Not talking about mundane issues that I solve day to day – but major issues I take the long view – I talk, read, and ponder over a period I hope I find enlightenment.

What makes critical reflection difficult?
Education is getting mandated programmes here same as in Vic – they require very little teacher intellectual engagement.

What would help you to critically reflect?
More time for us to share but also to be able to share continually on that same curriculum area, instead of jumping.

What would help you to experiment more in your work with Under Threes?
I need more theory to expose myself to differences because different thinking in the room helps.

What would help you to experiment more in your work with Under Threes?
A forum to talk and listen to others' struggles and I often struggled with the same things or still struggle.

If a 'Training Calendar' model continues to dominate opportunities for professional learning then many early childhood educators, like Cara, will still struggle to bloom intellectually and professionally. Their desires for an everlasting intellectual blooming sit in a landscape starved of time, opportunities for reflection, dialogue and collaboration. In such a landscape it is hard to imagine how Critically Knowing Early Childhood Communities could thrive. Yet it is possible to build Critically Knowing Early Childhood Communities if we are prepared to rethink the knowledge/power relations of existing approaches to professional learning and change that dominate much of the early childhood field. Specifically, we need to:

• recast our models of delivery;
• recast our target of 'development';
• recast the content of professional development.

Recast our models of delivery

We need to move away from single, isolated workshops and move towards strategic and integrated programmes that support professional learning. For instance, we know that one of the least effective ways to provoke learning and change in professional practices is using the one-shot injection. Cara reminds us of that, as did the women in the Trembarth Project. But, traditional research also reminds us of that. Consistently and persistently contemporary research on teacher learning and change suggests that the least effective way to excite learning and change in teachers is the one-off in-service workshop that is one of the most common forms of professional development. As Cooper and Boyd argue:

Single, isolated workshops do not help teachers effectively implement the strategies needed to meet the demands of today's students; in fact, they often add to the workload, confusion or guilt of teachers.

(Cooper and Boyd, 1997, p. 2)

Research shows that two months after teachers attend a one-off workshop, only 16–20 per cent of them have made any of the changes recommended (Cooper and Boyd, 1997, p. 2). Further, the teachers that did implement the changes were among the 20 per cent who were so committed and involved that they could have picked up the book and read the information in it and then implemented the change anyway (see Joyce and Showers, 1992, 1996; Glickman *et al.*, 1993).

Why should we continue a model that will probably only reach 20 per cent of staff, especially when those staff will probably learn what they need to know through reading anyway? Why use a model of 'quick fixes' that flood early childhood educators with new ideas and expect them to universally apply? What might happen if we moved to models of professional learning that rest on building the capacity and desire for lifelong learning within those who work with young children? Could we develop forms of professional learning that:

- reduce the workload of early childhood educators by actively helping them to restructure it?
- reduce the confusion about how best to act and why, by embracing diversity rather than assuming that there is just one best way to work?
- reduce educators' guilt about what they are not doing by making realistic assumptions about what is possible rather than assuming that anything is possible?
- enable early childhood educators to intellectually bloom by engaging with the 'big ideas'?

Increasingly, practitioners, teacher educators, professional trainers and academics are answering these questions by telling the same story of international best practice and wisdom about how to improve the quality of practices. They argue that learning can't and won't happen in one-off, isolated workshop sessions. The most effective learning happens when teachers are in small teams (or cluster groups) in which ongoing dialogue and planning can occur and, in which critical reflection is a key tool used to generate dialogue (Cooper and Boyd, 1997; Finch, 1999; Blase and Blase, 1998; Cochran-Smith and Lytle, 2001; Fleet and Patterson, 2001).

This approach to professional learning and development is described as 'building collaborative learning communities' and/or 'building communities of learners':

> Taken individually, each concept has incredible power and together, there is a synergy, a revolutionary force that we have not even begun to recognize yet in schools.
>
> (Global learning communities – online)

Consider Minerva's comments on the place of community in creating a culture of professional learning in work with schools in North West Tasmania:

> the critical factor is working collaboratively in a group where you feel comfortable to open up and share thoughts in an environment where there is no right answer
>
> (Minerva, early childhood educator, the Trembarth Project, journal entry 16 May 2002)

In summary: the most effective professional learning is collaborative, action-focused, dialogical and critically reflective. Could we can build such powerful, revolutionary collaborative learning communities in early childhood by recasting the target of professional development?

Recast the target of 'development'

To ignite a passion for equity and social justice in those who work with and for young children, I have argued elsewhere that we need to challenge the individualism built into much professional learning and into the very fabric of early childhood education (Mac Naughton, 2000). Individuals beavering away in individual centres cannot readily create the scale of change we need if our claim that we are working in the interests of all children is to have any credibility.

Creating change as an individual can be hard. It's hard to convince others to join you, it's hard to remember what you have learnt and it's hard to avoid retreating to the tried and trusted ways. It's hard not to wilt under the weight of sole responsibility for change. Persistently within the Trembarth Project teachers echoed these ideas emphasising the importance of time, dialogue and structural support for their learning. Sue expressed this clearly:

> The process for developing a culture of critical reflection will be a long slow process, as first there is a need to develop a climate of collaboration and sharing amongst the staff. This includes not only about teaching and learning but about having an input into school decision-making and planning processes as a collaborative team.
>
> (Minerva, early childhood educator, the
> Trembarth Project, journal entry 5 April 2002)

Alone, an individual has little chance of:

- rejecting or reassembling the knowledge learnt in their pre-service training that the tactics in the earlier chapters of this book advocate;
- convincing other people to break with early childhood traditions and come to know their will to truth;
- challenging their colleagues' social visions and educational practices and working with them to create a will to know differently, a will to know justly;
- discussing and negotiating their educational visions and practices with others committed to progressive social change and learning to deliberately practise for liberty.

My own research over several years now has shown that each of these changes is necessary to produce equity in and through what we do with young children in early childhood studies. Minerva's experiences in the Trembarth Project also reinforce the hard work that this involves:

> One of the hardest questions I think to ask teachers to consider is the one, 'Whose knowledge are you using?' in relation to their practices in working with young children. I think this can be a very powerful question to give teachers permission to really reflect on their own beliefs and whether their practices match what they believe. This question I think too has

the potential to support teachers to connect their emotions and feelings in relation to supporting their thinking.

(Minerva, early childhood educator, the
Trembarth Project, journal entry 3 July 2002)

The emphasis on the individual that underpins curriculum decisions in child-centred education also impedes work towards progressive social goals because:

• it dissuades individuals from questioning traditional views about how best to offer materials and equipment, especially when colleagues reinforce those views. It persuades instead towards a 'will to truth';
• it reveres the knowledge learnt in pre-service training as 'the truth' and in doing so reproduces regimes of truth that regularly silence equity and social justice visions;
• it defines people who publicly own and advocate a clear social change vision as odd, abnormal or just plain wrong. Being 'othered' in this way makes maintaining work for change a lonely journey.

There is much research to suggest that such attitudes unintentionally support conservative social goals and practices, and I believe we need to reconstruct how we work with educators to change this. Specifically, I believe that instead of seeking only to enhance individuals' skills – which has been shown to be ineffective – we should seek to build local communities of learners and network these communities across local, state and national borders. Learning with others can lessen the challenges of change by ensuring that you have support, encouragement and inspiration as you plunge into new ways of thinking and acting. I have worked and continue to work with a number of such local communities of learners. Several members of these communities have contributed to this book and it would not have been possible without them and the risks they have taken to know their work differently.

In each of these local communities of learners, educators are changing their relationships with the knowledge that informs their curriculum and pedagogical practices. A significant change enacted in these communities is a shift from individual responsibility for acquiring knowledge about their work to collective responsibility for critiquing and developing this knowledge. Community members have learnt to observe and think about others' work and to have others observe and think about their work. This has occurred because each member of the learning community explores their individual teaching decisions across a range of issues regularly with others in their learning communities. What this has looked like in each community has differed but the collective dialogic nature of the communities has not.

Within communities of learners, learning can be transformative, especially if members link their knowledge and practice through collaborative and critically informed action research (Cherry, 1998, pp. 31–32). Transformative learning is deep learning based on '"frame-breaking" changes in the way we think, feel and do things' (ibid.). Transformative learning, then, is learning with others to link knowledge and practice, to 'break frames' and to transform how we think and act. Cherry (1998) argues that organisations that successfully initiate collective learning are 'prepared to break, and re-create the mould in which they were doing business: if not the mould for the entire operation' (Cherry, 1998, p. 34). In early childhood studies breaking and re-creating the mould that generates and constrains our practices entails recasting our professional knowledge base – the content of our professional development. This book has focused on tactics to do this that express a turn to the poststructural.

Recast the content of professional development

This recasting involves a move away from acquiring *universal* truths and expert knowledge about children and a move towards producing *local*, critical knowledge drawing on Foucault's distinctions between the will to know and the will to truth.

As we have explored throughout this book, the will to truth is highly problematic because following Foucault, we have explored the idea that there is no such thing as truth. Foucault's argument that what we regard as the truth facts about (for example) child development is subjective, incomplete, multiple, contradictory *and* politically charged pushes us toward the 'will to knowledge' which is *potentially* productive yet dangerous in that all knowledge has an intimate relationship with power. The productivity of the 'will to know' is that it draws us to search beyond truth. Foucault talked of this search as an 'ordeal' (Miller, 1994, p. 280) because it was 'work done at the limit of ourselves'(Foucault, 1983, p. 47) but, if done, which places us in 'the position of beginning again' (Foucault, 1983, p. 47). Learning to meet and challenge our 'will to truth', deconstruction, rhizoanalysis and re-meeting histories are tactics towards placing us at 'beginning again'.

What could and would happen if the content of professional development in early childhood education were recast to help us work at the limit of ourselves and to thus begin again revitalised? Some people might say that the question of whether 'truth' exists is just something for the philosophers to consider. I disagree. In common with Foucault, I believe that the existence of truth is a fundamentally practical, political issue and this book has been premised on this belief.

Such a position is inevitably risky – people who take this position risk alienating others and being alienated from them. As Linda, an early childhood educator in the Trembarth Project, put it:

> There is no way to critically reflect and not put yourself at risk.
>
> (Linda, early childhood educator, the Trembarth Project, journal entry 16 May 2002)

However, I have spoken the 'truth' about early childhood education for nearly 30 years and yet we still can't persistently or consistently raise children respectfully, equitably and joyfully. Too many children still live in poverty, facing violence and injustices. The 'truths' of these we seem able to silence or ignore. In Australia these 'truths' include:

- The incidence of child abuse – physical, emotional and sexual – is thought to have risen over the last three decades with 26,025 substantiated cases of child abuse in 1997–1998 alone (Stanley, 2001).
- Children are more likely to live in families ranked at the lower end of the income distribution (ABS, 1999).
- The overall poverty rate among Aboriginal families is almost three times that among non-Aboriginal families. Half of all Aboriginal children were living in poverty in 1986, more than two-thirds were in near poverty and a fifth were in severe poverty. In all cases, these figures are well above those estimated for children in non-Aboriginal families (Saunders, 1996).

- Indigenous Australians suffer a higher burden of illness and die at a younger age than non-Indigenous Australians, and this is true for almost every type of disease or condition for which information is available (ABS, 1997).

In these circumstances, we can't continue to hold the same beliefs and maintain the same practices. We need new ways to know the child, to think about the child and to work with and for the child. We must take the risk of thinking the unthinkable and learn to deliberately practise for liberty. As this book demonstrates, early childhood educators and researchers are attempting to do just that and challenging the content of what needs to be learnt as an early childhood educator. Their challenges have troubled several 'truths' about the early childhood arena, including:

- child development is the only right and proper knowledge to guide our decision-making;
- development of the individual is the paramount and only right and proper goal;
- social injustice is someone else's responsibility;
- professionalism is about objectivity and social distance;
- equity issues are just for radicals.

Building critically knowing communities: the challenges and possibilities of learning for liberty

Troubling our truths troubles us. As discussed in Chapter 1 of this book, our truths provide certainty for our understandings and our practices. Is it fair, responsible and reasonable to trouble our truths without new ones to replace them? Should we ask each other to live with the uncertainty that a world without truth produces? Several people argue that we should, because in moments of ambiguity and uncertainty, transformative learning, creativity, change and innovation become possible.

Thus, Critically Knowing Early Childhood Communities don't imply or aim for a certain consensus among participants. Rather, they aim to encourage a positive dissensus (Lyotard, 1984) in which diversity flourishes, ruptures, reshoots, and produces desires to transform the disrespectful, the inequitable and the joyless in children's lives. When we shift individual professionals who hold the truth about children towards Critically Knowing Early Childhood Communities seeking knowledge about children, ambiguity and uncertainty become the art of constantly enlarging possibility and risking transformative change. If these Critically Knowing Early Childhood Communities exercised power in the Foucauldian sense through a 'net-like organization' in which individuals 'circulate between its threads' (Foucault, 1980, p. 98) to transform how we know and how we honour the child and honour equity, what could we achieve?

In what follows, a group of early childhood educators that have engaged in such work share their story of it. They established 'Curriculum Club' which as you will read challenges conventional understandings of what it is that early childhood educators should know and learn in order to 'do' early childhood curriculum. Sally Barnes initiated and is a member of Curriculum Club, and in what follows she explains how it came to exist and what has been gained to date through their efforts to learn differently and to learn collectively about early childhood curriculum. Sally's vignette highlights how coming to know your work differently takes time, it brings challenges and uncertainties and it brings excitement and possibilities for re-meeting what it means to be a professional in early childhood studies.

SALLY BARNES
Casting Critically Knowing Communities – Curriculum Club

In 2000, a small group of South Australian educators formed a professional learning group that has become known as Curriculum Club. Although the membership of that group has changed slightly over the past three years, it is a group that continues to meet on a regular basis to explore what it means to be an early childhood educator working in a kindergarten today. What follows is a short story about us!

Origins

A couple of years before we set up Curriculum Club, I had been working in State Office as a Birth to Age 4 Curriculum Officer. As an Early Years Curriculum Group, we had often discussed ways to make stronger connections between Curriculum as a State Office function and each of the education districts. At that time, there were many readers working in the curriculum department and we often shared books that we had just read. One day, in our discussions, the Curriculum Superintendent suggested that we form a kind of curriculum club that would be like a book club. Her idea was that an article or book would be read by all members of the group (as in a book club, only the article or book would be about early childhood curriculum) and then the group would meet once a month to discuss and debate what they had read. As a reader, I instantly liked the idea but at that time, South Australian education was about to undergo a major transformation. As a result, a clear opportunity to establish such a group never materialised. However, the idea stayed with me when I returned to the field although it took another two years before the group became a reality.

Four years ago, a fellow kindergarten director and I decided that we would initiate a different kind of professional learning group. This happened at a time of change in South Australia in early childhood curriculum. The South Australian Curriculum Standards and Account-ability framework (or SACSA as it is more commonly referred to), a birth to age 18 curriculum framework, had just been launched and educators were being offered an opportunity to establish their own networks with funding available to successful applicants.

Although it is true that Curriculum Club started at around the same time as SACSA arrived in kindergartens and schools for imple-mentation, it should not be assumed that SACSA was the driving force behind the establishment of this group. In fact, the move from idea to reality happened after a phone call that I had with a colleague who was to become one of the original members of the group. After talking for about two hours, she said 'You know, I love talking about curriculum and there is never any time to do that'. I knew that it was time to take action. Discussing my idea with my fellow director, we began planning for what was to become Curriculum Club.

Although SACSA was not the catalyst for Curriculum Club, it is true that when Curriculum Club became a reality, a new outcomes-based curriculum framework was launched in South Australia. The world of curriculum frameworks and outcomes-based education was not new territory for early childhood educators in South Australia since Foundation Areas of Learning, the previous curriculum frame-work, had been similarly organised. What was different with SACSA, however, was the fact that the early childhood definition of curric-ulum, a definition that had been carried forward from the first curriculum framework, Planning for Learning (which coincidentally was not an outcomes-based framework), into Foundation Areas of Learning was gone. Instead, a universal definition of curriculum was being applied to curriculum for children and students from birth to age 18 along with a universal and unquestioned acceptance of the benefits and appropriateness of outcomes-based education for all children and students.

As an early childhood educator, employed for the past 14 years in a variety of kindergartens throughout South Australia, I was troubled by this shift. I believed that early childhood education had traditionally conceptualised curriculum differently from school education and that there was still validity in many of those perspectives. As a kindergarten teacher and director, I, like others, had found that there was an imperfect fit between outcomes-based frameworks and my own approach to curriculum planning and programming. I struggled to 'do' SACSA, just like I had struggled to 'do' Foundation Areas of Learning, unable to reconcile my curriculum approach, where the curriculum was negotiated and co-constructed with children (and hence could not be cast in stone prior to meeting children) with an approach that allowed me to decide what the learning outcome would be before I had even met the child for whom I was making the plan or prior to the implementation of any experience.

Like many of my colleagues, I felt that important aspects of early childhood education were under attack and that the opportunities to argue differently about curriculum possibilities were limited or non-existent. In addition, a few years earlier, the DECS-funded project 'The Critical Teaching Project' had had a profound impact on my thinking and practice as an early childhood educator. In the process of creating this project (originally conceptualised as the documentation of examples of 'best practice' in programme planning) I had become increasingly aware of, and drawn to, the reconceptualist critique of early childhood education (and as a result, the original brief was eventually replaced with a critical and collaborative action research project). When I returned to the field I began to make serious attempts to take the reconceptualist critique from ideology to practice but as I did so I found myself becoming increasingly isolated in my team and in the broader early childhood community. As a result, I found myself clinging to those colleagues who could empathise with my struggles since they were reflective of their own. In the Critical Teaching Project, we had deconstructed our practice and then reconstructed it, only when it came back together it was different (even if it looked the same to those standing on the outside).

In my attempts then to build my curriculum practice from this critique, I felt thwarted by a curriculum framework that backgrounded issues of equity and social justice, and embedded precisely those concepts that I was finding increasingly problematic. Although it is a fact that SACSA asks educators to take equity issues into account when planning for children's learning, the idea that inequities are or can be embedded within a curriculum framework are effectively silenced. In the world of SACSA, equity is conceptualised either as an equal share of content for all children and students or the responsibility of the individual teacher or school to correct. With a growing awareness of how many of our own practices (and by own, I mean early childhood) entrenched inequities instead of overcoming them, such a narrow conception of equity bothered me deeply.

During this phase, I came across an article imploring teachers to reclaim assessment by rethinking notions of accountability. Written by Chris Gallagher in 2000 and published in *Phi Delta Kappan*, I found myself drawn to his reading of Gramsci's notion of hegemony (a concept of which I had only a very rudimentary notion at that time). Although Gallagher had applied these ideas to his critique of statewide assessment in the US, I found that I identified with many of his concerns. Likewise, I found that by taking the notion of hegemony as he had presented it, I could see that outcomes-based curriculum frameworks had come to represent curriculum hegemony in South Australian early childhood education, and that they manufactured consent and acceptance by being presented as the most obvious and logical direction for early childhood curriculum. Although I will admit that recognising outcomes-based curriculum frameworks as a form of curriculum hegemony did not fill me with a sense of calm and delight, I was excited as I read more of Gallagher's work. Again, drawing on the insights of Gramsci, he argued that within any hegemony, there are always fissures and thus 'the potential exists for people to exploit those fissures, disrupt hegemony, create spaces to act, and exercise power' (Gallagher, 2000, p. 504). Likewise, my own involvement in the the Critical Teaching Project had demonstrated to me the power and potential of working collaboratively with others. Inspired, Curriculum Club became a reality.

Some specifics

Curriculum Club has ten members, all of whom are women at this time, who meet every six weeks to discuss a research article, question, statement or book chapter which has been decided upon at the previous meeting. Having abandoned the idea that we can ever 'know' how to teach, we are committed to the notion that teachers should continue to be learners and that they should and can take responsibility for their own professional learning. We recognise that early childhood education is not a stable or consistent artefact to be reproduced for successive generations of South Australian children, but something that must develop and evolve if it is to be relevant in the context of children's lives today. As a result, our goal is to be aware of and informed by contemporary research and debates in early childhood education and to attempt to connect our current practice with current academic research and thinking. We seek to 'create a space' in which it may be possible to create new discursive realities or alternative ones to those that currently dominate the educational environment in which we work. The articles and chapters that we read and discuss are often difficult and challenging, stretching us to think beyond the 'regimes of truth' that currently construct our work and constitute our identities as early childhood educators. We are not interested in recipes or activity ideas and we do not seek consensus in our understandings. Rather, in our shared commitment to equity and social justice for all of the children with whom we work, we accept the belief that 'change lies not in our agreements but in our disagreements, because in our disagreements (dissensus) we argue about what is "the truth" and we question the dominant norms and values and seek to change them' (Bertens, 1995, cited in Hughes and Mac Naughton, 2000, p. 255). Having said that, however, there is no, and never has been any, obligation for members to incorporate systematic change to their practice (as, for example, an action research project would do). However, since we recognise that Curriculum Club is embedded in critical perspectives about knowledge and understanding, and since those critical perspectives arise 'from a tradition that emphasizes human autonomy and consciousness, [with an] approach to change and action [that] is concerned not just with "results", but with results that occur through transformed consciousness and experience' (Bentz and Shapiro, 1998, p. 152), many of us have found our practice problematised, challenged and changed.

Curriculum Club receives no financial support from DECS or any other groups. Although funding was available for educators creating their own Learner Educator Networks at the launch of SACSA, and we did apply for some funding, for a number of reasons we were not successful in accessing any of it. Disappointed at the beginning, we now recognise that we do not need money in order to meet with one another and that the independence of our group has been an important factor in its success. We are not 'duty-bound' to 'produce' a professional learning activity for others to copy (as was a condition of successful funding) and in our passion for equity and excellence, we do not feel that our critiques need to be limited only to those things that are outside of the bureaucracy in which we work. Instead we are committed to questioning how the structures and practices that we create and are created within, and are both constrained and liberated by, affect our attempts to ensure equity. We have also demonstrated that money is not the answer to every-thing and that educators do not have to wait for others to produce professional learning (a word I prefer to development) opportunities for them. A bureaucracy of 20,000 people cannot possibly know what every single educator needs but a small group of educators who know what they need can create exactly what they want!

Curriculum Club members meet after work (in their own time) for around two hours. Most members attend most meetings and the meet-ings are only open to members of the group. This was an important consideration (and in some ways makes the group exclusive), but because we knew that we wanted to be able to challenge and debate, we also knew that individuals needed to be in a safe and trusting environment to be able to do that. Food, as a means of building com-munity, is also an integral part of each meeting – as we debate, we eat. As a result, many of our conversations are dotted with calls to 'pass the forks' or questions such as 'Who ordered Chicken 22?'. These light hearted moments help to bring balance to discussions that can challenge long-held beliefs about children and teaching.

In conclusion

It was never a goal that Curriculum Club would help its members to finally know what to do. In fact, it was an initial point of agree-ment (Ah! So there was consensus on something!) that teaching was something that was unknown, intensely personal, contradictory and contextual. There was also an understanding among all members that understanding curriculum and teaching in that way was what made it interesting, intellectual and risky.

Lyotard (1984, cited in Dahlberg, Moss and Pence, 1999, p. 24) argues that by abandoning the grand narratives that characterise modernist understandings of the world, the path is opened for little narratives, 'forms of local knowledge, which are internal to the communities within which they occur, self-legitimating in that they determine their own criteria of competence, sensitive to difference and tolerant of incommensurability'. In taking this stance, we have accepted the postmodern idea that 'the world is always *our* world, understood or constructed by ourselves, not in isolation but as part of a community of human agents and through our active interaction and participation with other people in that community' (Dahlberg, Moss and Pence, 1999, p. 23). Likewise, we have rejected the idea that the power of bureaucracies (because we are all members of a large educational bureaucracy) is totalising or colossal. Instead, following Foucault, we see this power as breakable, pliable and able to change, with options for individuals about how they may choose to react and act (Dahlberg, Moss and Pence, 1999).

Within Curriculum Club, our discussions have taken us to new places and helped us to revisit old ones but the discussions that have begun in Curriculum Club have never stayed in just one place. As each member has interacted with colleagues outside of the group, members of her teaching team, bureaucrats, academics, and two blokes in the pub one Friday night, our discussions and tentative understandings have been enriched and challenged by a diversity of perspectives. Although at times we feel that we are an island of difference in a sea of conformity, we continue to share our discussions with others, to engage their interest in our debates and to incorporate their perspectives on a diverse range of challenges, since we believe that we are attempting to work, in Foucault's sense, from the 'bottom-up' to introduce change into the larger structure of power in which our work is embedded (Dahlberg, Moss and Pence, 1999).

When we created Curriculum Club, we took a risk. We did not know if this approach would work and, in all honesty, we did not know (or really even consider) if such a group could be sustained for a long period of time. After four years (and several phone calls over the past few days asking 'When are we meeting?'), these are considerations that we no longer have to make. The professional learning that has occurred within this group now spans a greater number of years than most of us spent in undertaking our undergraduate qualifications. I often wonder what I would have thought, if four years ago I had received a directive from the Chief Executive telling me that I needed to meet with ten people for two hours every six weeks to discuss and debate contemporary thought about early childhood education! Would I have looked forward to this event? Would it have sustained my interest? Would I still be there four years later? Is Curriculum Club 'the answer'? I have no idea, but what I do know is that I cannot imagine not meeting with this group of intelligent, imaginative and argumentative women for many more years to come.

For beginning learning again, for deliberately practising liberty

There is no single way to form a critically knowing community and the Curriculum Club is not the answer for all. But, what might be possible for early childhood studies if Curriculum Clubs and other iterations of critically knowing communities blossomed through the field and became:

- a key site for research with the child;
- a primary source for knowledge with the child;
- a main driver of quality assurance and improvement in early childhood studies;
- an active space for policy development and testing in early childhood studies;
- a leading arena for pre-service learning in early childhood studies?

Individual Critically Knowing Early Childhood Communities could expand their own ways of knowing and maintain their critical momentum through strategic coalitions with other communities, researchers, resource and advisory staff and tertiary trainers linking rhizomatically, re-meeting histories, deconstructing their wills to truth, reconstructing their practices for liberty.

This book invites you to create Critically Knowing Early Childhood Communities in your local area and to re-create yourselves as knowing learners, continuously and sustainably improving your understandings of the child in these changing times. Such efforts may bring a deeper and surprising knowledge of the child, intimately connected with many wisdoms and with a vision of ourselves as powerful agents of equity and innovation who can practise for liberty.

Could recasting the processes and content of professional learning in early childhood help us recognise our agency and our power to make a difference with and for children? As you reflect on that question, consider these words:

> Creating a crisis in people's thinking may be creative, opening up new possibilities and expectations, alternative enquiries and solutions, opportunities for new understandings and new ways of seeing, visions of accessible futures which neither reflect a nostalgic longing for the past nor assume a pessimistic outlook. It holds out the prospect that we as human beings are not powerless. Through empowerment and democracy we recognize the agency, richness and power of each of us – child and adult alike – and question the legitimacy of authority.
>
> (Dahlberg, Moss and Pence, 1999, p. 17)

The hope in this book is that it has created a crisis in your thinking, encouraging you to work with others as meaning makers for the deliberate practice for liberty, exploring new possibilities and expectations for how we are with the child, through recasting how we understand and practise meaning-making and professional learning in early childhood studies. This recasting needs to be directed at its models of delivery, its targets of development and its content. Critically Knowing Early Childhood Communities that are collaborative, inquiry-oriented, knowledge building, dialogical and change-oriented could offer us the opportunity to link what is so often produced as separate 'truths' – theory, practice and policy. Critically Knowing Early Childhood Communities could help us to re-imagine who the child is and how we act with children to honour them and to build an equitable and just world with them.

I started this chapter with a vision that I have built through the ideas, support and work of many people, several of whom are contributors to this book. I envisage people in the early childhood world drawing on the power and potency of collaborative learning. I see them using the unsettling tactics of a turn to the poststructural to transform how children are in our lives and how we are in theirs. I see them acting with, for and on behalf of children for greater equity in the lives of each one of us. I see them deliberately practising for liberty. I see its possibilities. And, as Sammy put it:

This is scary because now I have to do something.
(Sammy, early childhood teacher, Trembarth
Project, review session, February 2003)

The problem is not changing people's consciousness – or
what's in their heads – but the political, economic, institutional regime of the production of truth. ... The political
question   is truth itself.

(Foucault, 1984b, pp. 74–75)

Appendix: Research project summaries

This book draws on the experiences and efforts of several research projects in early childhood studies. They are described in summary form in this Appendix.

Creating and Sustaining Critical Reflection and Innovation in Early Childhood (the Trembarth Project)

This was a retrospective and prospective qualitative study of how teachers working in early childhood programmes take pedagogical decisions funded by the Margaret Trembarth Research Fund in 2001/2002. Please note that supplementary funding for the project was provided by the Department of Education, Tasmania's Flying Start programme.

Three questions guided the study:

- What mobilises early childhood staff to create and sustain innovation in and critical reflection on their programmes with young children? Specifically, what discourses and practices are associated with staff commitment to continuous curriculum innovation and critical reflection?
- How can critical reflection and pedagogical innovation best be practised, theorised and supported?
- What role can, and does, action research play in creating and sustaining pedagogical innovation and critical reflection in programmes with young children?

This project aimed to generate empirical data about:

- how early childhood staff in Australia understand and practise pedagogical innovation and critical reflection;
- how their understandings and practices are influenced by participating in action research.

The project tracked the pedagogical decision-making of 26 early childhood professionals in two ways:

- First it tracked 10 early childhood professionals who participated in an action research project for 6 months, collecting data through audio recordings and field notes of six whole group meetings and smaller response groups; formal interviews with participants; participants' journals; and participants' progress reports. This group was also interviewed 12 months after the final action research group meeting had been held. (This is referred to as Part A in what follows.)
- Second, I interviewed a group of 16 early childhood professionals *not* participating in the action research project but who had expressed an interest in and commitment to critical reflection on their practice. I interviewed them three times during a 12-month period. (This is referred to as Part B in what follows.)

This research was funded by the Margaret Trembarth Early Childhood Research Scholarship fund and the Flying Start programme, Department of Education, Tasmania. A report on the project was completed in July 2003 (refer Mac Naughton, 2003).

The project would not have been possible without the generous involvement of 26 early childhood professionals who contributed to the project. I would like to thank each of them for their time and commitment to the project. These participants will be referred to only by psuedonyms in this book in line with the University of Melbourne's Human Research Ethics Committee protocols.

Critical Reflection and Innovation in work with Under Threes (CRIUT)

This was a pilot study of how 12 teachers working in programmes with children under three take pedagogical decisions guided by the following questions:

- What mobilises early childhood staff to create and sustain innovation in their programmes with young children? Specifically, what discourses and practices are associated with staff commitment to continuous curriculum innovation?
- How can pedagogical problem-solving and innovation best be practised, theorised and supported?

It was conducted using an action research model over a three-month period. Research data was generated through audio-recordings of group meetings, interviews with participants at three points in the project, and participant journals.

The Critical Teaching Project (CTP)

I first used the 'Meaning Map' in a small professional learning project in 1999 funded by the South Australian Department of Education, Training and Employment. The project known as the Critical Teaching Project was initiated by Sally Barnes, a curriculum officer in the department, and supported by the then project officer Kerryn Jones (Jones, 2001). The project ran over six months and participants undertook a critical reflection project during this time. CTP participants were invited to find a concept or a practice that they wanted to understand more deeply and more critically and then to 'deconstruct' this concept or practice by asking the following questions of it and thus 'mapping' its meaning. Since then many other early childhood educators have used the 'Meaning Map' to tactically critically reflect on the meanings that construct their work.

The Preschool Equity and Social Diversity Project (PESD)

The aim of the PESD is to investigate and theorise the relationships between preschool children's understanding of social diversity and equity issues and their own gender, class and racial identity, directed by the following questions:

- What relationships exist between preschool children's understandings of cultural and 'racial' diversity and their own gender, class and ethnic identities?
- How can these relationships best be theorised?

The empirical data was (and continues to be) gathered in a qualitative field-based research study using semi-structured individual and group interviews of the participants and observations of their classroom play. These interviews between the researchers and 111 preschool children attending early childhood programmes explored how these children thought about and talked about cultural diversity and 'race' using 'anti-bias persona dolls'.

The PESD 'anti-bias persona dolls' were specially designed to present social diversity and equity issues to children in two ways. First, they vary in physical characteristics such as skin tone, hair texture and colour and so can physically represent diverse gender and race characteristics. Second, each doll has its own 'persona': a life history that details its 'race', ethnicity, family culture, gender and special interests in stories about the doll. The dolls acted as an icebreaker for initial interviews with children about cultural and racial diversity and offered a focus for three individual interviews with children and for story discussion interviews with groups of children about class, 'race' and gender.

Transcriptions of speech from two data sets from the initial 120 child interviews will provide the main source of data for this paper.

• Data Set 1 (N = 77) – Anglo-Australian children.
• Data Set 2 (N = 18) – children of immigrants to Australia from the Asia Pacific region.

In overview, children were asked in the initial interviews how they understood the differences and similarities between these dolls, which doll looked most like they did, which doll that they liked most and which doll they would like to come to their birthday party. They were also asked if they knew people that looked like the dolls, how they knew and what they knew about them. The children were also invited to ask the researchers questions about the dolls. The wider context of the project included the struggle of forces in the late 1990s that produced Hansonism, Australia's inhumane treatment of asylum seekers, and the Australian government's refusal to say 'sorry' to Indigenous Australians.

Bibliography

Aboud, F. and Doyle, A. (1996). 'Does talk of race foster prejudice or toler-ance in children?', *Canadian Journal of Behavioural Science*, 28(3), 161–170.

ABS (Australian Bureau of Statistics) (1997). *Statistical report on the health and welfare of Australia's Indigenous peoples.*

ABS (Australian Bureau of Statistics) (1999). *Children, Australia: A Social Report.*

ACEI (Association for Childhood Education International) (2004). *ACEI Position Paper, Preparation of Early Childhood Education Teachers*, published online by ACEI. Available at: http://www.acei.org/.

Adler Motaba, S. (2001). 'Racial and ethnic mirrors: reflections on iden-tity and voice from an Asian American educator', in S. Grieshaber and G. Canella (eds) *Embracing Identities in Early Childhood Education*, New York, Teachers College Press, pp. 148–157.

Alloway, N. (1995). *Foundation Stones. The Construction of Gender in Early Child-hood*. Carlton, Victoria: Curriculum Corporation.

Alloway, N. (1997). 'Early childhood education encounters the postmodern: what do we know? What can we count as true?', *Australian Journal of Early Childhood*, 22(2), 1–5.

Alloway, N. and Gilbert, P. (eds) (1997). *Boys and Literacy: Professional Development Units*. Melbourne: Curriculum Corporation.

Althusser, A. (1984). *Essays on Ideology*. London: Verso.

Alvermann, D. (2001). 'Researching libraries, literacies and lives: a rhizo-analysis', in E. St Pierre and W. Pillow (eds), *Working the Ruins: Feminist Poststructuralist Theory and Methods in Education* (pp. 114–129). London: Routledge.

Alvesson, M. (2002). *Postmodernism and Social Research*. Buckingham and Philadelphia: Open University Press.

Apple, M. (1990). *Ideology and Curriculum*, (2nd edn). New York: Routledge.

Aronowitz, S. and Giroux, H.A. (1985). *Education Under Siege: The Conserva-tive, Liberal And Radical Debate Over Schooling*. Massachusetts: Bergin & Garvey.

Ashcroft, B., Griffiths, G. and Tiffin, H. (1998). *Key Concepts in Post-Colonial Studies*. London: Routledge.

Attridge, D. (1995a). 'Singularities, responsibilities: Derrida, deconstruction and literary criticism' in Cathy Caruth and Deborah Esch (eds), *Critical Encounters: Reference and Responsibility in Deconstructive Writing* (pp. 109–110). New Brunswick, NJ: Rutgers University Press.

Attridge, D. (1995b) 'Ghostwriting' in A. Haverkamp (ed.) *Deconstruction is/in America*. New York: New York University Press.

Australian Government, Department of Multicultural and Indigenous Affairs (2004). *Fact Sheet 6: The Evolution of Australia's Multicultural Polices*. On-line, available at: http://www.immi.gov.au/facts/.

Averhart, C.J. and Bigler, R.S. (1997). 'Shades of meaning: skin tone, racial attitudes, and constructive memory in African American children', *Journal of Experimental Child Psychology*, 67, 363–388.

Bailey, G. and Gayle, N. (2003). *Ideology: Structuring Identities in Contemporary Life*. Ontaria, Canada: Broadview Press.

Ball, S. (ed.) (1990). *Foucault and Education: Disciplines and Knowledge*. London: Routledge.

Barnes, T.J. and Duncan, J.S. (1992). 'Introduction: writing worlds', in Trevor J. Barnes and J.S. Duncan (eds), *Writing Worlds: Discourse, Text and Metaphor in the Representation of Landscape* (pp. 1–17). London: Routledge.

Bartell, C.A. (2001). 'Bridging the diconnect between policy and practice in teacher education', *Teacher Education Quarterly*, 28, 189.

Belsey, C. (2002). *Poststructuralism: A Very Short Introduction*. Oxford: Oxford University Press.

Bennett, N. and Wood, E. (2000). 'Changing theories, changing practice: exploring early children's teachers' professional learning', *Teaching and Teacher Education*, 16(5–6), 635–647.

Ben-Peretz, M. (2001). 'The impossible role of teacher educators in a changing world', *Journal of Teacher Education*, 52, 48–56.

Bentz, V.M. and Shapiro, J.J. (1998). *Mindful Inquiry in Social Research*. Thousand Oaks, California: Sage Publications.

Berge, B.-M., with Ve, H. (2000). *Action Research for Gender Equity*. Buckingham: Open University Press.

Berger Hepworth, E. (1995). *Parents as Partners in Education: Families and Schools Working Together*, (4th edn), New Jersey: Merrill Prentice Hall.

Best, S. and Kellner, D. (1991). *Postmodern Theory: Critical Interrogations*. New York: Guilford Press.

Biesta, G.J.J. and Egéa-Kuehne, D. (eds) (2001). *Derrida & Education*. London/New York: Routledge.

Black-Gutman, D. and Hickson, F. (1996). 'The relationship between racial attitudes and social-cognitive development in children: an Australian study', *Developmental Psychology*, 32(3), 448–456.

Blase, J. and Blase, J. (1998). 'Inquiry and collaboration: supporting the lifelong study of learning and teaching', *International Electronic Journal for Leadership in Learning*, 2(7). Available online: www.ucalgary.ca/~iejll/volume2/Blase2_7.html.

Bleakley, A. (1999). 'From reflective practice to holistic reflexivity', *Studies in Higher Education*, 24, 315–330.

Bloch, M. (1992). 'Critical perspectives on the historical relationship between child development and early childhood education research' in S. Kessler and B. Blue-Swadner (eds), *Reconceptualizing the Early Childhood Curriculum: Beginning the Dialogue* (pp. 3–20). New York: Teachers College Press.

Boldt, G. (1997). 'Sexist and heterosexist responses to gender bending', in J. Tobin (ed.), *Making a Place for Pleasure in Early Childhood Education* (pp. 188–213). New Haven: Yale University Press.

Bottomore, T. (2002). *The Frankfurt School and Its Critics*. London and New York: Routledge.

Boud, D., Keogh, R. and Walker, D. (1985). 'What is reflection in learning?' in D. Boud, R. Keogh and D. Walker (eds), *Reflection: Turning experience into learning* (pp. 7–17). London: Kogan Page.

Bredekamp, S. (1987). *Developmentally Appropriate Practices in Early Childhood Programs serving Children from Birth through Age 8*. Washington, DC: National Association for the Education of Young Children.

Bredekamp, S. and Copple, C. (eds) (1997). *Developmentally Appropriate Practice in Early Childhood Programs* (revised edn). Washington, DC: NAEYC.

Brennan, F. (1998). *The Wik Debate: Its Impact on Aborigines, Pastoralists and Miners*. Sydney: University of New South Wales Press.

Brett, C. and Woodruff, E. (1997). 'Communities of inquiry among pre-service teachers investigating mathematics', paper presented at the Annual Meeting of the American Educational Association, Chicago, March. Session 5.13.

Brookfield, S.D. (1995). *Becoming a Critically Reflective Teacher*. San Francisco: Jossey-Bass Inc.

Brown, B. (1998). *Unlearning Discrimination in the Early Years*. London: Trentham Books.

Brown, B. (2001). *Persona Dolls and Young Children*. London: Trentham Books.

Burbules, N. and Berk, R. (1999). 'Critical thinking and critical pedagogy: relations, differences, and limits', in T. Popkewitz and L. Fendler (eds), *Critical Theories in Education: Changing Terrains of Knowledge and Politics* (pp. 45–65). New York: Routledge.

Burman, E. (1994). *Deconstructing Developmental Psychology*. London: Routledge.

Butler, J. (1990). *Gender Trouble: Feminism and the Subversion of Identity*. New York: Routledge.

Butler, J. (1997). *The Psychic Life of Power*, New York: Routledge.

Calderón, M. (1999). 'Teachers' learning communities for cooperation in diverse setting', *Theory into Practice*, 38(2), 94–99.

Campbell, D. (1992). *Writing Security: United States Foreign Policy and the Politics of Identity*. Minneapolis: University of Minnesota Press.

Campbell, S. (1999). 'Making the political pedagogical in early childhood education', *Australian Journal of Early Childhood*, 24(4), 21–26.

Campbell, S. (2001). 'The definition and description of a social justice disposition in young children', unpublished PhD thesis, University of Melbourne.

Campbell, S. and Smith, K. (2001). 'Equity observation and images of fairness in childhood', in S. Grieshaber and G.S. Cannella (eds), *Embracing Identities in Early Childhood Education: Diversity and Possibilities* (pp. 89–102). New York: Teachers College Press.

Campbell, S., Davis, K., Mac Naughton, G. *et al.* (2000). 'Reinventing knowledge/power relations in pedagogical practices: dimensions of action research for equity in early childhood education', paper presented at the tenth European Conference on Quality in Early Childhood Education, London.

Cannella, G.S. (1997). *Deconstructing Early Childhood Education. Social Justice and Revolution*. New York: Peter Lang Publishing.

Cannella, G.S. (1999). 'The scientific discourse of education: predetermining the lives of others – Foucault, education and children', *Contemporary Issues in Early Childhood*, 1(1), 36–44.

Cannella, G.S. (2000). 'Critical and feminist reconstructions of early childhood education: continuing the conversations', *Contemporary Issues in Early Childhood*, 1(2), 215–220.

Cannella, G.S. (2001). 'Natural born curriculum: popular culture and the representation of childhood', in J. Jipson and R. Johnson (eds), *Resistance and Representation: Rethinking Childhood Education* (pp. 15–22). New York: Peter Lang Publishers.

Cannella, G.S. and Grieshaber, S. (2001). 'Identities and possibilities', in S. Grieshaber and G. Cannella (eds), *Embracing Identities in Early Childhood Education: Diversity and Possibilities* (pp. 173–180). New York: Teachers College Press.

Carr, W. and Kemmis, S. (1986). *Becoming Critical: Education, Knowledge and Action Research*. Victoria, Australia: Deakin University Press.

Carter, K and Halsall, R. (1998). 'Teacher research for school improvement', in R. Halsall (ed.), *Teacher Research and School Improvement: Open From the Inside*. Buckingham: Open University Press.

Chandler, D. (2002). *Semiotics: the Basics*. London: Routledge.

Cherry, N. (1998). *Action Research: A Pathway to Knowledge and Learning*. Melbourne: RMIT University Press.

Cherryholmes, C. (1988). *Power and Criticism: Poststructural Investigations in Education*. New York: Teachers College Press.

Chow, R. (1993). *Writing Diaspora: Tactics of Intervention in Contemporary Cultural Studies*. Bloomington: Indiana University Press.

Clark, C., Moss, P., Goering, S. *et al.* (1996). 'Collaboration as dialogue: teachers and researchers engaged in conversation and professional development', *American Educational Research Journal*, 33(1), 193–231.

Cochran-Smith, M. and Lytle, S.L. (2001). 'Beyond certainty: taking an inquiry stance on practice', in A. Lieberman and L. Miller (eds), *Teachers Caught in the Action. Professional Development that Matters* (pp. 45–60). New York: Teachers College Press.

Cole, A. and Knowles, J. (1993). 'Teacher development partnership research: a focus on methods and issues', *American Educational Research Journal*, 30(3), 473–496.

Coole, C. (2002). 'The dialectics of the real', in S. Malesevic and I. MacKenzie (eds), *Ideology after Posstructuralism* (pp. 111–133). London: Pluto Press.

Cooper, C. and Boyd, J. (1997). 'A caring, competent and continuously improving teacher for every child in Australia: Dream or reality?', *Global Learning Community*. Available online: www.vision.net.au/~globallearning/pages/lfs/cb_article.html.

Coplan, R., Wichmann, C. and Lagacé-Séguin, D. (2001). 'Solitary-active play behaviour: a marker variable for maladjustment in the preschool?'. *Journal of Research in Childhood Education*, 15(2), 164–172.

Coyne, R. (1996). 'Deconstructing the curriculum: radical hermeneutics and professional education', *Edinburgh Architectural Research (EAR)*, 23, 1–24.

Cranton, P. (1996). *Professional Development as Transformative Learning: New Perspectives for Teachers of Adults*. San Francisco: Jossey-Bass Inc.

Creaser, B. (1995). 'Staff development', in B. Creaser and E. Dau (eds), *The Anti-Bias Approach in Early Childhood*. Sydney: Harper Education.

Creating and Sustaining Learning Communities: Connections, Collaboration, and Crossing Borders (1999). Available online: www.horizon.unc.edu/conferences/lc/.

Crowley, V. (1999). 'Towards a postcolonial curriculum for the new millennium', in B. Johnson and A. Reid (eds), *Contesting the Curriculum*. Sydney: Social Science Press.

Crump, A. and Ellwood, W. (1998). *The A to Z of World Development*. Oxford: New Internationalist Publications.

Dahlberg, G., Moss, P. and Pence, A. (1999). *Beyond Quality in Early Childhood Education and Care: Postmodern Perspectives*. London: Falmer Press.

Danaher, G., Schirato, T. and Webb, J. (2000). *Understanding Foucault*. Crows Nest, NSW: Allen & Unwin.

Danesco, E.R. (1997). 'Parental beliefs on childhood disability: insights on culture, child development, and intervention', *International Journal of Disability, Development, and Education*, 44(1), 41–52.

Darder, A (ed.) (2002). *Reinventing Paulo Freire: a Pedagogy of Love*. Boulder, Colorado: Westview Press.

Dau, E. (ed.) (2001). *The Anti-Bias Approach in Early Childhood* (2nd edn). Sydney: Addison Wesley Longman.

Davies, B. (1988). *Gender Equity and Early Childhood*. Canberra: Commonwealth Schools Commission.

Davies, B. (1989). *Frogs and Snails and Feminist Tales: Preschool Children and Gender*. Sydney: Allen & Unwin.

Davies, B. (1993). *Shards of Glass: Children Reading and Writing Beyond Gendered Identities*. St Leonards: Allen & Unwin.

Davies, B. (1994). *Poststructuralist Theory and Classroom Practice*. Geelong: Deakin University.

Davies, B. (2000). 'Eclipsing the constitutive power of discourse: the writing of Janette Turner Hospital', in E.A. St Pierre and W.S. Pillow (eds), *Working the Ruins: Feminist Poststructural Theory and Methods in Education* (pp. 179–198). New York: Routledge.

Davies, B. (2001). 'Eclipsing the constitutive power of discourse: the writing of Janette Turner Hospital', in E.A. St Pierre and W.S. Pillow (eds), *Working the Ruins: Feminist Poststructuralist Theory and Methods in Education*, (179–198). London: Routledge.

Deleuze, G. (1986). *Foucault*. Minneapolis: University of Minnesota Press.

Deleuze, G. and Guattari, F. (1987). *A Thousand Plateaus: Capitalism and Schizophrenia*. London: The Athlone Press.

Derman-Sparks, L. (1998) (published 2001). 'Education without prejudice: goals, principles and practices', paper presented to Respect: Education Without Prejudice, A Challenge For Early Years Educators In Ireland, 16 October. Published by Pavee Point Travellors Centre, Dubin, Ireland (22–31).

Derman-Sparks, L. (2001). 'Foreword', in E. Dau (ed.) *The Anti-Bias Approach in Early Childhood*. Melbourne: Longman.

Derman-Sparks, L. and the Anti-Bias Task Force (1989). *The Anti-Bias Curriculum*. Washington, DC: National Association for the Education of Young Children.

Derrida, J. (1976). *Of Grammatology*, trans. Gayatri Chakravorty Spivak. Baltimore and London: The Johns Hopkins Press.

Derrida, J. (1978). 'The retrait of metaphor', *Enclitic*, 5.

Derrida, J. (1983). 'The time of a thesis: punctuations', trans. K. McLaughlin in A. Montefiore (ed.), *Philosophy in France Today* (pp. 35–40). Cambridge: Cambridge University Press.

Derrida, J. (1992) cited in G. Biesta and D. Egea-Kuehne (eds), *Derrida and Education*, (176–185). London: Routledge.

Derrida, J. (1993). *Aporias*, trans. Thomas Dutoit. Stanford: Stanford University Press.

Derrida, J. (1997). 'A Conversation with Jacques Derrida', in J.D. Caputo (ed.) *Deconstruction in a Nutshell*. New York: Fordham University Press.

Derrida, J. (2002). 'Talking liberties. Jacques Derrida's interview with Alan Montefiore', in G. Biesta and D. Egea-Kuehne (eds), *Derrida and Education* (pp. 176–185). London: Routledge.

De Soto, L. (ed.) (2001). *The Politics of Early Childhood Education: Rethinking Childhood* (pp. 59–71). New York: Peter Lang Publishing Inc.

Dockrell, J., Lewis, A. and Lindsay, G. (2000). 'Researching children's perspectives: a psychological dimension', in A. Lewis and G. Lindsay (eds), *Researching Children's Perspectives*, (pp. 46–58) Buckingham and Philadelphia: Open University Press.

Doyle, A.B. and Aboud, F.E. (1995). 'A longitudinal study of white children's racial prejudice as a social cognitive development' *Merril-Palmer Quarterly*, 41(2), 209–228.

Dreyfus, H. and Rabinow, P. (eds) (1982). *Michel Foucault: Beyond Structuralism and Hermeneutics*. Chicago: University of Chicago Press.

Eaton, J. and Shephard, W. (1998). *Early Childhood Environments*. Watson, ACT: Australian Early Childhood Association.

Ebbeck, M. (1991). *Early Childhood Education*. Cheshire, Melbourne: Longman.

Ebbeck, M. (2003). 'Global pre-school education: issues and progress', *International Journal of Early Childhood*, 34(2), 1–11.

Ecclestone, K. (1996). 'The reflective practitioner: mantra or a model for emancipation?' *Studies in the Education of Adults*, 28(2), 146–161.

Education Review Office. (2000). *In-Service Training for Teachers in New Zealand Schools, 1*. New Zealand: Crown Copyright.

EYTARN, 2001. Membership leaflet. Early Years Anti-Racist Trainers Network, UK.

Feher, M. (ed.), with Naddaff, R. and Tazi, N. (1989). *Fragments for a History of the Human Body, Part III*. New York: Zone.

Finch, C. (1999). 'Using professional development to meet teachers' changing needs: what we have learned?' *Centerpoint no. 2*. Berkeley, CA: National Center for Research in Vocational Education. (ED 428 259).

Firestone, W. and Pennell, J. (1997). 'Designing state-sponsored teacher networks: a comparison of two cases', *American Educational Research Journal*, 34(3), 237–266.

Fleer, M. (ed.) (1995). *DAP Centrism: Challenging Developmentally Appropriate Practice*. Canberra: Australian Early Childhood Association, Inc.

Fleer, M. (2002). 'Research evidence with political currency: keeping the early childhood education agenda on the international agenda', *Australian Journal of Early Childhood*, 27(1), 1–7.

Fleet, A. and Patterson, C. (2001). 'Professional growth reconceptualized: early childhood staff searching for meaning', *Early Childhood Research and Practice*, 3(2). Online, available at: ecrp.uiuc.edu/v3n2/fleet.html.

Foot, H., Howe, C., Cheyne, B. *et al.* (2002). 'Parental participation and partnerships in pre-school provision', *International Journal of Early Years Education*, 10(1), 5–20.

Foucault, M. (1972). *The Archaeology of Knowledge*. London: Tavistock Publications.

Foucault, M. (1977a). 'Truth and power', in C. Gordon (ed.) *Power/ Knowledge: Selected Interviews and Other Writings 1972–1977. Michel Foucault* (pp.109–133). Sussex: The Harvester Press.

Foucault, M. (1977b). 'Two lectures', in C. Gordon (ed.) *Power/Knowledge: Selected Interviews and Other Writings 1972–1977. Michel Foucault* (pp. 78–108). Sussex: The Harvester Press.

Foucault, M. (1977c). 'Nietzche, genealogy, history', in D. Bouchard (ed.) (trans D. Bouchard and S. Simon), *Language, Counter-Memory, and Practice: Selected Essays and Interviews*. Ithaca: Cornell University Press.

Foucault, M. (1977d). *Discipline and Punish: The Birth of the Prison*, trans. A. Sheridan. New York: Pantheon.

Foucault, M. (1978). *The History of Sexuality. Volume 1: An Introduction*. New York: Vintage Books; London: Penguin.

Foucault, M. (1980a). *Power/Knowledge: Selected Interviews and Other Writings 1972–1977*. New York: Pantheon.

Foucault, M. (1980b). 'Prison talk', in C. Gordon (ed.), *Power/Knowledge: Selected Interviews and Other Writings 1972–1977* (pp. 37–54). New York: Pantheon.

Foucault, M. (1982). 'The subject and power', in H. Dreyfus and P. Rabinow (eds), *Michel Foucault: Beyond Structuralism and Hermeneutics* (pp. 208–226). Chicago: University of Chicago Press.

Foucault, M. (1983). 'What is enlightement?', in P. Rabinow (ed.), *The Foucault Reader*. Harmondsworth: Penguin.

Foucault, M. (1984a). *The Care of the Self: The History of Sexuality*. London: Penguin.

Foucault, M. (1984b). 'On the genealogy of ethics: an overview of work in progress', in P. Rabinow (ed.), *The Foucault Reader*. Harmondsworth: Penguin.

Foucault, M. (1985), *The Use of Pleasure, Volume 2 of The History of Sexuality*. New York: Pantheon.

Foucault, M. (1988). 'The ethic of care for the self as a practice of freedom', in J. Bernauer and D. Rasmussen (eds), *The Final Foucault*. Cambridge, Mass: MIT Press.

Foucault, M. (1989). *Foucault Live: Interviews, 1966–1984*. New York: Semiotext.

Foucault, M. (1994). 'Truth and power', in J.D Faubion (ed.), *Power: Essential Works of Foucault 1954–1984* (pp. 111–133). London: Penguin.

Foucault, M. (1997). *Ethics: Essential Works of Foucault 1954–1984*, vol. 1, ed. Paul Rabinow. London: Penguin.

Foucault, M. (1998). *Aesthetics, Method and Epistemology: Essential Works of Foucault 1954–1984*, vol. 2, ed. Janes Faubion. New York: New Press.

Fowler, H.W. and Fowler, F.G. (1990) *Concise Oxford English Dictionary*. Oxford: Oxford University Press.

Freire. P. (1970). *Cultural Action for Freedom*, trans. Myra Bergman Ramos. Middlesex: Penguin.

Freire, P. (1972). *Pedagogy of the Oppressed*, trans. Myra Bergman Ramos. Middlesex: Penguin.

Freire, P. (1996). *Pedagogy of the Oppressed*. London: Penguin.

Gallagher, C. (2000). 'A Seat at the Table. Teachers Reclaiming Assessment Through Rethinking Accountability', *Phi Delta Kappan*, March, pp. 502–507.

Gaudiano, E. and de Alba, A. (1994). 'Freire – present and future possibilities', in P. McLaren and C. Lankshear (eds), *Politics of Liberation: Paths from Freire* (pp. 123–141). London and New York: Routledge.

Gesell, A. (1952). *Infant Development: The Embryology of Early Human Behaviour*. London: Hamish Hamilton.

Gesell, A. and Ilg, F. (1943). *Infant and Child in the Culture of Today*. New York: Harper.

Ghandi, L. (1998). *Postcolonial Theory: A Critical Introduction*. Sydney: Allen & Unwin.

Gilroy, P. (1996). 'Route work: the black Atlantic and the politics of exile', in I. Chambers and L. Curti (eds), *The Postcolonial Question: Common Skies, Divided Horizons*, (pp. 17 – 29). Routledge: London.

Ginsburg, H. and Opper, S. (1969). *Piaget's Theory of Intellectual Development: An Introduction*. New Jersey: Prentice Hall.

Giroux, H. (1988). *Teachers as Intellectuals: Toward a Critical Pedagogy of Learning*. Massachusetts: Bergin & Garvey Publishers, Inc.

Giroux, H. (1991). 'Modernism, postmodernism and feminism: Rethinking the boundaries of educational discourse', in H.A. Giroux (ed.), *Postmodernism, Feminism and Cultural Politics: Redrawing Educational Boundaries* (pp. 1–59). New York: State University of New York Press.

Giugni, M. (2003). *Secret Children's Business: The Black Market for Identity Work*. Unpublished Honours thesis, The University of Western Sydney: Sydney.

Gleick, J. (1987). *Chaos*. Cardinal: Sphere Books.

Glickman, C. (1993). *Renewing America's Schools: A Guide for School-Based Action*. San Francisco: Josey Bass.

Global Learning Communities (2001). *Schools as Collaborative Learning Communities*. Online, available at: www.vision.net.au/~globallearning/.

Goldstein, L. (1997). *Teaching with Love: a Feminist Approach to Early Childhood Education*. New York: Peter Lang Publishing.

Gopaul-McNicol, S.A. (1995). 'A cross-cultural examination of racial identity and racial preference of preschool children in the West Indies', *Journal of Cross-Cultural Psychology*, 26(2), 141–152.

Gore, J. (1993). *The Struggle for Pedagogies: Critical and Feminist Discourses as Regimes of Truth*. London: Routledge.

Gore, J. (1995). 'Foucault's poststructulism and observational education research: A study of power relations', in R. Smith and P. Wexler (eds), *After Postmodernism: Education, Politics and Identity* (pp. 98–111). London: Falmer.

Gore, J. (1998). 'Disciplining bodies: on the continuity of power relations in pedagogy', in T.S. Popkewitz and M. Brennan (eds), *Foucault's Challenge:*

Discourse, Knowledge and Power in Education (pp. 231–251). New York: Teachers College Press.

Gore, J. (2001). 'Beyond our differences: A reassembling of what matters in teacher education', *Journal of Teacher Education*, 52, 123–135.

Greene, M. (1986). 'In search of critical pedagogy', *Harvard Educational Review*, 56(4), 427–441.

Grenz. S. (1996). *A Primer on Postmodernism*. Grand Rapids, Cambridge, MA: W.B. Eerdmans Publishing Co.

Grieshaber, S. (1997). 'Back to basics: the Queensland Year 2 Diagnostic Net', *Curriculum Perspectives*, 17(3), 28–38.

Grossberg, L. (1996). 'The space of culture, the power of space', in I. Chambers and L. Curti (eds), *Common Skies, Divided Horizons* (pp. 169–188). London: Routledge.

Grosz, E. (1990). 'Contemporary theories of power and subjectivity', in S. Gunew (ed.) *A Reader in Feminist Knowledge: Critique and Construct* (pp. 59–120). London: Routledge.

Grundy, S. (1982). 'Three modes of action research', *Curriculum Perspectives*, 2(3), 23–34.

Grundy, S. (1987). *Curriculum: Product or Praxis*. East Sussex: The Falmer Press.

Gunew, S. (1990). 'Questions of multiculturalism', in S. Harasym (ed.), *The Post-Colonial Critic* (pp. 59–66). New York: Routledge.

Habermas, J. (1972). *Knowledge And Human Interests*, trans. John Viertel. London: Heinemann.

Habermas, J. (1981). 'Modernity versus postmodernity', *New Left Critique*, Winter, 22.

Habermas, J. (1987). *Theory Of Communicative Action, Vol. 2: System And Lifeworld: The Critique Of Functionalist Reason*, trans. Thomas McCarthy. Boston: Beacon.

Hage, G. (1998). *White Nation. Fantasies of White Supremacy in a Multicultural Society*. Amandale, NSW: Pluto Press.

Hall, S. (1992). 'The West and the Rest: Discourse and Power', in Stuart Hall and Bram Gieben (eds), *Formations of Modernity*, (pp. 275–332). Oxford: Polity Press.

Hall, N. (1996), 'Why Mathematics Is Important', *Every Child*, 2(4), 4–5.

Hanson, Pauline (2002). *One Nation Policy Document: Immigration, Population and Social Cohesion*. Online, available at: www.gwb.com.au/onenation/policy/immig.html, accessed 21 November 2002.

Harasym, S. (ed.) (1990) *The Post-Colonial Critic: Interviews, Strategies, Dialogues*. London: Routledge.

Harry, B. (1992). 'An ethnographic study of cross-cultural communication with Puerto Rican-American families in the special education system', *American Educational Research Journal*, 29(3) 471–494.

Hartsock, N. (1990). 'Foucault on power', in. L. Nicholson (ed.), *Feminism/Postmodernism*. London: Routledge.

Haugaard, M. (2002). 'The birth of the subject and the use of truth: Foucault and social critique', in S. Malesevic and I. MacKenzie (eds), *Ideology after Poststructuralism* (pp. 157–170). London: Pluto Press.

Helford, E. R. (2002). '"My emotions give me power": The containment of girls' anger in Buffy', in R.V. Wilcox and D. Lavery (eds), *Fighting the Force: What's at Stake in Buffy the Vampire Slayer*, (pp. 18 – 34). Maryland: Rowman & Littlefield.

Henniger, M. (1999). *Teaching Young Children: An Introduction*. New Jersey: Merrill Prentice Hall.

Hirschfeld, L. (1995). 'Do children have a theory of race?', *Cognition*, 54, 209–252.

Honig, A.S. (1996) 'Early childhood education: Training for the future', *Early Child Development and Care*, 121, 135–145.

hooks, b. (1989). *Talking Back: Thinking Feminist – Thinking Black*. London: Sheba Press.

hooks, b. (1994). *Teaching to Transgress. Education as the practice of freedom*. London: Routledge.

hooks, b. (1996). *Killing Rage, Ending Racism*. London: Penguin.

hooks, b. (1997). *Wounds of Passion: A Writing Life*. New York: Holt.

hooks, b. (2000). *Feminism is for Everybody: Passionate Politics*. Cambridge: South End Press.

Huggins, R. and Huggins, J. (1994). *Auntie Rita*. Canberra: Aboriginal Studies Press.

Hughes, P. and Mac Naughton, G. (1999). 'Who's the expert: reconceptualising staff–parent relationships in early childhood', *Australian Journal of Early Childdhood*, 24(4), 27–32.

Hughes, P. and Mac Naughton, G. (2000). 'Consensus, dissensus or community: the politics of parent involvement in early childhood education', *Contemporary Issues in Early Childhood*, 1(3), 241–257.

Hughes, P. and Mac Naughton, G. (2000). 'Identity formation and popular culture: learning lessons from Barbie', *Journal of Curriculum Theorizing*, 16(3), 57–68.

Imel, S. (1998). 'Teaching critical reflection: trends and issues'. ERIC Alerts from the Clearinghouse on Adult Career and Vocational Education.

Indiana Professional Licensing Board, US (2004). *Licensing Rules for Early Childhood Teachers*. Available online at: http://www.in.gov/psb/, accessed 2 February 2004.

Jipson, J. (1998). 'Developmentally Appropriate Practice: Culture, curriculum, connections', in M. Hauser and J. Jipson (eds), *Intersections: Feminisms/Early Childhoods* (pp. 221–240). New York: Peter Lang Publishing.

Jipson, J.A. and Johnson, R. (eds) (2001). *Resistance and Representation: Rethinking Childhood Education*. New York: Peter Lang.

Johnson, D. (1992). 'Racial preference and biculturality in biracial preschoolers', *Merrill-Palmer Quarterly*, 38(2), 233–244.

Jones, K. (2001). 'The Critical Teaching Project'. Unpublished report, Department of Education and Children's Services, South Australia.

Joyce, B., Showers, B. and Weill, M. (1992). *Models of Teaching*. Sydney: Allyn and Bacon.

Kant, I (1958). *The Critique of Pure Reason: The Critique of Practical Reason and Other Ethical Treatises: The Critique of Judgement*. Chicago: Encyclopaedia Britannica.

Katz, L. (1996). 'Child development knowledge and teacher preparation: confronting assumptions', *Early Childhood Research Quarterly*, 11, 135–146.

Keedy, J. (1991). 'A strategy to develop teacher leadership for school restructuring: Teacher collegial groups', Annual Meeting of the American Association of School Administrators, New Orleans, LA.

Kelly, M. and Duckitt, J. (1995). 'Racial preference and self-esteem in black South African children', *South African Journal of Psychology*, 25(4), 217–223.

Kenway, J. and Willis, S. (1997). *Answering Back*. Sydney: Allen & Unwin.

Keohane, K. (2002). 'City life and the conditions of possibility of an ideology-proof subject: Simmel, Benjamin and Joyce on Berlin, Paris and Dublin', in S. Malesevic and I. MacKenzie (eds), *Ideology after Post-structuralism* (pp. 64–84). London: Pluto Press.

Kessler, S. and Swadner, B. (eds) (1994). *Reconceptualising the Early Childhood Curriculum: Beginning the Dialogue*. New York: Teachers College Press.

Kessler, S.A. and Hauser, M. (2000) 'Critical pedagogy and the politics of play', in L.D. Soto (ed.), *The Politics of Early Childhood Education: Rethinking Childhood* (pp. 59–71). New York: Peter Lang Publishing Inc.

KSI Research International Inc. (2003). Applied Research Branch Strategic Policy Human Resources Development Canada. 'Early Childhood Development in the Montreal study area (Quebec)', November 2003 SP-584–09–03 Executive Summary and SP-584–09–03 'Understanding the Early Years Early Childhood Development in the Montreal study area (Quebec)'.

Lather, P. (1991). *Getting Smart: Feminist Research and Pedagogy within/in the Postmodern*. London: Routledge.

Lawrence, R. (2000). 'Building a Learning Community', Global Learning Community.

Lawrence, V. (1991). 'Effect of socially ambiguous information on White and Black children's behavioural and trait perceptions', *Merrill-Palmer Quarterly*, 37(4), 619–630.

Longstreet, W. and Shane, H. (1993). *Curriculum for a New Millennium*. Needham Heights, MA: Allyn & Bacon.

Loomba, A. (1998). *Colonialism/Postcolonialism*. London: Routledge.

Losinsky, M. and Collinson, I. (1999). *Epistemological Shudder: The X-files, Myths and Mimetic Capital*. Paper presented at the University of New South Wales Post Graduate Conference School of English and Modern Languages. June.

Lubeck, S. (1994). 'The politics of developmentally appropriate practice: Exploring issues of culture, class and curriculum', in B. Mallory and R. New (eds), *Diversity and Developmentally Appropriate Practices: Challenges for Early Childhood Education* (pp. 17–43). New York: Teachers College Press.

Lubeck, S. (1998). 'Is Developmentally Appropriate Practice for everyone?', *Childhood Education*, 74(5), 293–298.

Luke, C. (ed.) (1996). *Feminisms and Pedagogies of Everyday Life*. New York: SUNY Press.

Luke, C. and Gore. J. (1992). *Feminisms and Critical Pedagogy*. London: Routledge.

Lynch, E.W. and Hanson, M.J. (1992). *Developing Cross-Cultural Competence*. Baltimore, MD: Paul H. Brookes.

Lyotard, J-F. (1984). *The Postmodern Condition: A Report on Knowledge*. Minneapolis: University of Minneapolis Press.

McCain, M and Mustard, F.J. (1999). *Reversing the Real Brain Drain: Early Years Study Final Report*. Canada: Publications Ontario.

McDermott, R.P. and Varenne, H. (1996). 'Culture, development, disability', in R. Jessor, A. Colby and R.A. Shweder (eds), *Ethnography and Human Development*. Chicago: University of Chicago Press.

Macedo, D. (1998). 'Foreword', in N.P. Freire, *Pedagogy of Freedom: Ethics, Democracy, and Civic Courage*. New York: Rowman & Littlefield.

McHoul, A. and Grace, W. (1993). *A Foucault Primer: Discourse, Power and the Subject*. Carlton, Vic.: Melbourne University Press.

MacIsaac, D. (1996). *The Critical Theory of Jürgen Habermas*. Accessed 2001 at www.physics.nau.edu/-danmac.

Mackintosh, C. (1998). 'Reflection: a flawed strategy for the nursing profession', *Nurse Education Today*, 18, 553–557.

McLaren, M. (2002). *Feminism, Foucault and Embodied Subjectivity*. New York: State University of New York Press.

McLaren, P. (1993). *Life in Schools: An Introduction to Critical Pedagogy in the Social Foundations of Education*. New York: Longman.

McLaren, P. (2000). 'Paulo Freire's pedagogy of possibility', in S. Steiner, H. Krank, P. McLaren *et al.* (eds), *Freirean Pedagogy, Praxis and Possibilities: Projects for the New Millennium* (pp. 1–22). New York and London: Falmer.

McLeod, J. and Yates, L. (2003). 'Who is "Us"? Students negotiating discourses of racism and national identification in Australia', *Race, Ethnicity and Education*, 6(1), 29–49.

Mac Naughton, G. (1993). 'Gender, power and racism: a case study of domestic play in early childhood', *Multicultural Teaching*, 11(3), 12–15.

Mac Naughton, G. (1995). 'A post-structuralist analysis of learning in early childhood Settings', in M. Fleer (ed.), *DAP centrism. Challenging Developmentally Appropriate Practice*. Canberra: Australian Early Childhood Association, Inc.

Mac Naughton, G. (1996). 'Is Barbie to blame: reconsidering how children learn gender', *Australian Journal of Early Childhood*, 21(4), 18–22.

Bibliography 231

Mac Naughton, G. (1998). 'Improving our gender equity "tools": a case for discourse analysis', in N. Yelland (ed.), *Gender in Early Childhood*. London: Routledge.

Mac Naughton, G. (1999). 'Early childhood review. curriculum issues in research and in action', discussion paper for consultation, Department of Education, Tasmania.

Mac Naughton, G. (2000). *Rethinking Gender in Early Childhood*. Sydney: Allen & Unwin.

Mac Naughton, G. (2001a). '"Blushes and birthday parties": telling silences in young children's constructions of "race"', *Journal for Australian Research in Early Childhood Education*, 8(1), 41–51.

Mac Naughton, G. (2001b). 'Silences and subtexts of immigrant and non-immigrant children', *Childhood Education*, 78(1), 30–36.

Mac Naughton, G. (2001c). 'Back to the future – young children constructing and reconstructing "White" Australia'. Keynote presented at the New Zealand Council for Educational Research 'Early Childhood Education for a Democractic Society' National Conference, Wellington, NZ, 26 October. Published conference procedings.

Mac Naughton, G. (2001d). 'Dolls for equity: foregrounding children's voices in learning respect and unlearning unfairness', *New Zealand Council for Educational Research Early Childhood Folio*, 5, 27–30.

Mac Naughton, G. (2001e). 'Challenging models of professional development in postmodern times'. Paper presented to the Australian Early Childhood Association Biennial Conference, Excellence for Children, Sydney, 18–21 July.

Mac Naughton, G. (2002). 'Innovations in working for social justice in early childhood', *WA SUPS State Conference 2002, Conference Proceedings*, Perth: Resource Unit for Children with Special Needs Inc., and Ethnic Child Care Resource Unit.

Mac Naughton, G. (2003). 'Eclipsing voice in research with young children', *Australian Journal of Early Childhood*, 28(1), 36–42.

Mac Naughton, G. (2004). 'Children, staff and parents: building respectful relationships in New Zealand and Australian early childhood contexts – the Australian context', *Australian Journal of Early Childhood*, 29(1), 1–7.

Mac Naughton, G. and Davis, K. (2001) 'Beyond "othering": rethinking approaches to teaching young anglo-Australian children about indigenous Australians', *Contemporary Issues in Early Childhood*, 2(1), 83–93.

McNay, L. (1992). *Foucault and Feminism*. London: Polity Press.

McTaggart, R. (1991). 'Principles for participatory action research', *Adult Education Quarterly*, 41(3), 168–187.

Mallory, B. and New, R. (1994). *Diversity and Developmentally Appropriate Practices*. New York: Teachers College Press.

Mangione, P.L. (ed.) (1995). *A Guide to Culturally Sensitive Care*. Sacramento, CA: California Department of Education.

Mansfield, N. (2000). *Subjectivity: Theories of the Self from Freud to Haraway.* Sydney: Allen & Unwin.

Marx, K. and Engels, F. (1965). *The German Ideology.* London: Lawrence & Wishart.

Massie, E. (1999). *Power of Persuasion.* New York: Pocket Books.

Mezirow, J. (1990). *Fostering Critical Reflection in Adulthood: A Guide to Transformative and Emancipatory Learning.* San Francisco: Jossey-Bass Publishers.

Miller, J. (1994). *The Passion of Michel Foucault.* Cambridge: Cambridge University Press.

Ministry of Education (MoE) (1996). *Te Whariki.* New Zealand.

Mooney, A., Munton, A.G., Rowland, L. *et al.* (1997). 'The development of materials to assess quality in group and family day care', *Early Child Development and Care,* 129, 27–42.

Munsch, R.N. (1980). *The Paper Bag Princess.* Sydney: Scholastic.

Munton, A.G. and Mooney, A. (1999). 'Improving quality of childcare provision through self assessment: Organizational characteristics of nurseries as predictors of the ability to plan and implement change', *Early Child Development and Care,* 148, 21–34.

Nandy, A. (1983). *The Intimate Enemy: Loss and Recovery of Self Under Colonialism.* Delhi: Oxford University Press.

National Child Care Accreditation Council (NCAC) (1993). *Quality Assurance and Improvement Handbook.* Canberra: Australian Government Publishing Service.

National Childcare Accreditation Council (NCAC) (2000). *Statistics of the QIAS.* Available online: www.ncac.gov.au/stats/progress.htm.

National Research Council and Institute of Medicine. (2000). *From Neurons to Neighbourhoods: The Science of Early Childhood Development.* Washington, DC: National Academy Press.

New South Wales Curriculum Framework (2002). *NSW Department of Community Service,* available online: http://www.nswcurriculumframework.asn.au/.

Oakton Early Childhood Education Centre (2004). Online, available at: http://servercc.oakton.edu/~levin/web/contactus.htm.

Ochsner, M. (2001). 'Developing reciprocity in a multi-method small-scale research study', in G. Mac Naughton, S. Rolfe and I. Siraj-Blatchford (eds), *Doing Early Childhood Research* (pp. 254–263). Sydney: Allen & Unwin.

O'Loughlin, M. (2001). 'The development of subjectivity in young children: some theoretical and pedagogical considerations', *Contemporary Issues in Early Childhood,* 2(1), 49–65.

Orton, F. (1989). 'Fred. on being bent "blue" (Second State): an introduction to Jacques Derrida/a footnote on Jasper Johns', *Oxford Art Journal,* 12(1), 35–46.

O'Shane, M. and Bickford, J. (1991). *Hand in Hand: Integrating Indigenous Education.* Australia: Department of Employment, Education and Training.

O'Sullivan, T., Hartley, J., Saunders, D. and Fiske, J. (1983). *Key Concepts in Communication.* New York: Methuen.

Parker, S. (1997). *Reflective Teaching in the Postmodern World: A Manifesto for Education in Postmodernity.* Philadelphia: Open University Press

Partington, G. and McCudden, V. (1993). *Ethnicity and education.* Wentworth Falls: Social Science Press.

Penney, J. (2003). 'Implementing developmentally appropriate practices in the classroom', *Childhood Education,* 80(1), 28–H–28–I.

Peters, M. (1999). 'Poststructuralism and education', *Encyclopedia of Philosophy of Education.* Available online: www.vusst.hr.encyclopaedia. poststructuralism.htm.

Phillipsen, L.C., Burchinal, M.R., Howes, C. *et al.* (1997). 'The prediction of process quality from structural features of child care', *Early Childhood Research Quarterly,* 12, 281–303.

Piaget, J. (1944/1995). 'Logical operations and social life', in L. Smith (ed.), *Sociological Studies* (pp. 134–157). London: Routledge.

Popkewitz, T. and Brennan, M. (1998). *Foucault's Challenge: Discourse, Knowledge, and Power in Education.* New York: Teachers College Press.

Potter, G. (2001). 'The power of collaborative research in teachers' professional development', *Australian Journal of Early Childhood,* 26, 8–13.

Pownell, E. (1960). *The World We Share.* Sydney: Shakespeare Head Press Ltd.

Pratt, M. (1985). 'Scratches on the face of the country: or, what Mr Barrow saw in the land of the bushmen', *Critical Inquiry,* 12(1), 138–162.

Pucckett, M., Marshall, S. and Davis, R. (1999). 'Examining the emergence of Brain Development Research', *Childhood Education,* 76(1), 8–12.

Prudhoe, C. (2003). 'Picture books and the art of collage', *Childhood Education,* 80(1), 6–11.

Putnam. J., Myers-Walls, J. and Love, D. (2003–2004). *Gender Development.* Online, available at: http:www.ces.purdue.edu/parentprovider/Child Growth-Development/GenderDEV.htm.

Quicho, A. and Rios, F. (2000). 'The power of their presence: minority group teachers and schooling', *Review of Educational Research,* 70(4), 485–528.

Rabinow, P. (1984). 'Introduction', in P. Rabinow (ed.), *The Foucault Reader.* New York: Pantheon Books.

Rabinow, P. (ed.) (1997). *Michel Foucault: Ethics, Subjectivity and Truth. Essential Works of Foucault 1954–1984. Volume I.* New York: The New Press.

Ramsey, P. (1991). 'The salience of race in young children growing up in an all-White community', *Journal of Educational Psychology,* 83(1), 28–34.

Read, K., Gardner, P. and Mahler, B. (1993). *Early Childhood Programs: Human Relationships and Learning.* Brace Javonovich, Forth Worth, TX: Harcourt.

Reid, A. and Johnson, B. (1999). 'Introduction', in A. Reid and B. Johnson (eds), *Contesting the Curriculum* (pp. x–xvii). Sydney: Social Science Press.

Rizvi, F. (1998). 'Higher education and the politics of difference', *Australian Universities' Review*, 41(2), 5–6.

Rodd, J. and Clyde, M. (1990). 'Ethical dilemmas of the early chldhood professional: a comparitive study', *Early Childhood Research Quarterly*, 5, 461–474.

Roe, D. (2001). *Autism Spectrum Disorder and Young Children*. Watson, ACT: AECA.

Rose, N. (2001), *Governing the Soul*. London: Routledge.

Roman, L.G. and Linda E. (eds) (1997). *Dangerous Territories: Struggles for Difference and Equality in Education*. London: Routledge.

Rowley, C. (1986). *Recovery: The Politics Of Aboriginal Reform*. Ringwood, Victoria: Penguin.

Royle, N. (2002). 'What is deconstruction?', in G. Biesta and D. Egea-Kuehne (eds), *Derrida and Education* (pp. 1–13). London: Routledge.

Ryan S. and Oschner, M. (1999). 'Traditional practices: new possibilities. Transforming dominant images of early childhood teachers', *Australian Journal of Early Childhood*, 24(4), 14–20.

Sarup. M. (1988). *An Introductory Guide to Poststructuralism and Postmodernism*. Hemel Hempstead: Harvester Wheatsheaf.

Said, E. (1978) *Orientalism: Western Conceptions of the Orient*. New York: Pantheon Books.

Saunders, P. (1996). *Income and Welfare Special Article – Poverty and Deprivation in Australia (Year Book Australia, 1996)* (ABS Catalogue No. 1301.0).

Saussure, F. de (1959). *Course in General Linguisics*, eds C. Bally, A. Sechehaye and A. Riedlinger, trans. W. Baskin. New York: Philosophical Library.

Schecter, S. and Parkhurst, S. (1993). Ideological divergences in a teacher-research group. *American Educational Research Journal*, 30(4), 771–798.

Seckold, C. and Campbell, S. (2003). 'Everybody helps on the farm: gender issues in rural early childhood settings', *Everychild*, 9(2), 6–7.

Silin, J. (1995). *Sex, Death and the Education of Children: Our Passion for Ignorance in the Age of AIDS*. New York: Teachers College Press.

Silin, J. (1999). 'Speaking up for silence', *Australian Journal of Early Childhood*, 24(4), 41–45.

Sleeter, C. and McLaren, P. (1995). 'Introduction: exploring connections to build a critical multiculturalism', in C. Sleeter and P. McLaren, *Multicultural Education, Critical Pedagogy and the Politics of Difference* (pp. 5–28). New York: State of New York Press.

Smith, D. and Lovat, T. (1990). *Curriculum: Action on Reflection*. Sydney: Social Science Press.

Smith, K. (2000). 'Reconceptualising the role of parents in observation', *Australian Journal of Early Childhood*, 25(2), 18–21.

Smith. K. (2003). '*The Paper Bag Princess, Harry Potter* and *Buffy the Vampire Slayer*: Exploring popular culture texts to create new co-ordinates for observation as a political practice for social justice'. Paper presented at Honouring the Child Honouring Equity 3 Conference. Melbourne University. November.

Spencer, L. and Krauze, A. (2000). *Introducing the Enlightenment*. Cambridge, UK: Icon Books.

Spivak, G. (1988 [1985]) 'Can the subaltern speak?' Reprinted in Cary Nelson and Lawrence Grossberg (eds) *Marxist Interpretations of Culture* (pp. 271–313). Basingstoke: Macmillan Education.

Spivak, G. (1990). 'The post-modern condition: the end of politics?' (with G. Hawthorn, R. Aronson, J. Dunn), in S. Harasym (ed.), *The Post-Colonial Critic* (pp. 17–34). New York: Routledge.

Spivak, G. (2002). 'Deconstruction and cultural studies: Arguments for a deconstructive cultural studies', in G. Biesta and D. Egea-Kuehne (eds), *Derrida and Education*, (pp. 14–43). London: Routledge.

Stanley, J. (2001). *Centenary Article – Child Health Since Federation (Year Book Australia, 2001)*. Australian Bureau of Statistics.

Stanley, L. (ed.) (1997). *Knowing Feminisms: On Academic Borders, Territories and Tribes*. London: Sage Publications.

Strike, K. (1993). 'Professionalism, democracy and discursive communities: Normative reflections on restructuring', *American Educational Research Journal*, 30(2), 255–275.

Swepson, P. (1995). 'Action research: understanding its philosophy can improve your practice'. Available online: www.scu.edu.au/schools/gcm/ar/arp/philos.html.

Szente, J. (2003) 'Teleconferencing across borders: promoting literacy – and more – in the elementary grades', *Childhood Education*, January.

Taylor, P. (1993). *The Texts of Paulo Freire*. Buckingham: Open University Press.

Theilheimer, R. and Cahill, B. (2001). 'A messy closet in the early childhood classroom', in S. Grieshaber and G. Cannella (eds), *Embracing Identities in Early Childhood Education: Diversity and Possibilities* (pp. 103–113). New York: Teachers College Press.

Thompson, P. (1999). 'How doing justice got boxed in', in B. Johnson and A. Reid (eds), *Contesting the curriculum*, (pp. 24 – 42). Sydney: Social Science Press.

Thompson, R. (2001). 'Development in the first years of life', *The Future of Children*, 11(1), 21–33.

Trinh, Minh-ha T. (1990). *Woman, Native, Other: Writing Postcoloniality and Feminism*. Bloomington, IN: Indiana University Press.

Valdivia, R. (1999) 'The Implications of Culture on Developmental Delay'. The Council for Exceptional Children. *ERIC EC Digest #E589*. The ERIC Clearinghouse on Disabilities and Gifted Education (ERIC EC).

Van Ausdale, D. and Feagin, J.R. (1996). 'Using racial and ethnic concepts: the critical case of very young children. *American Sociological Review*, 61, 779–793.

Viruru, R. and Cannella, G.S. (2001). 'Postcolonial ethnography, young children, and voice', in S. Grieshaber and G. Cannella (eds), *Embracing Identities in Early Childhood Education: Diversity and Possibilities* (pp. 158–172). New York: Teachers College Press.

Walkerdine, V. (1981). 'Sex, power and pedagogy', *Screen*, vol. 38, 14–24.

Walkerdine, V. (1982). *Girls and Mathematics*. London: Virago.

Walkerdine, V. (1984). 'Developmental psychology and the child-centred pedagogy', in J. Henriques, W. Holloway, C. Urwin *et al.*, *Changing the Subject* (pp. 153–202). London: Methuen.

Walkerdine, V. (1988). *The Mastery of Reason: Cognitive Development and the Production of Rationality*. London and New York: Routledge.

Walkerdine, V. (1989). *Counting Girls Out*. London: Virago.

Walkerdine, V. (1990). *Schoolgirl Fictions*. London: Verso.

Walkerdine, V. (1992). 'Progressive pedagogy and political struggle', in C. Luke and J. Gore (eds), *Feminisms and Critical Pedagogy* (pp. 15–24). London: Routledge.

Walkerdine, V. and Lucey, H. (1989). *Democracy in the Kitchen: Regulating Mothers and Socialising Daughters*. London: Virago Press.

Weedon, C. (1997). *Feminist Practice and Poststructuralist Theory*, (2nd edn). Oxford: Basil Blackwell.

Weiner, G. (1994). *Feminisms in Education: An Introduction*. Buckingham: Open University Press

Willerman, M., McNeely, S. and Koffman, E. (1991). *Teachers Helping Teachers: Peer Observation and Assistance*. New York: Praeger.

Wolf, J.M. and Walsh, D.J. (1998). 'If you haven't been there, you don't know what it's like: doing day care', *Early Education and Development*, 9(1), 29–47.

Wong, C. (2002). 'Heidegger's and Derrida's notions of language and difference', *Quarterly Literary Review Singapore*, 1(2), available online: http://www.qlrs.com/issues/jan2002.

Woodrow, C. and Brennan, M. (2001). 'Interrupting dominant images of childhood: critical and ethical issues', in J. Jipson and R. Johnson (eds), *Resistance and Representation: Rethinking Childhood Education* (pp. 22–43). New York: Peter Lang Publishers.

World Bank (2002). *Why Invest in ECD?* Online, available at: http://www. worldbank.org/children/whyinvest/ (accessed on 1 November 2002).

Wroe, A. and Halsall, R. (2001) 'School self-evaluation: measurement and reflection in the school improvement process', *Research in Education* 65 (May): 41–52.

Yin, R. (1994). *Case Study Research: Design and Methods*, (2nd edn). London: Sage Publications.

Yost, D, Sentner, S. and Forlenza-Bailey, A. (2000). 'An examination of the construct of critical reflection: implications for teacher education programming in the 21st century', *Journal of Teacher Education*, 51, 39–49.

Index